W9-ANA-590

TECHNICAL COLLEGE OF THE LOWCOUNTRY
LEARNING RESOURCES CENTER
POST OFFICE BOX 1288
BEAUFORT, SOUTH CAROLINA 29901-1288

BRITISH DRAMA
BEFORE 1660

TWAYNE'S
CRITICAL HISTORY
OF
BRITISH DRAMA

Kinley E. Roby
SERIES EDITOR
Northeastern University

The opening of the *Second Shepherds' Play* (*Alia Eorundum*) from the Towneley plays, Huntington MS HM 1. f. 38r. (fifteenth century). *Reproduced by permission of the Huntington Library, San Marino, California.*

British Drama

Before 1660

A Critical History

Jennifer R. Goodman
Texas A & M University

Twayne Publishers • Boston
A Division of G. K. Hall & Co.

TECHNICAL COLLEGE OF THE LOWCOUNTRY.
LEARNING RESOURCES CENTER
POST OFFICE BOX 1288
BEAUFORT, SOUTH CAROLINA 29901-1288

British Drama before 1660
Jennifer R. Goodman

Copyright 1991 by G. K. Hall & Co.
All rights reserved.
Published by Twayne Publishers
A division of G. K. Hall & Co.
70 Lincoln Street
Boston, Massachusetts 02111

Copyediting supervised by Barbara Sutton.
Book design and production by Gabrielle B. McDonald.
Typeset in 10 point Bembo
by Huron Valley Graphics, Inc. of Ann Arbor, Michigan.

First published 1990.
10 9 8 7 6 5 4 3 2 1

The paper used in this publication meets the minimum requirements
of American National Standard for Information Sciences—Permanence
of Paper for Printed Library Materials, ANSI Z39.48-1984.

Printed and bound in the United States of America.

Library of Congress Cataloging-in-Publication Data⊗™

Goodman, Jennifer R. (Jennifer Robin), 1953–
British drama before 1660 : a critical history / Jennifer R. Goodman.
    p.   cm. — (Twayne's critical history of British drama)
    Includes bibliographical references and index.
    ISBN 0-8057-8953-7 (alk. paper)
    1. English drama—Early modern and Elizabethan, 1500–1600—History
and criticism.   2. English drama—17th century—History and
criticism.   3. English drama—To 1500—History and criticism.
    I. Title.   II. Series.
    [PR651.G66   1990]
    822.009—dc20   90-41056
                                                        CIP

CONTENTS

ACKNOWLEDGMENTS

For permission to reproduce the page from the Towneley plays manuscript (Huntington Library MS HM 1) I am grateful to the trustees of the Henry E. Huntington Library and Art Gallery, San Marino California. I would also like to thank Daniel H. Woodward, the librarian, and Kay Peterson, library assistant, for their help in obtaining this illustration.

For permission to reproduce a 1980 slide of the Harvard Theatre Collection model of Shakespeare's First Globe Playhouse I would like to thank Harvard College Library, and in particular Dr. Jeanne T. Newlin, curator of the Harvard Theatre Collection.

For the Ben Jonson frontispiece (*Workes,* London: Will Stansby, 1616) I am indebted to the Rare Book Collection of the O. Meredith Wilson Library of the University of Minnesota. I would especially like to thank John Jensen of the Rare Book Collection for all his help and good advice. Professor Harry Roe of the Centre for Medieval Studies of the University of Toronto has also gone out of his way to assist me with the problem of illustrations, and I would like to thank him here, together with the helpful staff of the Poculi Ludique Societas of the same university.

My mentors in the fields of medieval drama and stage history, Professor John Leyerle of the University of Toronto and Dr. Jeanne T. Newlin of the Harvard Theatre Collection, have offered me continuing support and much kind encouragement, as has my distinguished colleague Professor Harrison T. Meserole of the World Shakespeare Bibliography project at Texas A & M University. Finally, I would like to thank Professor Gwynne Evans of Harvard University, who introduced me to Restoration drama in his seminar on the age of Dryden. None of these eminent scholars and dedicated teachers should be held responsible for any idiosyncratic opinions, errors, or oversights that may have crept into this volume, but I do want to thank them for much inspiration.

CHAPTER I

INTRODUCTION

The Oxford English Dictionary defines *drama* as "a composition in prose or verse, adapted to be acted upon a stage, in which a story is related by means of dialogue and action, and is represented with accompanying gesture, costume, and scenery, as in real life." This definition identifies the elements that set drama apart from all other branches of literature. Drama unquestionably qualifies as a form of literature. Without it English literature would shrink beyond recognition. The written text or script stands as a primary component, the most permanent phase of the evanescent dramatic event. Yet drama is, with few exceptions, written to be performed. That purpose inspires the writer and shapes every aspect of the work of dramatic literature. The written form is inert, perhaps tangential. The stage, the actors and their audiences, speech and action, costume, scenery, and music bring the drama to life.

Drama is the most composite and transitory of the arts. No two performances can be identical. Time and chance constantly enforce changes, impossible to record but perceptible to every witness. This temporal variance helps to lend the theater its inherent fascination. Its complexity and continual change present the historian of the drama with immense challenges. How can a single work of art that implicates poetry and prose, speech and song, music and dance, art and architecture be adequately represented in an expository prose description? Only with extreme difficulty. The multidimensional nature of dramatic art creates many of the problems that perplex the students of that art.

Initially, drama springs from powerful, primitive human impulses. Impersonation, the temporary assumption of the identity of another being, is its central element—a spontaneous, irresistibly appealing feature of child's play through the ages. Impersonation is a way of expressing the self and exploring the outer world, a tool for discerning the relationship between self and world by bringing them into conjunction on a hypothetical plane. Drama appears in the most solemn human rituals early in the history of civilization, adding a new depth of experience to religious ceremonies and festivals. At the same time, drama retains its status among the most frivolous human activities. The play element helps to render dramatic activity perennial in human history. It also brings drama under attack from critics of all periods who feel that human life should be relentlessly serious, and who react against dramatic play as aberrant or deceptive. As a literary form, the drama is acutely responsive to social and political stimuli, making it perhaps the most topical of all literary genres. Still, the crudest drama often contrives to express the timeless concerns of its human creators.

The critical history of British drama to 1660 presents the same basic challenges as any history of drama. It also offers its own local difficulties. Balancing the components of drama so as to give a fair picture is especially important in presenting the rich literary, visual, architectural, and musical evidence of the fourteenth through seventeenth centuries in Britain. The dramatic text must remain the central piece of evidence, but the text should function as a guide to visualizing the complete production, not as a self-sufficient work of art. At the same time, the importance of the literary artifact must not be slighted.

When does the history of drama in Britain begin? With the first play or with the first theater? Each is a landmark, but neither marks the beginning of dramatic activity in the British Isles, which must go back far beyond recorded history. The trail vanishes in the mists of archaeological conjecture. The Roman theaters, the first major complex of public stages in Britain, offer tangible architectural evidence of drama in Britain from the first to the fourth centuries, but evidence of actual dramatic performances is almost nonexistent. Specific evidence of performances remains fragmentary until the tenth century, when the appearance of Latin liturgical drama coincided with the monastic reform movement that produced the *Regularis Concordia*. The first biblical plays in vernacular languages associated with England do not appear until the twelfth century, and then their language is French. The first unmistakably Middle English dramatic fragments belong to the early fourteenth century. Under these circumstances it seems appropriate to devote the second chapter of this study to the emergence of drama in Britain and to reexamine the early, fragmentary evidence.

If the history of British drama in this period must begin by struggling to find its beginning point, its conclusion presents a different problem. The restoration of Charles II in 1660 brought with it the triumph of new forms of drama and theater, tied to European neoclassical aesthetics. This direction is unquestionably new in British dramatic history. Here the student must decide how drastic the change is and what survived of the earlier native tradition.

Geographically it is important to remember that British drama before 1660 was not limited to London and its environs; throughout the period surveyed in this volume, key dramatic events took place across Britain. A compact study of this kind cannot be comprehensive, but it should aim for representative coverage of the territory.

Within these limits of time and space the historian of drama must discuss a wide range of dramatic literature, extending well beyond the categories defined by Aristotle or the classic plays of the Elizabethans. Students of early British drama must become acquainted with unfamiliar shaping principles that lent the native dramatic tradition its distinctive character. The calendars of the church and the agricultural year powerfully influenced the dramatic forms that developed in response to specific celebrations. While it is neither appropriate nor desirable for a compact overview of this type to claim to cover everything, it should at least essay to be inclusive or representative. This study focuses, then, on dramatic literature in the context of its performance, as the product of individual artists at specific places and times, but also as part of the overall history of drama in Britain.

THE STUDY OF EARLY BRITISH DRAMA: RECEIVED IDEAS

When, as in John Dryden's "Essay of Dramatic Poesy" of 1668, Restoration students of the theater looked back at the dramatic history of Britain, they saw the drama as an ancient, classical art that reemerged, inspired by Greek and Roman models, in the England of Elizabeth. Its major British exponents were Shakespeare, Jonson, Beaumont, and

Fletcher, playwrights marred only by their lack of courtly polish and failure to adhere strictly to neoclassical principles of design. "The incomparable Shakespeare" is already firmly ensconced on his pedestal. As for "all those credulous and doting ages from Aristotle to us," they are cheerfully dismissed from the minds of Dryden and his friends. The history of British drama, as of 1668, is short and sweet.[1]

Indeed, the relics of medieval drama that had survived the Reformation received little scholarly attention before the medieval revival of the nineteenth century. Dryden's adjectives, "credulous" and "doting," reflect prejudices against the thought and culture of the Catholic Middle Ages born of more than a century of conflict between Catholic and Protestant. The linguistic unfamiliarity of medieval Latin, French, and Old and Middle English, the technical difficulty of reading manuscript sources, and the deliberate or inadvertent destruction of most of those sources all combined to alienate the English-speaking world from its late-antique and medieval roots. The truncated outline of the history of drama implied in Dryden's essay satisfied most scholars through the romantic period; it retains its popularity as a system of received ideas still afloat in programs of general education.

With the rediscovery of the Middle Ages, propelled by Horace Walpole and later by Sir Walter Scott, came a new interest in early British literature. The wandering minstrel, Anglo-Saxon scop, or Celtic bard became an alluring figure, and strenuous efforts were made to provide new editions of medieval texts that survived in manuscript. The Towneley Plays were first edited for the Surtees Society by James Gordon and Joseph Hunter in 1836, the earliest complete edition of any medieval play cycle. Performance records began to be ferreted out as matters of antiquarian interest.

Critical expertise in the interpretation of these medieval dramatic records was much slower to develop. David Mills dates the beginning of scholarly analytical criticism of medieval drama to the mid-1960s. This pattern contrasts strikingly with the history of the study of the text of Shakespeare, which had been a lively enterprise ever since Nicholas Rowe's scholarly 1709 edition of the plays. Shakespeare's contemporaries had also benefited from his popularity, while Shakespeare's Jacobean and Caroline successors were somewhat less fortunate in their critics. Stanley Wells identifies A. C. Bradley's *Shakespearean Tragedy* of 1904 as

4

marking an important shift from literary to academic analysis of Shakespeare. G. Blakemore Evans stresses the importance of the bibliographical techniques developed by scholars like R. B. McKerrow, A. W. Pollard, and J. Dover Wilson in the first decade of the twentieth century for the establishment of texts along scientific principles.[2] While their work was centered on the Elizabethan and Jacobean periods, their basic ideas influenced editors of earlier and later texts as well.

When E. K. Chambers published *The Medieval Stage,* a clear chronological pattern had been established to explain the history of the drama in Britain. This scheme seems to have been an early product of the persistent desire to make the study of literature scientific. Elaborated by the Victorians, its salient features are noticeable as early as Sir Walter Scott's *Essay on Drama* of 1819, written for the *Encyclopaedia Britannica.* This evolutionary view of dramatic history in Britain traces the native drama back to a single cell, the *Quem quaeritis* trope recorded in the *Regularis Concordia* of ca. 965–75, the earliest extant dramatic text of the British Middle Ages. Before this time, no doubt, there were folk plays, and before them the decadent death struggles of Roman drama. But from the initial dialogue and impersonation interjected by the *Quem quaeritis* into the liturgy for Easter Sunday stems full-fledged liturgical drama. From then on the history of British drama becomes the history of the emancipation of the stage from the control of the church, six centuries of "progressive secularization." According to this model, liturgical drama was first expelled to the churchyard, then relegated to the control of the trade guilds. Morality plays like *Everyman* represent a further estrangement of drama from ritual. This theory of progressive secularization renders the medieval mystery play and morality play obsolete, each in its turn, to be replaced by a classically inspired Renaissance professional theater whose culminating point is Shakespeare. From this pinnacle the drama descends into the decadence of James I's reign and the emasculation of his son Charles I's before plunging into the abyss of the Puritan interregnum. The closing of the theaters in 1642 by parliamentary order fittingly ends the story.[3]

This well-established view of the development of drama in Britain has all the geometry of a triangular plot diagram: expository action beginning slowly, rising to a climax, and then descending to its conclusion. Its parallels with the biological evolution and extinction of a species have proven similarly satisfying to the nineteenth- and twentieth-century intelligence. It is no surprise that this model has entrenched itself so firmly in British literary history.

Since the late 1950s a series of challenges has shaken the established pattern. New evidence and ways of examining evidence, together with new critical viewpoints, have rearranged the history of drama. A narrative account of British drama up to 1660 written in 1989 must differ in many respects from accounts of 1909, perhaps most in its basic overview of the subject. So many received ideas have been called into question that the terrain now looks much different than it did even fifty years ago. Scholars must explore newly available evidence and reevaluate older concepts. Dismissed until recently as a period that produced no masterpieces of dramatic art, the Middle Ages have increasingly been recognized as a period of great theatrical inventiveness and sophistication. A new understanding of the artistic principles that shape the surviving works allows today's readers to appreciate the dramatic power of the Corpus Christi cycles and the morality plays, along with that of the liturgical drama and court and civic pageantry. Medievalists no longer remark defensively that the playwrights of the English Middle Ages produced great theater if not major works of dramatic literature; these dramas are both. The growing interest in early plays on the part of contemporary directors underlines affinities between the symbolic staging of medieval drama and experimental modern theater. Appreciating medieval British drama as vital in its own right, we also recognize the intimacy of its connection with the Elizabethan stage.

It is currently postulated that the medieval liturgical drama, the scriptural drama of the clerics, and the moralities developed along their own lines, each separate from the Corpus Christi cycles and from secular entertainment. This model replaces the evolutionary, single-track image of medieval dramatic history, wherein one genre succeeded another, with a series of parallel dramatic developments, interlaced like plot lines in a thirteenth-century romance, or like a bundle of fiber-optic telephone cables.

In recent years the Middle Ages have assumed special importance in the history of stagecraft. David Bevington and others have demonstrated the ways in which medieval dramaturgy shaped the early Tudor and Elizabethan theater's sense of time, space, form, and dramatic structure. The same pioneering scholars have stressed the continuing importance of the hall as a place of performance, and of symbolic spaces and visual emblems as key features of staging from the Middle Ages into the seventeenth century. A new perspective has also changed our view of the end of medieval religious theater. The Corpus Christi cycle is seen today not as decayed or obsolete but at the height of its popularity in the mid-sixteenth century.[4] The Coventry plays were last performed in 1580, four years after Burbage's Theatre was erected in Shoreditch. This energetic revision of medieval and Renaissance dramatic history automatically reshapes the history of British drama.

A new vision of the foundations of British dramatic tradition also gives us a new standpoint from which to reassess the Elizabethan and Jacobean periods. Shakespeare and his contemporaries become the heirs of a lively native tradition. The humanists' redefinition of drama along classical lines still registers its influence but can no longer obliterate the often contradictory British heritage of theater and dramaturgy.

A similar process of revision affects our estimation of drama after Shakespeare, of Jacobean and Caroline drama in particular. Martin Butler has been most influential in calling for a new look at dramatic literature on the eve of the English civil war. As in the study of the medieval stage, the evolutionary approach is coming under attack here. In response to his provocative reevaluation, an effort is now being made to suppress hindsight and see the politically active authors of Charles I's reign—Brome, Massinger, Shirley, Davenant—with fresh eyes. Butler argues that the 1642 closing of the theaters was announced as a temporary measure, one of many cancellations of performances in moments of crisis recorded since the thirteenth century. The eighteen years of the Puritan interregnum also proved a less complete theatrical blackout than is often imagined. Surreptitious productions, arrests of actors, and Davenant's successful redefinition of his entertainments to evade the law all testify to a compulsion on the part of players and audiences to continue. At the same time, these reflections should not lead us to neglect the power of the antitheatrical tradition from the Roman Empire to 1660. Suspicions of drama remained ingrained in Christian thought; Tertullian, the original archenemy of the Roman stage, found able successors among the disciples of John Wyclif and Martin Luther. Antitheatrical critics offer valuable evidence of the role of drama in British society and of the tension between its advocates and its opponents.[5]

DRAMA IN BRITISH SOCIETY AND POLITICS

Drama has always responded with alacrity to the currents of social and political change. The history of drama is inseparable from the intellectual, political, social, and economic histories of late antique, medieval, and Renaissance Britain. Reined in by state censorship, the drama of the Roman empire intensified sociopolitical conflicts through its inevitable gravitation toward the forbidden ground of satire: the comic Christian became a staple of late Roman farce. The social role of the stage in remote provinces like Britannia echoed that in Rome, Constantinople, or Gaul. A form of government-supported entertainment that still maintained clear religious connections, late Roman drama satisfied the public's need for spectacular amusement, often cruel or obscene, often delicately sophisticated. On the available evidence, Roman Britons were more likely to cheer a gladiatorial combat or a bull baiting than a troupe of traveling mimes or a revival of a comedy by Plautus. The late Roman stage's probable lack of literary distinction has always disappointed its students. Still, its social and political importance should be stressed. Attendance at the local theater or amphitheater was a fact of civic life; performances brought the community together and advertised the benificence of the town authorities who subsidized the production. As theatrical buildings fell into disuse across the province, it proved a disquieting symptom of the breakdown of Roman civilization in Britain.[6]

In the age of transition following the gradual withdrawal of Roman troops from Britain, it is almost impossible to trace the bands of traveling mimes, clowns, and musicians who are presumed to have transmitted the Roman theatrical tradition to the performers of the Middle Ages. We can hypothesize that they existed, as one factor in the preservation of our Greco-Roman dramatic heritage. Some scholars, like Allardyce Nicoll, have gone much further in their re-creations of these troupes and their activities. But the rise of drama within Christian ritual is a much more visible element in the history of the early medieval stage. Specialists insist properly that liturgical plays should be seen in the context of the entire church calendar, the annual sequence of celebrations evoking the lives of Jesus and the saints. This succession of events, superimposed on the preexistent agricultural calendar, still lends the Christian year its own dramatic unity. It is also important to remember that, for the Anglo-Saxons and many of the Normans who conquered them, vernacular poetry was composed primarily for public performance. The performer might be a professional poet and singer or an embarrassed amateur like the cowherd Caedmon. In either case the dramatic element in what we now consider non-dramatic literature demands attention. It could even be argued that most Old English poetry should properly be considered a form of drama.[7]

The lack of evidence makes it difficult to speculate about the nature of twelfth- and thirteenth-century British drama, let alone its social role. Liturgical plays continued to be produced in churches across the British Isles, within and beyond monastic communities. Biblical drama was also performed outside the church, both in Latin and in French, usually by clerics and often for lay audiences. The lost play of St. Katherine and the later surviving plays of Adam and of the Resurrection belong to this phase of dramatic activity. Indications of court revels and civic pageants begin to appear, testifying to interest in a variety of dramatic entertainments. Imitations of Latin comedy evidently amused some late twelfth-century courtiers and scholars. While it is difficult to reconstruct the performances of the traveling entertainers of this period, it seems possible that they included short farces like *Dame Sirith*. Village folk plays continue to disturb the ecclesiastical authorities. All of these hints share the haphazard, maddening charm of wildflowers appearing in the lawn. Dramatic events crop up unexpectedly in chronicle histories, account books, episcopal regulations. They are invariably suggestive and appealing, but difficult to connect in a coherent pattern. Dramatic activities were familiar, pervasive, and sometimes considered improper. Identifiable dramatic texts may have remained part of an oral or impromptu theater, for the most part beneath the dignity or expense of a permanent record on parchment. Equally, some texts have no doubt been lost.[8]

Certain factors that hold true for the entire period up to 1660 do seem to be developing by the twelfth century. Amateur drama appears as a key element in popular and aristocratic recreation, appropriate to festive occasions. Wickham and other scholars stress the calendar as the key to the development of dramatic genres, with the festivities of Christmas and the New Year emerging as the location for courtly revels, and the old planting and harvest celebrations demanding dramatic recognition across social ranks. Professional drama gravitates into the hands of versatile, mobile groups of entertainers who are primarily musicians but also on occasion dancers, acrobats, storytellers, actors, puppeteers, and animal trainers. With the attachment of performers to particular noble patrons, more than evident by the turn of the thirteenth century, the ground is prepared for the professional companies of the age of Shakespeare. We also observe the emergence of the clerically trained playwright and performer, sometimes a student and sometimes even a nun or abbess. The first identifiable woman playwright in Britain was Katherine of Sutton, abbess of Barking in 1363–76. Finally, political pageants intermingle royal households and civic authorities. At the end of the thirteenth century Edward I demonstrated his appreciation of the prestige value of pageantry in international politics; the records of his court festivities also reveal an enjoyment of entertainment and entertainers on a truly royal scale.[9]

From the fourteenth through the sixteenth century we find ourselves on surer ground because of the increasing volume of surviving evidence. Haphazard events resolve themselves into clearer pictures. On the political level we can see princes exploiting drama to enhance their own policies while entertaining their households. Edward III and Richard II were particularly gifted in self-dramatization. Sydney Anglo has studied the Tudors' development of this medium of political expression, which continues through the most theatrical cult of Elizabeth into the elaborate court performances of the Stuarts. Drama retains its celebratory function in amateur and professional activities, extending from domestic games, mummings, and revels to large-scale public drama. Drama also functions as an international medium of cultural exchange and diplomatic communication through tournaments and dramatic displays for the reception of foreign visitors. Thus in the course of two centuries drama became a vehicle for religious, political, and social comment across the British Isles. By the later fourteenth century the governing bodies of provincial centers like York and Coventry had discovered in the Corpus Christi cycles of mystery plays an effective form of communal activity and a powerful symbol of corporate identity, economic power, and shared faith. On the village level, companies of amateur or semiprofessional players might visit neighboring parishes as a fund-raising activity, perhaps with a religious play, perhaps with a play of Robin Hood. Towns, aristocrats, prelates, and members of the gentry found it desirable to retain professional players in their service. The popularity of drama in all these social and political settings, from the individual household through the larger community, allowed it to play a unifying role in society. It was also, potentially, a powerful subversive force. Assassins festively disguised as mummers lurked in the vicinity of Henry IV. Not surprisingly, ecclesiastical and secular authorities attempted to control the dramatic impulses of society at large. After 1530 regulations became rapidly more stringent. Scripts were censored, the content of performances specified, theaters closed, and actors and playwrights imprisoned. The history of British theatrical legislation bears witness to the governing powers' serious regard for drama as a social and political force.[10]

The religious drama of the Middle Ages celebrated a shared faith, defining the community of believers and excluding outsiders. With the Reformation there entered a Protestant polemical drama, championed by John Bale. As successive British monarchs through the sixteenth and seventeenth centuries changed their religious and political orientations and as their subjects debated their own position within the new system, the plays of professional companies and public pageantry offered a flexible and sophisticated medium for discussion. The effect of theater as moral experience also created controversy. Performance records confirm the drama's attraction for audiences across Britain. At the same time, official and unofficial complaints indicate that many serious-minded Britons continued to view drama as pernicious. The ancient antitheatrical debate remained lively up to the Restoration, when it merely entered a new stage.[11]

THEATERS IN BRITAIN, 100–1660

ARCHITECTURE AND STAGING. One of the most powerful concepts for the modern student of theater is the notion that
theatrical architecture or space conditions dramatic form. The history
of theatrical architecture in Britain begins imposingly with the Roman theaters and amphitheaters of the first through the fourth century. First timber, later in some cases masonry structures, they might
accommodate up to eight thousand spectators. The theaters, D-
shaped, with provisions for a curtain slot and stage buildings behind
the playing area, were better adapted for dramatic performances, but
like the circular Roman amphitheaters they might accommodate pantomime, religious ceremonies, and military or gladiatorial games
with equal facility. In this adaptable quality they foreshadow the
Elizabethan public playhouses, the next major group of specialized
public theatrical buildings in Britain.[12]

The chief theaters of the earlier Middle Ages were halls and
churches. Liturgical drama through the Reformation was sensitively
oriented within the symbolic space of the church building. Indoor
secular drama through 1660 was most often performed in halls: in
palaces, manors, church houses with upper rooms, guildhalls, refecto-
ries of monastic establishments, schools, universities, or the London
Inns of Court. Halls might be constructed with specialized features to
facilitate entertainments. A raised minstrel gallery and a platform for
the high table were both useful to performers. The ability to control
audience access to such enclosed interior spaces seems to have proved
especially attractive to professional companies. The indoor "private"
theaters of the Elizabethan and Jacobean periods were hall theaters,
first set up within the shells of the Blackfriars and Whitefriars religious
houses.[13]

Medieval outdoor theater took place in a wide variety of locations.
Stages might be improvised in fields and gardens, in the streets and
market squares. Two basic schemes of staging predominated. Pageant
wagons seem to have been used in processional presentations of certain civic cycles, notably at York and Coventry. A series of wagons,
often mounted with elaborate scenery or machinery, carried players
through the city, with designated stops to allow performance of each

pageant before a new audience. Alternatively, open-air performances might take place in defined, often circular playing areas, with strategically placed scaffolds as raised stages for key groups of characters. The celebrated staging diagram for the morality play *The Castle of Perseverance* indicates a staging arrangement of this type; the Cornish *Ordinalia* and the N-town passion play call for similar presentations. Informal booth stages of boards raised above ground level on barrels or some other type of support, backed by a curtained enclosure, may have allowed smaller scale performances at fairgrounds and other temporary locations. In any outdoor performance, controlling access and collecting fees from the audience created major difficulties for the theatrical entrepreneur. Plays supported by towns, trade guilds, or religious confraternities had other economic problems. For the professional company the ideal solution was to find an enclosed space, preferably a weatherproof indoor facility. Failing this venue, an outdoor enclosure of some type helped to insure that only paying members of the public could see the performance. The architecture of the London playhouse of the age of Elizabeth is in part a response to this issue.[14]

Much attention has been focused on the architecture of one particular form of British theater, the public Elizabethan playhouse. The history of these structures begins with the construction of Burbage's Theatre in 1567 and ends with the disappearance of the Red Bull around 1664. Of the eight or so open-air London playhouses constructed during the reigns of Elizabeth I and James I, the most celebrated is of course the Globe, where most of Shakespeare's plays were first performed. The origins, structure, interior arrangements, decor, and mode of operation of the Elizabethan playhouses have proven a matter of controversy. Only one visual representation of the interior of any Elizabethan playhouse, Johannes de Witt's 1596 sketch of the Swan Theatre has been identified. Otherwise researchers depend on financial records and deductions from the plays themselves. It is clear that each theater had its own distinctive features. Modern scholars' reconstructions also vary noticeably one from another. The recent London excavations on the site of the Rose playhouse promise to shed light on the design of at least one playhouse. Still, the basic configuration of the Elizabethan public theaters seems clear. A circular arena at the center of the structure, with its platform stage, was surrounded by three galleries of tiered seats for affluent spectators; less affluent members of the public stood in the central arena on three sides of the raised stage. The Fortune's platform stage was twenty-seven and a half feet deep by forty-three feet wide, and probably stood five feet above ground level. The stage was sometimes set up on trestles so that it could be removed to allow bear or bull baiting in the central area. All or part of the stage was protected from the elements by a projecting roof, the "heavens," supported by pillars. At the rear of the stage some type of "inner stage" or "discovery space," screened by a curtain, could be opened to reveal hidden persons or objects. Behind that was the actor's "tiring house," or dressing room. Actors came onstage through doors at the left and right. An acting space on the upper level, equipped with windows, allowed characters to appear "above." Higher still was accommodation for musicians and special effects. As many as three thousand spectators might attend each performance. As with all open-air theaters, the Elizabethan playhouse's usefulness was limited by the weather.[15]

Overall, the history of British drama to 1660 emphasizes the importance of the hall as a primary location for dramatic events. The hall did not fade into obscurity with the appearance of the public playhouses; it would dominate British theater design into the future. The study of drama in the chapters to come reflects the shaping power of the physical space upon the performance it contains.

SCENERY AND COSTUME. When Roman drama was enacted in the six known public theaters of the province of Britannia, it took place before a fixed stage building, perhaps representing for its audiences a row of town residences or a mansion. The amphitheaters lacked this particular amenity; theatrical performances were staged in the central area, perhaps with the aid of temporary platforms. Aside from evidence of the raised wooden stage itself, fragmentary buildings, and indications of a slot for a curtain at St. Albans, few clues survive of Roman scenic technique in Britain. The most striking article of theatrical costume would have been the tragic or comic mask: eight examples have been recovered at various archaeological sites across Britain, the three fragmentary masks of grotesque old men salvaged in London being the most identifiable in character.[16]

Any traveling mimes who survived the collapse of Roman authority in the West necessarily developed a portable dramatic tradition. Its

TECHNICAL COLLEGE OF THE LOWCOUNTRY
LEARNING RESOURCES CENTER
POST OFFICE BOX 1288
BEAUFORT, SOUTH CAROLINA 29901-1288

scenery and costumes, like its drama, have so far proven irrecoverable.[17]

The earliest liturgical plays rapidly developed scenic effects and costumes to designate performers and symbolic locations within the larger setting of the church building. Pamela Sheingorn has studied the development of the Easter Sepulchre in England, a temporary or permanent re-creation of Jesus' tomb at Jerusalem that was often used in dramatizations of the Deposition and Resurrection. The Easter Sepulchre became a popular feature of English churches, with important dramatic functions. The *Regularis Concordia* Easter rites use a "likeness of a sepulchre" on the altar. Into this space the cross wrapped in a linen cloth, a symbolic representation of the body of Jesus, is reverently placed. The brothers who take part in the *Quem quaeritis* dialogue at the tomb wear ecclesiastical vestments: the angel wears an alb and carries a palm branch, while the three Marys wear copes and carry thuribles with incense. On finding the tomb empty they display the linen shroud to the congregation as visual evidence of the Resurrection. This austere, symbolic enactment of the scene uses familiar ecclesiastical costumes and properties to create a dignified visual effect.[18]

By the twelfth century British theater had clearly become more visually elaborate. The *Ordo representacionis Adae* (known popularly as the *Jeu d'Adam* or *Mistère d'Adam;* in English "Ceremony for Representing Adam") specifies multiple locations necessary for the production, with an eye to visual hierarchy and scenic impact. The Garden of Eden is a raised space on the church steps, enclosed with curtains to represent a wall. Above this wall appear the shoulders of Adam and Eve and the trees, leaves, and fruit of the garden. The production employs the church itself as the dwelling of God and the choir as commentator on the action. Events also take place on an intermediate level, possibly a platform, and on an open playing area below the steps. Devils run across this space into the audience and drag characters off to "the gates of hell," equipped with materials to produce smoke and pots to clash at appropriate times. These multiple settings confront the audience with the cosmic geography of the play and invest a familiar locale with profound dramatic significance. Costumes for this production are no longer purely ecclesiastical: God wears a dalmatic and a stole, but Adam and Eve appear in secular costume.[19]

Records of the Corpus Christi cycles and of court and town pageantry from the fourteenth through the sixteenth centuries testify to
the resourcefulness and sophistication of the artisans who created these
impressive spectacles. These documents reflect the development of an
extensive system of visual conventions as an important theatrical
means of communication. A series of compact scenes might be poised
on a string of pageant wagons or deployed over an open playing area,
recalling contemporary maps of the universe. Alternatively, in the case
of a royal entry, the scenes might appear along the path of a procession, so that the visiting dignitary passes through a succession of
varied settings. Even where scenery apparently remained simple, in
the portable productions of small professional troupes, visual effects
invariably played a key role in staging. The *Interlude of the Clerk and the
Girl* (*Interludium de clerico et puella*) requires a weeping dog; the student
moral play *Mankind* focuses special attention on the fantastic fashions
of the vices and on a stupendous devil's mask. Guild records and
financial accounts of court pageants both stress the importance of
visual effects in the British theater of the later Middle Ages and the
early Tudor period.[20]

The visual resources of Elizabethan theater have been much debated. It is often assumed that Shakespeare and his contemporaries
relied little on scenery, that in fact Elizabethan professional productions
made up in verbal splendor for their drab appearance. But Glynne
Wickham in particular has attacked the concept of a spartan Elizabethan
theater. He stresses the role of the court Revels Office as a source of
scenic devices for professional productions at court as well as for its own
masques and tournaments. Even in the public theaters it seems clear that
lively scenic effects were both possible and desirable. Costume was
unquestionably expensive and important: in 1602 a black velvet gown
cost the theatrical entrepreneur Philip Henslowe more than the script of
Thomas Heywood's *A Woman Killed with Kindness*.[21]

With the advent of Inigo Jones as a designer of court masques in
1604, new techniques of staging and a new visual philosophy of the
theater appeared in England. Wickham discusses the collision of the
new representational stage and the old emblematic drama of poetry
and symbol, an argument that found expression in the conflict between Jones and his collaborator Ben Jonson. On the technical side

Jones's skill in Italian scenic innovation brought the proscenium arch, framing exquisitely detailed stage pictures, to his English court audience. Revolving screens and sliding panels arranged in perspective allowed as many as five scene changes in a single performance, while turntables rotated three-dimensional scenic devices before the eyes of the spectators. This dazzling array of special effects was complemented by elaborate costumes, also of Jones's design. Many of these technical developments found their way onto the professional stage in the course of the seventeenth century: Jones's work prepared the way for the Restoration theater. It also reflected and supported new audience expectations for visual brilliance and representational specificity. Martin Butler's research suggests that a sizable popular audience continued to demand conservative Elizabethan stage conventions at least through 1642. At the same time the sumptuous scenery of court drama created new expectations, especially for the indoor theaters of the later seventeenth century.[22]

BRITISH AUDIENCES AND THEIR CHARACTER. The British audience has remained essential in the development of drama in Britain throughout its history. Drama is normally written to be performed, most often as the work of authors acutely alert to the nature and taste of their specific audiences. Audiences in Roman Britannia might include the local officials who sponsored the drama; it is fair to assume that the aedile Marcus Ulpius Januarius attended performances on the stage he contributed to his town of Petuaria, if only from a sense of his official duty. He might have been the most prominent or affluent member of the audience, but the performance was not staged for his exclusive enjoyment as much as for the community at large. While private indoor performances would be for a socially limited group at a banquet or other celebration, the public theater catered to the citizenry of major provincial centers from Kent to Yorkshire, en masse. While we have no evidence that favorite players attracted followings in Britain as they did in Rome or Constantinople, gladiators evidently did; this allegiance suggests that minor segments of the provincial populations may have been just as fanatical about their entertainment at some of the powerful theatrical factions of the major Roman cities.

Throughout the Middle Ages the liturgical drama not only took place within male, female, or double monastic communities, but was also enacted by members of the clergy for lay congregations. Likewise, amateur village, town, or court dramas of celebration—May games or Christmas revels—brought together the members of specific communities as participants and spectators.

The records of the later Middle Ages bear witness to the wide appeal of the theater for both popular and elite audiences, and often for mixed social groups. Street theater gave the widest access to dramatic events. Royal personages attended Corpus Christi cycle performances—Elizabeth I inspected four of the Coventry pageants in 1567—but so did the dregs of society; maintaining civic decorum preoccupied the organizers. A similar degree of access allowed wide audiences to glimpse civic pageantry free of charge while simultaneously stimulating local economies. Exclusive events were also staged among the upper classes: small-scale interludes flourished between courses at banquets, and private parties conducted mummings for their own amusement. Schoolboys and university scholars experimented with both classical and devotional theater. The exceptional hermit or anchoress might be denied any glimpse of drama; the more strenuous followers of Wyclif might deplore attendance at religious or secular plays as woefully inappropriate to a serious-minded Christian. But the majority of medieval and early Tudor Britons could freely experience and often participate in many forms of drama.[23]

The debate over the Elizabethan audience continues. In 1941 Alfred Harbage describes Shakespeare's public as made up largely of London citizens, workers, and tradesmen. Ann Jennalie Cook's 1981 study concludes instead that Elizabethan theaters attracted the privileged: members of the peerage, the gentry, merchants, lawyers, clergymen, yeomen. She rejects the generally accepted distinction between patrons of the more expensive indoor theaters and of the public playhouses as another Restoration misconception about the Elizabethan stage. In 1984 Martin Butler retorted that plays were an inexpensive and tempting form of entertainment for a wide range of Londoners up to 1642, one that spectators were reluctant to forgo under the Commonwealth. By contrast, the Restoration theater became much more exclusive. Butler points out that while London in the 1630s supported six playhouses, during the Restoration it struggled to maintain two. Different theaters, as Butler observes, attracted different audiences. Court drama remained the most exclusive; the elegant Blackfriars theater under the King's Men came a close second. The Red Bull and the Fortune amused vulgar audiences in the 1630s, as did their rival the Curtain, described in 1613 as "an infamous place in which no good citizen or gentleman would show his face." Other stages, like the Globe, brought together elite and popular spectators. Within the theaters these groups were divided geographically and economically. In the playhouses the privileged spectator took his or her seat in the gallery and the underprivileged stood in the yard surrounding the stage. At the indoor theaters the positions were reversed, with the elite close upon the stage and the less affluent to the rear. The need to hold the interest of a heterogeneous audience, made up of courtiers and brewers in varying proportions, helped to lend the drama of later sixteenth- and seventeenth-century England its richness and complexity.[24]

THE SOCIAL STATUS OF THE ACTING PROFESSION. Roman professional actors were often slaves, actually owned by their troupe's producer. The actor's social status was only marginally higher than the actress's—she was almost invariably a prostitute as well as a player. The actress or dancer Verecunda is the only Roman player whose name appears on a British inscription. Imperial legislation for a time forbade men of senatorial rank to marry actresses. Actors might also be wildly popular and affluent figures, flamboyant stars, the objects of popular cults across an imperial touring circuit. Nonetheless, an actor could become a Christian only by renouncing the theater, as a few did. In the late Republic an equestrian playwright was degraded by being forced to appear onstage in his own play. The theatrical dabbling of aristocratic amateurs like Nero did nothing to elevate the status of the actor, and late Roman intellectuals seem to have found drama unattractive as a literary medium.

Distinction needs to be made among professional, semiprofessional, and amateur performers during the fourteenth through sixteenth centuries—a distinction more evident in social status than in skill or experience. The players of the Corpus Christi cycles were often expensive professional performers, whether actors or musicians. Small professional troupes of the later Middle Ages sought respectability through engagements as liveried members of noble households;

and although the professionalization of the stage increased at a steady pace, they held essentially the same position when Shakespeare became a member of Lord Pembroke's Men. They were still nomadic; M. C. Bradbrook's *The Rise of the Common Player* credits the London theaters with raising the status of the players, allowing them to attain social respectability and in some famous cases the status of gentleman. Like Shakespeare and his brother, many players were sons of tradesmen. James Burbage, the builder of the theater, was a carpenter before he joined Leicester's Men. Edward Alleyn's father was an innkeeper. Marlowe sprang from a Canterbury family of tanners and shoemakers. From start to finish of the period covered in this volume, acting remained a "base trade," from which only a few talented performers managed to leap to more privileged strata of society.[25]

THE DEVELOPMENT OF ACTING STYLES ON THE BRITISH STAGE

Across so many years of the history of British drama one would expect acting styles to vary along with the tastes, cultural backgrounds, and training of actors. No style is likely to dominate any era to the exclusion of all others, though styles may be limited to particular troupes or genres or attain differing degrees of prestige. Acting technique involves stage movement and business, vocal production and direction of speech. We clearly know more about such matters regarding the seventeenth century than we do regarding the first.[26]

What little we do know of the late Roman stage suggests that broad physical comedy retained a following, sometimes in improvised farces, sometimes in revivals of earlier plays. While the popularity of outdoor theaters and masks suggests that declamation and the large gesture might have been mandatory, evidence for indoor performances reveals Roman pantomime as a refined, balletic art, perhaps more dance than drama. A strong pornographic element in dramatic spectacle invariably scandalized the imperial moralist.

Liturgical drama like that of the *Regularis Concordia* demands restraint in impersonation, to protect the decorum of the ceremony. The twelfth-century stage directions of the *Ordo representacionis Adae* require precise enunciation, close attention to the pace of the speeches,

and appropriate gestures, sometimes formal and dignified and sometimes exuberant. Adam and Eve throw themselves to the ground in an
agony of grief; Cain rushes at Abel like a madman.

As the Corpus Christi cycles develop in the later fourteenth century, regulations setting high standards for their performance appear
in municipal sources, together with fines for substandard work. The
best-known references to acting style in the cycle plays record the
ranting of villains like Herod and Pilate, flamboyant declamatory characterizations geared to street theater. Yet the cycle plays demand a
wide range of acting styles, from the dignified eloquence of God
through the comic verisimilitude of the aged wrights Noah and Joseph. The appeal of slapstick is evident on more than one occasion, as
in the Croxton *Play of the Sacrament*'s doctor scene and in the antics of
the "vices" in *Mankind*. The juxtaposition of solemn exaltation and
sheer "game" lends many late medieval plays their special dramatic
sophistication.

Varied styles of acting seem also to have flourished side by side in
the theaters of the late sixteenth and earlier seventeenth centuries.
Analysis here is limited by the available evidence, as Daniel Seltzer
notes. Some critics have maintained that most Elizabethan acting
should be described as formal; others, that its main effects would have
been perceived as naturalistic. Edward Alleyn and the Admiral's Men
are associated with a declamatory style, ideal for Marlowe's thunder-
ing tragedies. Richard Burbage expended similar histrionic energy in
roles like Othello and Richard III, but seems to have mastered a
greater range of nuances. The boy companies, like the Children of
Paul's or the Children of the Chapel Royal at Blackfriars, seem to have
cultivated complex shifts from naturalistic to burlesque styles. The
very use of boy actors for female roles in adult acting companies left its
mark on the theater of this period. On the Jacobean and Caroline
stages of the court, the private theaters, and the public playhouses,
extremes of style crystallized. Popular taste seems to have approved
the broadest Elizabethan acting techniques as late as the surreptitious
"drolls" of the Commonwealth. Simultaneously the continental taste
of the court supported radical experiments in detailed visual representation. The implications of these general stylistic comments for the
study of British drama should become clear in the chapters that follow.

CHAPTER II

EARLY DRAMA IN BRITAIN

The drama of medieval Britain weaves together many strands. Primitive ritual; classical theater; Christian, popular, and literary drama; and Roman, Celtic, Anglo-Saxon, and Norman elements all join in its development. Indeed, over the past three decades scholars have been struggling to balance these disparate ingredients. Theoretical studies have connected the drama with innate human impulses toward play, religion, and combat. The cycle of seasons has also been identified as a key factor in the development of early drama. In early societies agricultural festivals inspired dramatic celebrations, which perhaps merged later with religious festivals that evoked their own dramatizations. This chapter attempts to trace these disparate strands in the earliest British dramatic events. In the process it must define the terms *drama, theater,* and *dramatic literature.* It must also ask a series of basic questions: Who were the earliest performers and audiences in Britain? What kind of performances did they participate in, and where did they perform? Did classical traditions continue to be influential after the departure of the Romans from Britain, or did the Middle Ages in fact represent a fresh start for the theater?

Like the chapters that follow, this one follows a middle course between topical and chronological modes of presentation. Many types of drama existed simultaneously, as Roman and folk traditions theoretically overlap in the era comprising the beginning of this chapter. Other elements recur throughout this volume—the protean role of traveling entertainers and the continuing presence of popular rituals, for instance.

This chapter focuses on the earliest British drama, up to the start of the fourteenth century. Two fundamental problems present themselves at once. First the investigator must decide where the history of drama in Britain ought to begin. Second and most important, the student must remain sensitive to the limits as well as the potential of the surviving evidence of the earliest British drama.

The late antique and early medieval periods gain much of their mystery from our knowing so little about them. Students of the period must focus on the facts that can be securely established and resist the temptation to link them. What relics survive from this earliest period of British drama resemble a collection of scattered tesserae from a large mosaic. At the moment it cannot be completely reassembled, nor can the original picture be identified with total certainty. This chapter can only collect the pieces and tentatively approximate their relations to one another.

THE EMERGENCE OF DRAMA IN BRITAIN

One alluring impossibility would be to begin the history of British drama as early in the history of the settlement of the British Isles as archaeology permits. Tantalizing hypothetical reconstructions envision impersonation and drama in the rituals of prehistoric Britain. Indeed, anthropological models for the study of early drama have appealed to many scholars ever since Sir James Fraser's *The Golden Bough* first explored this possibility.[1] Animal impersonations were probably important in ancient rituals across Europe. Cave paintings of dancers wearing antlers may reflect performances in which hunters mimed their own actions and those of their prey to ensure future success. They also suggest the impersonation of sacrificial animals or of antlered gods. A variety of prehistoric sites in the British Isles, from the great circles of standing stones at Stonehenge and Avebury to others less celebrated, may well have been designed in the late Neolithic and Bronze Age periods as awesome settings for ritual events, lending them a strong dramatic elements. The intended functions of these monuments remain a matter of perennial debate. Inigo Jones, architect and designer of masques to the court of James I, asserted that they were Roman theaters. Special lighting effects, derived from the site's orientation to the heavens, might have contributed to the theatrical quality of the events that took place there. These effects suggest early links between ritual and key events of a primitive agricultural calendar, particularly the summer and winter solstices. Whatever the function of the central spaces, the processional avenues associated with these monuments (at Avebury fifty feet wide and a mile long) tell us that communal religious processions attracted the British from an early period. Processions continued to be important in medieval and Renaissance drama. The twentieth century's fondness for parades is only the latest phase of this ancient form of theater.

Practically, though, the history of drama in Britain can only begin with the first substantial body of evidence—that is, with the Roman occupation of Britain after Caesar's arrival in 54 C.E. The scattered clues tell more about the physical conditions of Roman provincial theater than they do about drama specifically. Specialists can only propose the sketchiest inferences about the dramatic performances that took place in the Roman theaters of Britain. The first definite dramatic texts that can be tentatively localized in Britain remain those of tenth-century liturgical dramas, while the first play that looks like a play to twentieth-century readers is probably the French or Anglo-Norman *Ordo representacionis Adae* of about 1146–74.

ROMAN ANTECEDENTS. Two basic problems face the student of Roman drama in Britain: the first is deciding what it consisted of in the first place, and the second is estimating its impact on later periods. Ian Lancashire portrays the Roman theater as a vital shaping influence on the long-term development of British drama (x–xi, xxxi). To evaluate this suggestion, it seems important to find out what of the Roman theatrical tradition penetrated to this farthest outpost of empire between the initial Roman incursions of 54–55 B.C.E. and the departures of Roman forces at the end of the fourth century of the common era. Between those dates, Rome stationed a substantial body of troops in Britain to control the Celtic tribes, particularly on the western and northern frontiers. The communities of this outlying province developed as points of intersection for military personnel, immigrants, and natives and as distribution centers for trading and manufacturing enterprises and agricultural estates. These contracts brought together native British religions, the official imperial cult, Mithraism, and eventually Christianity. In towns and major country estates, Roman Britons might enjoy the amenities of central heat and public baths, as well as theatrical entertainment. Their taste in mosaic might run to Virgilian allusions or to allusions to the wild beast combats of the amphitheater. To the north and west, beyond Roman control, the tribes of Scotland, Wales, and Ireland maintained a way of life that combined hunting, fishing, and agriculture.[2]

That the Roman and perhaps the Celtic subjects of the province of Britannia, from Kent to Yorkshire and west at least as far as Dorchester, did assemble to view dramatic spectacles from before 60 C.E. until late in the fourth century seems well established by archaeological evidence. These findings allow us to begin to appreciate the range and resources of Roman theater in Britain.

Collingwood defines three basic types of Roman theatrical structures: the circus, the amphitheater, and the theater proper. Each had its own specialized functions. The circus, an elongated oval structure in which seats surrounded a central track, was designed for chariot racing (*ludi circenses*). No circus has been found in Britain, though the interest in chariot racing gleaned from other sources suggests that it did occur.

The amphitheater, a circular or elliptical arena surrounded by seats for spectators, was generally used for military displays, legionary training, gladiatorial combats, executions, or animal baitings. Remains of amphitheaters associated with legionary headquarters and civil centers have been definitively identified at Cirencester, Dorchester, Frilford, Silchester, Caerwent, Chester, Chichester, and Caerleon. These British facilities were most often not the massive freestanding stone amphitheaters of Italy or Southern France, but circular or oval arenas surrounded by earthworks, surmounted by timber or stone seats for between three and eight thousand spectators. Most recently, the excavation of the amphitheater at London (Roman Londinium) has added to the pattern. Probably an elliptical structure whose inner dimensions measured about seventy meters by fifty meters, it was discovered in the course of construction work near the London Guildhall, adjacent to the remains of the Roman Cripplegate fort. By far the most common type of Roman theatrical building in Britain, these amphitheaters remind us that the military was strongly represented in the Roman British population. Gladiators seem to have been the most popular entertainers in Britain throughout the period of Roman settlement; names and images of fighters in action have been recovered.[3] The amphitheater at Dorchester, remodeled from a Neolithic stone circle, Maumbury Rings, continued in use for animal baitings through the Middle Ages.

The basic Roman theater was a D-shaped structure, with a semicircle of tiered seats facing a stage house set behind a flat acting space. A curtain might be raised from a curtain slot to hide the stage. Of particular individuality is the theater at Verulamium. It seems to have been remodeled twice, changing its configuration from that of the standard D-shaped theater, backed by its stage house, to the circular central arena of the amphitheater. Other ruins at Verulamium reveal an ambitious building program: the town boasted a forum, a triumphal arch outside the theater, and a temple nearby. Similar combinations of theater and amphitheater appear elsewhere in more than twenty buildings north of the Alps. They may testify to economic constraints on the part of a community less affluent than Cirencester, to changing tastes, or perhaps to local ingenuity. At Gosbecks near Colchester the largest theater yet found in Britain was part of a complex that also included a fairground and a native shrine. The mid-second to the early third century seems to have been a period of theatrical renovation in Britain, coinciding with the reigns of Hadrian and the Antonines in Rome. By the end of the fourth century the theater at Verulamium was evidently disused, except as a rubbish dump. Ian Lancashire observes that such major public theatrical structures were not to be built again in Britain until the Elizabethan era.

The theater sites are interesting in themselves. All were Roman cantonal capitals. Roman theater was not centered in London, but dispersed throughout municipal centers across the province, where theaters were supervised by local authorities. As Lancashire notes, Britain through the mid-sixteenth century presents a similar picture. A second possible parallel between Roman and medieval theater lies in the persistent link between the stage and religious celebration. The Gosbecks site was evidently associated with a pre-Roman native sanctuary of continuing popularity outside the planned Roman *colonia,* which also had its theaters. The structure at Verulamium stood near the major cross-country thoroughfare of Watling Street. Here, too, a native temple was located behind the theater. The physical proximity of these Roman theaters to shrines of various types associates drama with religious festivals and rituals. Perhaps, as in Rome, dramatic performances were mounted as part of the festivities. This characteristic ties in with the medieval drama's frequent connection with religious festivals.[4]

Besides these three types of public arenas, late Roman literary references suggest that smaller private performances involving mime, pantomime, and music also took place in, for instance, the banqueting halls of villas. Such activities would find affinities in the later history of drama in Britain.

What type of performances did the Romans witness in Britain? This aspect is much more difficult to determine than the nature of their theatrical buildings. Even at Rome, imperial drama is paradoxically difficult to reconstruct. Almost no dramatic texts and few reliable accounts of performances survive from the late Roman theater, though the buildings themselves have had a disproportionate influence on ancient stage history. Students of Roman theater in the days of the republic complain of the opposite problem; they possess texts but little reliable evidence for contemporary theater buildings. Provincial Roman theater is even more difficult to reconstruct. Tydeman notes that the variety of Roman entertainments challenges current definitions of drama: Roman *ludi* might be the sporting or athletic games of the circus and amphitheater, gladiatorial combats, wild beast hunts or animal baitings, dance, mime, pantomime, or spoken drama. We associate the later Roman theater with grandiose special effects like those recorded in accounts of Nero and Heliogabalus and in Apuleius's *Golden Ass* of the late second century. We hear about imperial theater from largely antitheatrical sources, notably Tertullian's *De Spectaculis*. Tertullian (Quintus Septimus Florens Tertullianus, ca. 155–ca. 222), probably the founder of Latin Christian literature, argues with characteristic vehemence concerning the extreme immorality of all forms of Roman spectacles and the impropriety of Christian attendance at such events. Prophetically, Tertullian anticipates a more appropriate spectacle for a Christian audience—the thrills and chills of the Last Judgment. This last is an exceptionally unpleasant passage, driving home the ultimate force of Tertullian's rhetoric, but it also looks forward unmistakably to the religious drama of the Middle Ages.[5]

The social role of theater continued to be important under the empire, as theatrical buildings were continually built and rebuilt in Britain from the earliest days of Roman occupation to the early 300s. Expatriate Romans and Romanized Celts of both sexes evidently expected to witness state-supported performances or athletic events as a part of the civic calendar. The pleasure of attending free public spectacles was ingrained in the Roman way of life. Indeed, Tertullian reveals the attractions of the emperial stage, circus, and amphitheater for literate, committed Roman Christians of the second century. His argument is so urgent, as he admits, because a noticeable body of Christians still enjoys attending these events (*De Spectaculis*, 27:292–93). Distant provincial productions might be less gorgeous than those at Rome, just as British theatrical buildings seem to have been notably less monumental than those at Rome or in Roman enclaves around the Mediterranean (*De Spectaculis*, 7:250–51). Nevertheless, they remained a persistent feature of life in Britain up to the end of the province's connection with Rome, when the breakdown of town government and economic collapse contributed to the disappearance of organized municipal theater.

The drama that these theaters presented might vary radically in type and quality. Students of the period recognize that theatrical presentations had changed a great deal since the days of the republic and the Roman comic playwrights Plautus (ca. 254–184 B.C.E.) and Terence (ca. 195–159 B.C.E). Their plays, adapted from the Greek New Comedy, were still revived, perhaps for performance by the mimes who had become popular in the empire. The discovery of eight tragic or comic masks in sites across the country certainly implies that some types of masked theatrical performances were known in Britain. Generally, however, comedies and tragedies modeled from Greek originals seem to have gone out of fashion under the late republic and early empire. It seems unlikely that Seneca's tragedies, so influential in the drama of the English Renaissance, were written for the public stage.[6] Writing for the theater had become a degrading activity, beneath the notice of elegant Roman literati. Roman audiences of the late republic and the early empire were beginning to demonstrate a preference for mime, or pantomime. In pantomime a masked dancer acted out scenes based on mythology, while a chorus sang the words. Roman mime seems to have been the province of small troupes of barefoot, most often unmasked actor-acrobats, male and female. Under the empire they performed in the public theaters, but their art was immensely adaptable. Some of the earliest records of performance in the Greco-Roman orbit describe small traveling mime troupes with their portable stage, perhaps simply a curtain. They might play in private houses, in the marketplace, or anywhere they could find an audience. This flexibility helped to make the mime the longest lived as well as the oldest type of Roman theater. Although literary mimes were also composed, the skits that were staged seem to have been contrived by anonymous scriptwriters, or improvised by the performers themselves. The sole surviving Greek mime script presents a lascivious wife, played by the chief mime, attempting to seduce her slaves; it recalls the short interpolated stories of the *Golden Ass,* which would have made excellent mimes. Adultery and its farcical or melodramatic consequences seems to have been a frequent theme of these pieces.[7]

Who performed and who financed Roman drama in Britain? Two inscriptions give us minor clues. One commemorates the aedile Marcus Ulpius Januarius and his gift of a stage for the theater at Brough-on-Humber (Petuaria) around 140–44 C.E. This local official's donation reflects the continuing responsibilities of civic officials at Rome and elsewhere to provide free public entertainment. A second inscription, a graffito scratched on a potsherd found at Leicester, tells us that Verecunda (Maloney translates her name as Modesty) the *ludia* loves Lucius the gladiator. Was Verecunda a dancer or an actress? It is impossible to tell. Her name reminds us that traveling mime troupes did include female performers, although Roman comedy and tragedy, like that of Greece, was presented by masked male actors. By contrast, the *archimimus* might be an *archimima,* a woman. (The most celebrated instance of a female performer in the Roman tradition remains the Byzantine mime Theodora [ca. 500–47 C.E.]. Procopius's notorious account of her performances leads Glynne Wickham to describe her as "a striptease go-go dancer." Her attractions contributed to her marriage to the emperor Justinian and her enthronement as empress.) Members of a school of gladiators popular in Britain were depicted in action on glass cups. These souvenirs remind us that more than twice as many amphitheaters as theaters have been found in Britain (Maloney, 48). Military shows, gladiatorial combat, and animal baiting may well have been the most popular forms of entertainment in Roman Britain. All of these performers were either slaves or members of the lowest classes, strictly controlled by their managers or trainers, and regarded with great dubiety by society at large. As Theodora's case indicates, a mime might attain wealth and supreme power without ever attaining respectability.

The rise of Christianity may well have hastened the end of the Roman theater. The closing of Roman theaters in some ways parallels the closing of British theaters in 1642 (discussed in chapter 4 of this volume). But in both cases there are complicating factors. The Roman experience and its discussion by the early church certainly supplied a precedent for later antitheatrical reactions. Tertullian's remarks sufficiently indicate the reaction of Christian authorities to the Roman stage, though he also indicates that the theater had Christian patrons. After the empire adopted Christianity as its official religion in 378, it might be expected that the traditional spectacles of Rome would be abruptly discontinued. In fact, they were kept on by popular demand, in spite of increasing official disapproval. The fifth-century monk Telemachus was stoned by an irate audience when he tried to stop the gladiatorial games; in response, a ban against public theater was put into effect (Bevington, *Medieval Drama*, 3). Nevertheless, the factions of the circus, "Blues" and "Greens," maintained political and social power in Rome and Byzantium. Their riots at the beginning of the sixth century threatened public safety in both Constantinople and Rome. The last circus games were held at Rome by the Gothic commander Totila around the mid-sixth century. In 500 C.E. Choricius of Gaza wrote his defense of the actor's profession, and later in the sixth century Justinian, who had closed the theaters, rescinded the law that barred men of senatorial rank from marrying women of the stage (*scenicae mulieres*), in all probability so that he himself could marry the fascinating Theodora.

The tension between church and stage was clear. Mimes mocking the Christian sacraments were evidently performed, and in the fifth century the church excommunicated all performers of mimes (Beare, 232). The church objected most strenuously to the amphitheater as the center of Christian persecution under Nero and Diocletian. The ancient and continuing ties between pagan festivals and theatrical performances were equally damning, as was the immorality that had disgusted many Roman intellectuals, Christian or pagan. Tertullian also distrusts the seductive power of spectacle itself and its imitation of nature, as did later iconoclasts, notably in the English Reformation. British evidence of either Roman Christianity or of friction between church and stage is equally thin. The sporadic appearance of private chapels and participation in church controversies suggests that by the early fourth century Britain had a lively if somewhat heretical Christian community; it had, after all, produced that persuasive heretic Pelagius, much to St. Augustine's annoyance. Bede's note that St. Alban was scheduled for execution in an arena at Verulamium hints that in Britain, too, martyrdom and Roman spectacle might be inextricably linked.

The evidence does indicate that the church and Christian intellectuals played an important role in the suppression of Roman public theater. Other factors were also at work. With the economic decline of Roman Britain in the late fourth and fifth centuries and the influx of Germanic tribes from overseas, life in Britain was transformed. Theaters and amphitheaters stood empty as local governments collapsed and communities dispersed. Whether their response to the pressure of Anglo-Saxon migration and imperial decay was flight, resistance or compromise, the Roman Britons faced radical changes. Roman towns and country villas would give way to new patterns of settlement, sometimes overlapping and sometimes ignoring the precedents of the past four hundred years.

Certain elements of Roman theater and theatrical practice did survive into the early Middle Ages. First and perhaps most importantly, the Middle Ages took their theatrical vocabulary from the Romans. *Ludus* transmits its ambiguities to the Old English *pleg* and the modern English "play." As in Latin a *ludus* can be any sort of game or drama, so "play" preserves the connections among recreation, entertainment, and the performer's mimicry. *Theatrum* becomes our "theater," by way of medieval usages that apply the term to brothels and figurative theaters as well as to the literal playing place, the Old English *plegstowe*. As for the Latin terms for performers, *mimus, scurra,* and *histrio,* they are an endless source of frustration to scholars interested in their precise interpretation.[8]

Next in importance, perhaps, for the future of drama, are the manuscripts of Roman plays that transmitted the works of Terence, Seneca, and less commonly Plautus to medieval readers. It is no longer necessary to wait until the sixteenth century to witness the enthusiastic reception of Latin drama among the educated classes of the British Isles. An eleventh-century booklist from Keynsham Abbey refers to a manuscript of Terence, possibly belonging to Worcester Priory. A twelfth-century Terence manuscript from St. Albans (Bodleian Library MS Auct. F.2.13) is illustrated with images of theatrical masks and masked actors in performance. In 1370 the Augustinian friars of York had copies of Terence and Seneca. The abbey of Bury St. Edmunds had copies of Plautus and Terence in the twelfth or thirteenth centuries. Dover priory had a Terence by 1389 (British Library MS Royal 15.A.12).[9] As they were read and recopied these manuscripts passed along ideas about the construction of Roman drama and notions about its performance. They also inspired imitation in new Latin comedies by lettered authors. The German nun Hrotsvitha of Gandersheim wrote six Christian comedies around 960. *Babio,* possibly by Walter Map, dates from the late twelfth century. Whether the learned writers of such pieces intended them to be performed is still debated. As performances or as literary exercises, they did transmit the traditions of Greek New Comedy and the Roman *palliata* to medieval readers. In the English Renaissance Terence's lucid style would make him a principal textbook of humanist education. Plautus was always less accessible, with his colloquial language and metrical virtuosity.

As for the physical remains of Roman theatrical structures, the Anglo-Saxon reaction to Roman monuments was cautious in the extreme. Many Roman buildings stood empty, regarded by suspicious Germanic settlers as *eald enta geweorc,* the ancient handiwork of giants. Poems like *The Ruin* recall some of the awe and dubiety that Roman remains evoked in Anglo-Saxon poets. Londinium was not reinhabited until Alfred's day, though a new community grew up alongside it. On the other hand, an assembly place at the Northumbrian royal seat at Yeavering of around 605–40 suggests that one Anglo-Saxon royal house was ready to model a theatrical site on the disused Roman theaters. What was it used for? We can only speculate.

TRAVELING ENTERTAINERS. Traveling entertainers remain important in the development of British drama up to 1660. The

omnipresence of nomadic mimes, dancers, singers, acrobats, and puppeteers has been documented throughout the early Middle Ages. Regrettably for the purpose of stage history, it has not been well enough
documented, considering the importance of such itinerant performers
to theorists of the history of drama. Their relationship with stationary
forms of theater is never easy to establish, yet from time to time the
entire theatrical future is seen as resting in their hands, as perhaps
indeed it did. At both ends of the chronological period covered by this
volume, after the disappearance of the Roman stage and after the
closing of the theaters in 1642, drama in Britain is left to these incon-
spicuous and allegedly disreputable practitioners.

The presence of wandering entertainers is made apparent by a
variety of church prohibitions, in a period when the church's literacy
makes it our principal source of information. Monastic communities
are warned not to receive traveling players or to witness their performances, though monastery account books reveal that they did. The
same sources are less useful when it comes to determining these players' identities. They could be mimes, in groups or individually. They
could also be native entertainers, Anglo-Saxon scops or Celtic bards,
who might chant or recite poetry to musical accompaniment, most
often a harp. The legend that King Alfred disguised himself as a wandering entertainer in order to spy on his Danish enemies does not
specify the type of entertainment the king proposed to provide.
Ogilvy discusses theatrical terminology and the difficulties inherent in
its interpretation at this period. Learned readers knew and used classical theatrical terms, but it is not always easy to determine whether
they used them as references to contemporary reality or as learned
allusions. Only on rare occasions do we meet an individual performer
or obtain some account of a performance.

Whatever their origin, it seems clear that these performers' official
status was low. The church thought little of them. They inherited many
of the legal disabilities that had crippled their predecessors under Roman law. Practically, distinctions were made among performers. The
more proficient or opportunistic might secure the patronage of some
powerful individual and might be rewarded with land or other impressive gifts. Taillefer, who was attached to William the Conqueror, sang
one of the songs of Roland before the Norman troops assembled at

Hastings in 1066 and completed his performance by charging the Anglo-Saxon ranks; the sources describe him as a *histrio,* an actor.[10] From the fourteenth-century Statute of Laborers on, government regulations attempted to control these irregular wanderers. A distinction is drawn in that statute between "minstrels of honor" and less prestigious performers, just as later, under Elizabeth, a legal distinction divided players with aristocratic patrons from those who were unconnected. The "minstrel of honor" might be attached to an aristocratic household, or he or she might be distinguished simply by superior skill, character, or reputation. Chambers suggests that this distinction reflects the differing social rank of the degraded Roman mime and the Anglo-Saxon scop, an essential and respected member of a Germanic prince's court.

The repertory of these traveling entertainers varied as widely as the individual performers. By the early fourteenth century minstrels might be acrobats or tightrope walkers, jugglers, dancers, puppeteers, musicians of varying degrees of skill, singers, storytellers, poets, and performers of dramatic or semidramatic pieces. Our difficulties in determining how closely the minstrel approaches the player lie in the fact that almost no detailed descriptions of their performances have been recorded. One or two references suggest that mime remained a staple of minstrel performance; imitating a drunkard or fool seems to have been perennially popular.

It might be partially true that discussions of minstrels intrude in the history of the drama because they confuse the issue. It is also true that such performers might indeed include dramatic works in their repertory. If so, they must be admitted either to be engaged marginally in drama or else to fall into the realm of lost literature or improvisation. Later in the Middle Ages, we encounter professional entertainers as participants in dramatic events, if only because of their musical expertise. The experience of the medieval traveling entertainers is also noteworthy because it sets important precedents for the traveling companies of professional actors of the fifteenth and sixteenth centuries and their connections with noble or affluent patrons.[11]

The relationship between those performances and our concept of drama is equally difficult to determine. E. K. Chambers and Allardyce Nicoll have argued that the fifteenth-century farce, particularly in France, and the commedia dell'arte in Italy should be seen as continuations of Roman tradition, after centuries of subliterary existence as a staple of popular performance. This reasonable supposition is not easy to prove, and perhaps not capable of proof.

THE PERFORMANCE OF VERNACULAR LITERATURE AND THE FOLK PLAY

Chambers see *chansons de mal marié* as possible folk plays dramatizing the misery of wedlock. How far can a reasonable definition of drama be stretched? Drama in most cases implies the impersonation of characters and the distribution of roles at least between two performers, or does it? In this early period, it is tempting to extend the definition of drama to include orally performed works we now classify as nondramatic. *Beowulf*, sung or chanted to music in the halls of Anglo-Saxon England, must have been a powerful experience for its audience. But was it drama, or even opera? The great Old English elegies, *The Wife's Lament*, *The Seafarer*, and *The Wanderer*, all present first-person dramatic monologues. In *The Dream of the Rood* the Cross appears in a dream vision and engages in dialogue with the narrator. How far can one afford to go in this direction? Other Old English works have been read as dramatic fragments, for instance an Exeter Book dialogue of Joseph and Mary. The many charming Old English riddles involve verbal impersonation, as the speaker describes himself and invites his audience to "say what I am called." How much impersonation was involved in the performances of the scops and Celtic bards? Is the work of a single entertainer by definition nondramatic? It may be important to remember that the vernacular literature of the Middle Ages was most often a performed literature, whether recited, sung from memory, acted out, or read aloud to an audience.

By the mid-sixth century Anglo-Saxon kingdoms had replaced British communities over much of England. By the late sixth century, the effort to convert these heathen centers to Christianity was well under way. Augustine of Canterbury's conversion of King Æthelbert of Kent in 597 was only the first major blow in a protracted struggle to establish the Roman church in northern Europe. The complementary activities of Celtic missionaries from Ireland brought a sophisticated insular dimension to the effort, apparent in Northumbrian culture and later significant for the revival of European learning encouraged by Charlemagne. All this does not immediately connect with the history of drama, still the province of straggling mimes and minstrels.

A master stroke of Pope Gregory the Great's missionary policy was the decision to preserve pagan shrines, converting them to Christian churches along with their congregations. Because the people were accustomed to resort to these locations, the new religion offered a reassuring geographical familiarity. In his letter of 601, reported in Bede's *Historia Ecclesiastica,* Gregory suggested that the people might still be permitted to hold their customary festivals, though the occasion would be a Christian saint's day rather than a pagan holiday. Overt acts of pagan worship, images of gods and sacrifices to them, would not be tolerated. General celebratory gestures could survive. This strategy proved effective, though certain disadvantages would gradually become apparent. The local populations did indeed continue to resort to their accustomed haunts and to conduct their festivities there on nominally Christian occasions. The church became the center of village celebrations, as the pagan temple had been before it. Inappropriate festivities later proved hard to control. Mandates from ecclesiastical authorities attempted to restrict dancing and other *ludi* in church precincts.

But what were these *ludi,* whether pagan survivals or Christian games? Theorists from Fraser on have envisioned a lively tradition of folk drama in Britain, dating back to prehistoric times. These Celtic or Germanic, tribal or village activities have proven difficult to reconstruct. Reliance on anthropological data from primitive societies elsewhere is always appealing but also potentially fallacious. Mummer's plays and sword dances collected from a variety of locales across Britain point to folk plays and ceremonies as important seasonal events in the village calendar. It is clear that the village agricultural calendar shaped the lives of most inhabitants of the British Isles well beyond the period covered by this volume and into the twentieth century. Seasonal ceremonies that can be reconstructed or that in some cases are still performed often include mock combat, the death and resurrection of a champion, the choice of a seasonal king or queen, and other rites intended to ensure the continuing fertility of the land. Their performance contributed to the "luck" of the village, to the communal agricultural economy, and to the social fabric of the community. The ecclesiastical calendar of the medieval church deliberately overlapped the agricultural calendar and encompassed these key events of the village life.

A hypothetical village calendar in pre-Roman Britain would be built around four key points in the agricultural year. A festival celebrating the end of winter and the beginning of spring agricultural activity would be celebrated near the vernal equinox on 15 March. Its timing might vary according to the weather; the rite was presumably more closely tied to specific agricultural tasks than to astronomical events. The autumnal equinox on 15 September would coincide with a village harvest festival. The summer solstice on 23 June, the Celtic Beltane, would be celebrated as the longest day of the year, with a "midsummer watch." The winter solstice on 23 December became the occasion of a winter festival. Bede gives the Old English name for Christmas eve as *Modranicht,* evidently a night associated with some type of female spirits.[13] Roman holidays were from early times occasions for public theatrical presentations. The major festivals were the Megalensia on 4–10 April; the Floralia from 28 April to 3 May, when the female mimes of Rome were to appear naked; the Apollinares of 6–13 July; the Romani of 4–9 September; and the Plebei of 4–17 November. These dates perhaps reflect the more temperate climate of the Mediterranean (Beare, 154). Any comparison of Roman and primitive agricultural calendars should also include three celebrated Roman holidays influential in the development of medieval Christmastide customs: the Saturnalia beginning on 17 December, the Mithraic feast of the unconquered sun (*Sol Invictus*) on 25 December, and the Roman New Year of the Kalends of January, when masking and the exchange of symbolic presents took place.

The calendar of the Christian year successfully adapted features of both these pagan predecessors. The medieval British year customarily began in March, with the feast of the Annunciation (25 March). The sequence of church festivals leading up to Easter punctuated the spring season: Shrovetide (Carnival or Mardi Gras) offered a last burst of high spirits before the forty days' abstinence of Lent. Easter was and still is a moveable feast, whose calculation preoccupied clerical scholars, including the Venerable Bede. Set on the first Sunday after the first full moon after 21 March, it can fall as early as 22 March or as late as 25 April. Easter's date determines the dates of a series of major festivals: Ascension Day and the Rogation Days that follow it, Pentecost (Whitsun), and Trinity Sunday. In 1311 a new feast of the church, Corpus Christi, held on the Thursday after Trinity Sunday, would prove vital in the history of medieval drama in Britain (see chapter 2). All of these spring and summer festivals attracted earlier forms of celebration from the native agricultural calendar.

Processions to gather garlands of new greenery ("Maying"), the appearance of troupes of "peace-egging" village mummers at Easter, bonfires at midsummer, all testify to the integration of pagan customs into the Christian year. Harvest festivities in the fall and winter feasts of dead ancestors or Roman New Year customs in midwinter also became attached to church festivals. Hallowmas (1 November, our All Saint's Day; Martinmas or Martlemas on 11 November; the feast of St. Nicholas on 6 December; and especially the twelve days of Christmas beginning with Christmas itself on 25 December and ending with Twelfth Night (Epiphany), the feast of Christ's baptism, on 6 January, all became occasions for rejoicing. The history of drama in Britain developed within the calendar of the church. As in the ancient world, festivals continued to generate drama.

The calendar of the church structured life in Britain through 1660. It was crucial in the rise of liturgical drama, to be discussed in the following section of this chapter. But it also determined the seasons when folk dramas would take place in agricultural communities across the British Isles. Much of this popular ceremony was imitative. Garlands might represent the rebirth of the year or the fertility of the harvest. Bonfires and the ritual extinction and rekindling of lights imitated the decline and renewal of the sun. Processions involving traditional disguises or impersonations might occur in the spring or at midwinter, later giving rise to aristocratic masquerades and the court masques of the sixteenth and seventeenth centuries. In spring the "Jack in the Green," a man in a wicker frame covered with leaves, was a popular performer. The hobby horse, a man dressed as a horse, and the Bessy, a man dressed as a woman, might appear at more than one time a year. Sword dances or morris dances with death and resurrection story lines, Easter or Christmas mummers' plays, the "king games" and later the Robin Hood plays of May all qualify as folk drama. Several of these ceremonies involved the selection of a king or queen of the festival, the "king of the bean" or a twelfth-day king or queen at Christmas, a king or queen of May (later Robin Hood and Maid Marian), and a harvest king or queen in the fall. Evidence that several of these types of performance appeared early in the Middle Ages comes, again, from the thirteenth-century ecclesiastical prohibitions of "games of king and queen," or the *inductio Maii*.

Circular or processional dancing, feasts, and "ales" were welcome on every occasion. Of these popular festivities, May and Christmas games, the sword dance, and the mummer's play proved especially significant in the history of the drama. They require some further description.

May games might take a variety of forms. The *inductio Maii* of Bishop Robert Grosseteste of Lincoln's 1244 prohibition might be almost any ritual celebrating the arrival of spring. Later this rite would occasion garlanded festival processions including the usual catalogue of village grotesques—hobby horse, Bessy, and all. The "Jack in the Green" who appears in these seasonal processions may represent the ultimate spring garland, Chambers's "worshiper decked in his god," or a fertility god. His relatives include the Green Knight of *Sir Gawain and the Green Knight,* the leaf-covered wild man or wild woman of medieval folklore and romance, and Robin Hood in his Lincoln green. Later chapters will discuss the Robin Hood plays that developed from the popular festival. Robin Hood, Chambers suggests, replaces an earlier king or queen of May, the ruler of the feast, perhaps as in those "games of king and queen" that Bishop Walter de Chanteloup of Worcester rejected in his *Constitutions* of 1240 (*Medieval Stage,* 1:91). The fifteenth-century testimony of Sir Thomas Malory and the *Très riches heures du duc de Berry* both state that the most elegant enjoyed similar May games. The cavalcade of riders decked in green leaves on the *Très riches heures* calendar page for May could be acting out a private French aristocratic love game, but if so it markedly resembles town and village spring festivals across Europe.

Christmas games included many activities familiar to western countries today and reminiscent of pre-Christian customs. Evergreen garlands and games relating to them—mistletoe or the rivalry of the holly and the ivy—commemorate the death and renewal of the year. The exchange of presents may be a relic of the Roman New Year's celebration. Of particular interest to students of drama are the mummer's plays, frequently held at Christmas, and other games involving masks; these are precursors of masques and disguisings that increased in popularity from the fourteenth century into the seventeenth. Bands of maskers might roam city streets at this season, to the distress of those responsible for law and order.

The Middle English romance *Sir Gawain and the Green Knight* evokes many varieties of Christmas game, interlude, and diversion that might entertain an English court of the later fourteenth century. Clerical sports of the season included the Feast of Fools, when the minor clergy took over the cathedral, and a more popular institution in England, that of the boy bishop, who presided over cathedral, monastery, and school festivities on Childermass (Feast of the Holy Innocents). At a time when most monastic communities and major churches had schools, this children's performance seems to have gained favor as an attractive and appropriate festivity for schoolchildren during the Christmas season. As early as 1222 there was a Feast of Boys at Salisbury, one of the most influential English cathedrals. A procession of choirboys (sometimes elaborately costumed as clerical dignitaries), visits to local magnates to collect contributions, special services, a sermon delivered by the boy or child bishop himself, and a concluding feast were all standard features of this event. Convents might also choose a child abbess on this occasion. Such activities combined elements of popular festivals with social reversal, impersonation, and liturgical drama.[14]

A sword dance is described in Tacitus's *Germania* as a characteristic amusement of young Teutonic barbarians. There it involves naked youths leaping across a mass of spear- and sword points to entertain their fellow tribespeople. The description recalls the sword dance familiar from Scotland. A different sword dance, practiced widely in the north of England, recurs across Germany, Italy, Spain and Sweden. In this performance, five to seven male dancers holding swords interweave them to form intricate figures. At the climax of the performance a star or ring of swords is placed around the neck of one of the dancers, sometimes a character wearing a foxtail, described as the "fool." After this symbolic execution a comic "doctor" may appear to revive the "beheaded" dancer. This plot and these characters find parallels in the morris dances of southern England. The familiar hobby horse and Bessy are often worked into the performance as well. Chambers suggests that such dances represent a mock sacrifice, perhaps the symbolic death and revival of the year.

The English mummer's play bears a strong family resemblance to the sword dance. The same characters appear, but the dance is replaced by a mock combat in which one of the characters dies, to be revived by the "doctor." This drama is prefaced by a man with a broom who sweeps a circle on the floor to mark the performance space. It continues with the presentation of the characters, usually including the fool, the Bessy, the hobby horse, and a black-faced man. The character of St. George, perhaps attracted from medieval St. George processions like the one at Norwich, is prominent among the dramatis personae of the extant examples. The performance normally ends with a collection from the audience. Most often the mummer's play is associated with Christmas, though it was also performed at Easter. A surprising number of texts have been recorded, but unluckily they are all late; the earliest example goes back to the late eighteenth century. Their confused state suggests to Professor Wickham that this early tradition was seriously disrupted by the Puritans.

Any of these celebratory activities might be used for local fundraising. A skilled team of dancers or mummers might visit neighboring villages to collect funds for their home parish or for a village feast. Volumes of Records of Early English Drama (REED) completed so far have documented many instances of this practice.

The folk drama is not often seen as the central force in British dramatic history. All indications point to the drama of the church as the most influential factor in the rise of medieval theater. Still, two features of the folk drama do demand attention. First, it reinforces the connection between dramatic performance and the calendar, whether religious or agricultural. Second, it depends on local initiative and local talent; this theater is anything but a sophisticated, cosmopolitan, professional endeavor. Again in Britain we find drama dispersed across the countryside, not emanating from some central source. Both these features reappear in the cycle plays of the medieval towns.

THE DEVELOPMENT OF CHRISTIAN LITURGICAL DRAMA

Roman Christianity was reintroduced to England in 597, when Augustine of Canterbury converted the Anglo-Saxon king of Kent. The remnants of the Celtic church, exiled to Wales, Brittany, and Ireland, had already made an impact on Scotland and northern England and on the Continent. At the Synod of Whitby in 664 the merits of Celtic and Roman practices were debated, and the Roman party under the leadership of St. Wilfrid triumphed. The Roman calendar and Roman liturgy would henceforth govern the British church. On the continent the Roman form of the liturgy did not replace the Frankish "Gallican" ritual until 750. C. Clifford Flanigan and other scholars describe the Gallican form of the liturgy as a dramatic, expressive rite; they suggest that its suppression may have prompted dramatic additions to the Roman liturgy, as clergy tried to supply an expressive element missing in the new services.

The role of the Christian calendar in village life, briefly discussed earlier in this chapter, was incidental to that calendar's chief objective, to fix a schedule for the services and festivals of the church. Events in the life of Christ and feast days of saints shaped not only the Christian year but also the daily schedule of services, giving names to the seven canonical hours of the ecclesiastical day. This ecclesiastical sense of time pervaded medieval society. The rhythm of medieval life set by the church persisted into the sixteenth and even the seventeenth century. The history of drama is also a history of the church.

To understand the drama of the medieval church, it is vital to understand the liturgy. The basic pattern of worship of the medieval church developed from standard Jewish practice during Jesus' lifetime. The central ceremony of the mass grew out of the account of the Last Supper in Mark 14:22–27, in all probability a Passover Seder. In the original Mass the eucharist of bread and wine, the body and blood of

Christ, were presented to the faithful. The apostles continued to observe three periods of prayer at the third, sixth, and ninth hours of the day. Four new services were added later, possibly to assist the monastic aspiration to recite the entire Book of Psalms daily. From the sixth century on, seven canonical hours were standard: matins, technically a midnight service but regularly rescheduled, lauds at sunrise, prime at six in the morning, terce at nine, sext at noon, none at three in the afternoon, vespers (evensong) at sunset, and compline at nine in the evening. Every priest or member of a religious house was required to celebrate or read these services each day: lay practice varied with the devotion of the individual. Then specific psalms, hymns, and passages from the Scriptures or from the church fathers proper to each service began to be collected in breviaries. This development simplified life for clergy who would otherwise have had to collect six or seven books in order to perform services, in an age when a book—a manuscript written on parchment—represented the value of a herd of sheep or cattle. The breviary recorded, in the *Proprium de tempore,* the whole service for each day according to its position in the year. It also gave special services for the festivals of particular saints, the *Proprium sanctorum,* and for other special services. These special services have come to occupy the major part of the church calendar.

In Britain the task of the liturgical historian is complicated both by major shifts and by local variation. After 1066 the upper level clergy imported by William the Conqueror instituted their own Anglo-Norman liturgy, adapted locally according to the quirks of the institution that performed it. The liturgy developed at Salisbury Cathedral, *The Use of Sarum,* was widely adopted, but other major centers had their own procedures. The details of ecclesiastical practice reflected in medieval religious drama are proving of particular interest to scholars who hope to use them to trace the geographical origins of particular plays.

O. B. Hardison powerfully states the case for regarding the Mass itself as sacred drama, "encompassing all history and embodying in its structure the central pattern of Christian life on which all Christian drama must draw" (Hardison, 79). It re-creates the life and sacrifice of Christ, with the celebrant taking the central role of Christ and the attendant deacons and subdeacons, acolytes and lay congregants all participating actively. Many services offered dialogue through responses, two choirs or speakers answering one another. The pageantry of ecclesiastical processions, the vividly colored and embroidered vestments of the clergy, incense and light all made an intense sensory appeal to the faithful (Bevington, *Medieval Drama*, 4). Developments in ecclesiastical architecture also contributed to church drama. As Honorius of Autun observed around 1100, churches, with symbolic locations like the altar and the long central nave for processions, were after all the theaters for this performance. In the ninth century Amalarius, Bishop of Metz (780?–850) interpreted the Mass as a drama representing the life of Christ. At the same time, an opposition party objected to heightened dramatic style and visual content in church services. The Cistercians of the twelfth century were not alone in taking this stance, though their pronouncements are the best known today. St. Bernard of Clairvaux's tirade against the church ornament of the Benedictine house of Cluny was only the most flamboyant of these critiques. The English Cistercian Ailred of Rievaulx objected to theatrical gestures and vocal effects as employed by priests of his acquaintance. This tension between those striving to enhance the drama of the liturgy and those who found such enhancements repugnant continued into the Reformation and well beyond it.

Drama grew at the heart of the liturgy of the early medieval church. Several theories account for its reemergence. The trope proved a key element in this movement. Tropes were musical embellishments of the vowels of certain key words—the "A" of "Alleluia" is most commonly proffered as an example. Bevington cites Notker Balbulus, the ninth-century monk of St. Gall, who observed that words had been added to these originally wordless musical embellishments to help the singers memorize them.

Medieval liturgical drama coalesced around the most important occasions in the church calendar—Easter first, then Christmas. Bevington and Pamela Sheingorn link the Western monastic rites reenacting the events of Holy Week with those performed from an earlier date in Jerusalem itself. There, according to pilgrims' accounts, the bishop and the people commemorated Christ's entry into Jerusalem on Palm Sunday, with a procession in which the bishop took the part of Christ. English evidence is essential here: The *Regularis Concordia* contains perhaps the earliest authoritative description of a liturgical dramatization of the visit to the sepulchre. The *Regularis Concordia* itself stands as a key document of the English monastic reform movement of the tenth century. This monastic code was drafted at the Synodal Council held by King Edgar (944–75) at Winchester under the leadership of St. Dunstan, archbishop of Canterbury, Oswald of Worcester, and Æthelwold, archbishop of Winchester. There English abbots and abbesses, together with advisors from Ghent and Fleury, agreed to enforce a stricter interpretation of the Rule of St. Benedict and eliminate lay control of monastic houses. These reforms brought England into line with ecclesiastical movements that had been sweeping Europe for some time.[16]

Among its many recommendations for the improvement of British monasticism, the *Regularis Concordia* suggested appropriate ceremonies for Easter Week. These were described as practices already adopted elsewhere, perhaps in France. In analyzing these ceremonies, it is important to look at them in sequence. Like the later cycle drama of the fourteenth through the sixteenth centuries, these dramatizations of the liturgy were not single, isolated "plays." They were part of a larger whole, whether a cycle of religious plays or the drama of sacrifice and redemption during Holy Week, the climax of the Christian year. The events of the week should properly be analyzed as a unit. The climactic ceremonies of Good Friday, Saturday, and Easter Sunday were to follow a week in which church decorations and lights would gradually be removed. For the Mass of the Presanctified on Good Friday the *Regularis Concordia* prescribes an *Adoratio crucis* (Adoration of the Cross). Here the Cross is set before the altar, supported by two deacons, one on each side, who chant the "Reproaches" of Christ on the Cross: "*Popule meus, (quid feci tibi?)* [My people, (what have I done to you)] . . . *Quia eduxi vos per desertum.* [Because I have led you through the desert.] . . . *Quid ultra (debui facere tibi, et non feci?)* [What more should I have done for you, that I have not done?]" (Bevington, *Medieval Drama*, 14–15). Two subdeacons standing before the Cross respond in Greek, and the brethren respond in Latin, repeating "Holy God . . . have mercy upon us." This dialogue evokes the typological parallel that links the events of Easter to the Exodus. The ceremony reaches its climax when the two deacons turn toward the clergy and present the unveiled Cross, with the words "*Ecce lignum crucis*" (Behold the wood of the Cross). Then the famous hymn of Venantius Fortunatus, "*Pange lingua gloriosi proelium certaminis*" (Sing, O tongue, the glorious battle), is sung, and the abbot and all the junior and senior brethren of the choir on the right hand prostrate themselves three times before the Cross, the abbot reciting the seven penitential psalms and prayers celebrating the Cross "*cum magno cordis suspirio*" (with deep, heartfelt, sighs).

The rite of the *Depositio crucis,* the symbolic interment of the Cross that immediately followed the *Adoratio,* is based on a practice already performed by "certain religious men" and "worthy of imitation." The intent of the ceremony is "to strengthen the faith of the unlearned multitude and of neophytes." Frustratingly, the wording does not identify either the *quorundam religiosorum* who were already performing the ceremony or the *indocti uulgi* whose faith it was to strengthen. The *indocti uulgi* might suggest an audience beyond the immediate monastic community, or it might refer simply to the wide range of levels of sophistication to be found within any normal monastery or convent, a microcosm of the exterior society that encompassed learned and illiterate, aristocrat and peasant, lay brothers and sisters and novices. Most important is that statement that this ceremony is intended to strengthen the faith of the ignorant or inexperienced Christian. We shall meet this motivation for religious drama later in the annals of British performance, together, of course, with its counter-argument—that such graphic depictions of matters of faith confuse rather than aid the unwary believer. Varying theories of religious psychology, to use a wildly anachronistic term, lie at the root of the debate. Here the *Regularis Concordia* states its authors' faith in the value of visual correlatives, of physical depiction, as a guide to the highest mystery of the church. By seeing the cross placed in its Easter sepulchre, the most naive witness will be prepared to understand the entombment and the resurrection of Christ.

For the *Depositio,* "a likeness of the sepulchre," surrounded by curtains, is placed on an altar. Is this the high altar, usually at the east end of the church, or another altar? The text does not clarify the important matter of location. After the *Adoratio* has been completed, the same two deacons who supported the Cross initially wind it in a linen cloth and carry it away, intoning the appropriate antiphons, "In peace, in this very place," "He shall dwell," and "My flesh shall rest in hope." When they reach the sepulchre, the Cross is laid within, "as if the body of our Lord Jesus Christ had been buried." Then they say the antiphon, "After the Lord was buried, the tomb was sealed; stationing the soldiers who were to stand guard over him." This description does imply some processional movement by the deacons carrying the Cross away from its location in the *Adoratio* to its resting place on the altar.

After the Cross is placed in the sepulchre prepared for it, and the curtain drawn, two or more appointed members of the community take their places to stand watch, conceivably symbolizing or counterbalancing the soldiers of the final antiphon of the *Depositio* ceremony. During their vigil they sing psalms. Sometime in the course of the night, before the bells ring for matins on Easter Sunday, the sacristans raise the Cross from its sepulchre and restore it to some frustratingly unspecified "appropriate place." This *Elevatio crucis* is followed by the *Visitatio sepulchri* itself.

In this final, most clearly dramatized ceremony, the *Regularis Concordia* assigns the part of the angel at Christ's tomb to one of the brethren, while three others represent the three Marys. The service itself provides "cues" for the participants. They are to dress during the reading of the third lesson. The angel wears an alb and carries a palm frond. He enters first, unobtrusively, and seats himself at the sepulchre. The three Marys appear during the third responsory, wearing copes and carrying thuribles with incense. The thuribles' presence and the scent of the incense recall that the Marys were bringing myrrh to embalm the corpse of Jesus. The text specifies that they should wander about, as if looking for the tomb, and that the angel should greet them in a melodious, moderate tone. The dialogue that ensues follows the familiar lines of the *Quem Quaeritis* trope, with the angel asking the Marys, "Whom do you seek?" and the Marys responding, "Jesus of Nazareth." "He is not here," the angel says, "he is risen as he had prophesied; go, announce that he has risen from the dead." After the Marys turn and state their message to the choir, the angel calls them to view the empty tomb. He is instructed to lift the curtain and display the vacant sepulchre, with the linen cloth that had been used to shroud the Cross left inside. The Marys place their thuribles in the sepulchre, take the cloth, and stretch it out to display it to the assembled brethren, displaying it as an emblem of the Resurrection. They then sing the antiphon "The Lord is risen from the tomb" before they spread the cloth on the altar. The ceremony ends with the prior starting to sing the *Te Deum,* and all the bells ringing at once, both manifestations of communal rejoicing.

This sequence of ceremonies incorporates several degrees of dramatization of the liturgy. The *Adoratio* and the *Depositio* employ exchanges between groups of singers, vocal expression, action, symbolic locations, and visual symbols. The Cross, the pillow on which the cross is laid, the Easter sepulchre with its curtain, and the cloth that symbolizes Christ's shroud all function as effective visual cues in these linked ceremonies. The *Visitatio sepulchri* comes the closest to fully developed liturgical drama: here the four brethren are assigned specific roles, appropriate costumes and properties, lines and actions. The three monks who impersonate the Marys are the first of our acquaintance in a long line of male actors who undertake female roles. By contrast, the *Elevatio crucis* is not even a ceremony, and certainly not a public event. The raising of the Cross from its tomb is done behind the scenes, a matter for the stagehands. Since there were no known eyewitnesses to the Resurrection itself, the early church had no scriptural source for an appropriate ritual, though later in the Middle Ages the *Elevatio* nevertheless developed its own public ceremonials. The *Regularis Concordia* thus provides an attractive illustration of the varying degrees to which the liturgy could choose to employ dramatic techniques.

The *Regularis Concordia* text leaves many tantalizing unanswered questions, both about the ceremonies it describes and about the state of liturgical drama in Britain. The European influence on the *Regularis Concordia* suggests that the ceremonies it advocates are more likely to be continental than English in origin. It is questionable whether they were ever performed in Britain before the *Regularis Concordia,* or whether they ever took root there to any great extent. The introduction to the *Depositio* in particular hints that this is an especially unfamiliar ceremony, presented to British monastic institutions on a purely conditional or experimental basis. The text does not attach the ceremonies it describes to specific locations within the church, at least not as well as modern students of liturgical drama would like. Carol Heitz and Elie Konigson have focused attention on the western end of the church, the Westwork, as the locale for the celebration of Easter in the Gallican rite, and by extension as the place where much of the later Easter drama would occur. Without more specific evidence from architecture, archaeology, or the documents concerned, it remains difficult to visualize the Easter drama of the *Regularis Concordia*. That the Winchester Troper of 978–80 includes a version of the *Quem quaeritis* dialogue suggests that the monks of Winchester were prepared to go at least that far in the dramatization of their Easter liturgy.

Interestingly, the evidence for this ceremonial is monastic; the contemporary practices of the secular clergy may or may not have included such dramatic rituals. The great monastic centers of the continent would continue to stand in the forefront of the development of church drama through the twelfth and thirteenth centuries. The Fleury playbook, Benediktbeuern, Hildesheim, Hildegard of Bingen's convent on the Rupertsburg, and Monte Cassino all bear witness to the continuing efflorescence of drama in the monasteries of France, Germany, and Italy over the next three hundred years. The *Regularis Concordia* should perhaps be read as evidence for the already substantial international prestige of these continental centers and their liturgical practices in the tenth century. In the seventh century British monastic learning had been a principal source of inspiration for the "Carolingian renaissance," the celebrated renewal of learning and church discipline under Charlemagne. Now it was the turn of continental monks and nuns to influence the British, recovering from their dire experiences during the Danish and Norwegian Viking raids of 787–885.

Pamela Sheingorn's impressive study inventories the physical remains of Easter sepulchres in English churches, together with other evidence for Easter ceremonies in England from their liturgical beginnings through the sixteenth century. She establishes that the story of the drama of the Easter services did not end with the *Quem quaeritis* but continued to develop astonishing new variations until the Reformation brought it to a violent halt. Other occasions also developed appropriate liturgical performances, which are documented in Karl Young's *Drama of the Medieval Church*. Each one bears witness to the delicate and complex interaction of liturgy and drama during this key phase of British history.

TWELFTH- AND THIRTEENTH-CENTURY CHURCH DRAMA. Ever since Charles Homer Haskins described the "Twelfth-century renaissance" in 1927, scholars have been divided over the appropriateness of the term *renaissance* as a descriptive term for the flowering of learning and artistic activity that graced that marvellous century. There is no debate over the marvels themselves. Lively developments in politics and all fields of cultural life make the twelfth century an alluring area of study for medieval specialists. Today it is one of the most celebrated periods of the Middle Ages, thanks in part to repeated popularizations in the theater and on film, from *Ivanhoe* and *Becket* to *The Lion in Winter*. This was the age of Abelard and Heloise, Thomas Becket and Henry II, Eleanor of Aquitaine, the troubadour poets of Provence and the question of courtly love, St. Bernard and the Cistercian monastic reform movement, the rise of the University of Paris and of scholastic philosophy, Chrétien de Troyes and the French Arthurian romances, the newest Gothic architecture, and the Latin Goliard poets.

Twelfth-century Europe produced many masterpieces of church drama; after centuries of oblivion, twentieth-century audiences are rediscovering the most celebrated, the Beauvais *Ludus Danielis* (*The Play of Daniel*) and Hildegard of Bingen's *Ordo virtutum,* through modern reenactments, fueled by the growing enthusiasm for early music and musical instruments. The Fleury playbook displays the richness of the drama that embellished the liturgy at this major French monastic center. Some of this religious drama seems to have been associated with schools, as are certain of the secular Latin plays like *Babio,* modeled on Terence, that survive from northern France and perhaps England during this period. Some writers of the period seem to have confused the methods of production of Roman pantomime with those of the drama proper, imagining that the play was recited while actors carried out the appropriate actions in dumb show. Still others, like the philosopher John of Salisbury, show themselves to be interested and knowledgeable on the subject of Roman theatrical techniques.[17]

The masterpieces of church drama during the twelfth century seem to have been written and performed by clerics, whether schoolboys and their masters, university-level students, or older monks, priests, and nuns. The principal language employed is still Latin, the international language of scholarship and religion throughout the Middle Ages and early Renaissance. Some Latin plays, like the *Lazarus* and *St. Nicholas* plays of the scholar Hilarius or the Benediktbeuern Christmas and passion plays, contain vernacular refrains. Less frequently still, we begin to encounter plays entirely in the vernacular. William the Conqueror's victory of 1066 had replaced the upper echelon of native English aristocrats and prelates with their French-speaking Norman counterparts. The linguistic consequences of this infusion of prestigious speakers and writers of Norman French were striking. The French of the conquerors of England was altered enough to become an identifiable dialect, Anglo-Norman. Old English, the language of the conquered majority of the population, developed in the course of the later eleventh and twelfth centuries into early Middle English.

The earliest plays that can be associated with England are in Latin, Anglo-Norman, or both French and Latin. This fact in itself suggests that the clergy were writing and performing the plays, primarily for clerical or courtly audiences. As David Bevington points out, these plays are not designed to instruct the simplest believer in the fundamentals of biblical history. For the most part, they require an educated, often a learned audience. This observation is not intended to imply that there were no sophisticated clerics and aristocrats whose native language was English; but such persons would also be well trained in French and Latin. Whatever drama was being performed in early Middle English has left few if any traces. This suggests several possibilities: that it was improvised or orally composed rather than written, that the audience for complex religious dramas in English did not yet exist, or simply that such works have been completely lost. Late twelfth- and thirteenth-century Middle English literature does contain elements that would lend themselves to dramatic performance. Narratives like Layamon's *Brut* are amply provided with powerful speeches and moments of interaction between characters. The debate poem *The Owl and the Nightingale* elegantly differentiates its quarreling birds in their styles of argumentation and dialogue.

The early *fabliau* of *Dame Sirith,* as Martin W. Walsh argues, may indeed have been performed as a play, like its close relative, the fragmentary *Interlude of the Clerk and the Girl* (*Interludium de clerico et puella*) of around 1300–25. If so, it bears witness to the development of the interlude as a dramatic form as early as 1272–83, the estimated date of Bodleian Library MS Digby 86, in which that poem appears. As Professor Wickham notes, scholarship is most familiar with the early sixteenth-century "Tudor interlude," a form of short dramatic entertainment most often composed by humanist schoolmasters for performance by their pupils. In fact, the Latin *interludium* and the English "enterlude" can be traced back into the fourteenth century. The interludes may be moral or immoral in their subject matter, but they tend to be brief, designed for small, mobile troupes of professional actors and for indoor performance, typically between the courses of a feast. Many more examples of this influential type of drama survive from the fourteenth through the sixteenth centuries (Wickham, *Medieval Theatre*, 169–75). Walsh's study tentatively links the interlude's earliest appearance in England with the minstrel's repertory and techniques; he also sees it as influenced by the Latin "elegaic comedies" of the twelfth century.[18]

Dame Sirith and the *Interlude of the Clerk and the Girl* both present the same story. "Wilekin," the clerk, courts a young wife, "Margery" (or the "girl" of the later version), who properly rejects his advances. He is then advised to approach an old woman, Dame Sirith (or Mome Elwis), who agrees to assist him in return for an appropriate reward. She feeds her dog pepper and mustard and carries the weeping animal on a visit to the young woman. The dog, Dame Sirith explains tearfully, is actually her daughter, transformed into this very bitch by a clerk whose love she had spurned. Shocked, the young woman hurries to surrender her chastity to her gleeful suitor. In her final speech Dame Sirith offers to solve the audience's love difficulties, for a similar fee. While the northern *Interludium* only preserves a section of dialogue, *Dame Sirith* gives the entire story with rudimentary narrative links to connect the extensive speeches of the three characters. These links give *Dame Sirith* the look of a nondramatic narrative, or of a piece for a solo performer. Nevertheless, Walsh analyzes *Dame Sirith* as a dramatic work and finds it eminently suited for performance by a troupe of three minstrels, with a trained dog figuring prominently in the cast.

The records assembled by Ian Lancashire give us some idea of the types of twelfth- and thirteenth-century dramatic works that have been lost, as well as of their authors and performers. An alluring reference in the *Gesta Abbatum monasterii Sancti Albani* (*Lives of the Abbots of St. Albans;* 1:73, cited in Lancashire under "Dunstable") tells us that early in the twelfth century (ca. 1100–19) a certain Geoffrey, engaged as a schoolmaster at Dunstable in Bedfordshire, borrowed ecclesiastical robes from St. Albans for a play of St. Catherine that he had organized. It has been suggested that the play might have been produced for Henry I at his nearby palace of Kingsbury Regis. In any case, the play was performed, but the robes were destroyed in a fire, and the embarrassed Geoffrey presented himself as a monk in their stead. The writer notes that for this reason Geoffrey, when he came to be abbot, took care to provide St. Albans with especially opulent vestments. This record shows how school, monastery, and court might all be linked by the same performance. It also suggests that plays dramatizing the lives of saints were developing in England, as we know they were on the Continent. No St. Catherine play survives, though an incomplete Anglo-Norman life of St. Catherine from 1080–1120 shows signs that the story might well have been dramatized. A troupe of "St. Catherine's players" did perform in fifteenth-century Bristol on the eve of St. Catherine's feast day (Lancashire, 89, n. 406). Around the mid-twelfth century (ca. 1149–54) Lawrence, prior of Durham, composed a dramatic *peregrinus* dialogue, *Rithmus Laurentii de Christo et eius discipulis.* The statutes of Lichfield Cathedral in the days of Bishop Hugh of Nonant (1188–98; revised in the thirteenth and fourteenth centuries) stipulate that a Christmas shepherds' play (*Officium pastorum*), an Easter Sunday *Visitatio sepulchri,* and a *peregrinus* scene for Easter Monday should continue to be appropriately and honorably represented there.

A single actor's part from this group of plays may be preserved in the "Shrewsbury Fragments," perhaps the earliest fragments of religious drama in the English language. In 1196 Eynesham Abbey in Oxfordshire was accustomed to present an Easter Resurrection play. It sounds very much like a variant of Pamela Sheingorn's Type III *Visitatio sepulchri,* beginning with the dialogue of the three Marys and the angel and adding scenes of Peter and John and of Christ's appearance to Mary Magdalene. In 1279 there is a reference to children's performances for the Feast of the Holy Innocents at Barking Abbey in Essex; the nuns were instructed to take charge of the production instead so that the event did not deteriorate into a disorderly game (*ludibrium*).

British records of the religious drama outside monastic settings become more extensive in the thirteenth century than they had been earlier. These documents indicate that performances were associated with cathedrals and churches all across the country. Liturgical plays continued to be enacted inside the churches, whereas other performances took place outside. About 1220 a Resurrection play was executed by masked performers in St. John's churchyard at Beverley in Yorkshire. By around 1260 the three Marys were definitely in evidence at matins on Easter Sunday at Norwich Cathedral. Lincoln Cathedral was evidently a stronghold of the Feast of Fools from before the time Bishop Robert Grosseteste prohibited it in 1236 until at least 1390, when the archbishop of Canterbury remarked on the clerks' *ludos* on the same occasion. A Middle English homily of about 1250 describes a St. Nicholas play to be performed afterward. A 1283 reference mentions that the clerks of Gloucester performed a miracle play of St. Nicholas at Christmas and chose a boy bishop. Religious drama could also occur in secular locations, organized either by clerics like Geoffrey of St. Albans or by laymen. In 1298 a play of St. Magnus, mounted by the Fishmongers' Guild of London as part of the pageantry to celebrate Edward I's victory over the Scots, looked forward to the celebrated guild cycle plays of the fourteenth and fifteenth centuries. In 1307 the harper and "king of heralds" James de Cowpen is reported to have presented miracle plays before Queen Margaret of France either at Lanercost Priory in Cumberland or at Carlisle.

The surviving play texts that can be connected with England in the twelfth century were all written for religious occasions. Two are fragments of vernacular plays. The most famous of these is the Anglo-Norman (or French) *Ordo representacionis Adae*. A second Anglo-Norman play, *La seinte Resureccion* (The Holy Resurrection), has a better claim to be located in Britain, since one of the two manuscripts in which it survives was copied at Christ Church, Canterbury; it has been dated around 1275. One of Abelard's students, the "wandering scholar" Hilarius, wrote in Latin and French; his references elsewhere in his manuscript to English acquaintances suggested to scholars that he might have been English himself, though it is clear that he lived at Angers. In all three cases, the links with Britain are regrettably tenuous, resting on details of dialect, manuscript provenance, and other forms of somewhat circumstantial evidence. It nevertheless seems appropriate to reexamine them here, with these qualifications in mind, in order to build up a clearer picture of what twelfth-century drama in England might have been.

Earliest in date of the texts to be considered in this section is the brief manuscript of around 1130 that contains the miscellaneous works of Hilarius. Hilarius's manuscript includes three plays: a Daniel play *Suscitatio Lazari*, (*The Raising of Lazarus*) and *Imago Sancti Nicolai* (*The Image of St. Nicholas*). Its sixteen leaves also preserve a surprising variety of miscellaneous poetry. "Wandering scholars" are by definition hard to locate geographically. The twelfth century was their heyday, but they persist through the Middle Ages and into the Renaissance as familiar figures, more or less disreputable, university students at one time or another, usually discreditable members of the minor clerical orders, often unscrupulous in their literary virtuosity. (François Villon is a fifteenth-century specimen, perhaps the most renowned of the breed. The "university wits" of Elizabethan London might be regarded as their sixteenth-century descendants.) Hilarius links his biblical plays to the liturgy, though he offers alternative connections depending on whether the play is performed at matins or at vespers. His Daniel play, entirely in Latin, has marginal annotations giving additional names, which has suggested to scholars that either Hilarius had collaborators, perhaps fellow students, or this group was somehow concerned in a performance of the play. Like the better known Beauvais play that is its closest relative, Hilarius's Daniel play would lend itself to sumptuous staging effects. Its two main incidents, Daniel's solution of the mystery of the handwriting on the wall at Belshazzar's feast (here he is Baltasar), and Daniel in the lion's den, both require special effects—the hand of God appearing above the king's throne, and the lions that spare Daniel but tear his detractors to shreds. Grandiose processions, sumptuous garments, and a sham battle in which Darius kills Baltasar enliven the production. Hilarius includes an incident from the Apocrypha, in which the aged prophet Habakkuk is told to carry his mowers' dinner to

Daniel in the lion's den at Babylon, and is miraculously transported there by an angel pulling him by the hair. This scene might well be played for comic effect.

Hilarius's other two plays are further individualized by the effective use of French refrains. Like Daniel, these are constructed with careful symmetry. In *The Raising of Lazarus* Mary and Martha express their grief in Latin and French. The barbarian who entrusts his treasure to the statue of St. Nicholas is given a marvelous tirade when he discovers his belongings have been stolen; it culminates in his frenzied beating of the icon. Of courses, Nicholas appears to the robbers and induces them to restore the stolen goods. Distinctively here Nicholas also appears to the barbarian and instructs him to direct his thanks and belief to the true God.[19]

The twelfth century brings us the first known play associated with Britain, though we are still a century before the first surviving Middle English dramatic work. The *Ordo representacionis Adae* has been identified as an Anglo-Norman work, possibly written and performed in Britain and dated between 1146 and 1174. The evidence for its dialect and location are not as strong as one could desire. The text itself is of immense interest as the earliest known example of a play explicitly intended to be performed outside a church—on the church steps in fact—rather than in the interior. The playwright makes adept use of this location to set up a stage with multiple locations and a clear hierarchy. The play uses the vernacular throughout, punctuated by antiphons and readings in Latin. The stage directions are also in Latin, suggesting a French-speaking clerical author and cast and probably a secular, French-speaking audience. Because of its use of vernacular speech, its external setting, and its presentation of the Fall of Adam and Eve followed by Cain's murder of Abel and a procession of prophets (*Ordo prophetarum*) foretelling the birth of Jesus, the *Ordo representacionis Adae* looks forward to the English mystery cycles of the later Middle Ages. Indeed, from time to time it has been called a "proto-cycle." While not entirely independent of the liturgy, the play combines features that might permit it to be performed either before Lent or in Advent.

The *Ordo representacionis Adae* has been long acclaimed for its command of domestic realism. Henry Adams in *Mont St. Michel and*

Chartres and Erich Auerbach in *Mimesis* both admire the author's depiction of the lively interaction between Adam and Eve and their effectively contrasted personalities. Few critics have been able to resist the fascination of this Eve. From the start the outdoor setting is employed with skill. The decor of paradise suggests the walled garden and also permits costume changes onstage—for instance, Adam's assumption of his fig leaves. An ingeniously constructed serpent climbs the tree to tempt Eve. Throughout, devils run in and out of "Hell mouth" below the church steps and dart in, gesticulating appropriately, among the spectators.[20]

The second major episode, the story of Cain and Abel, has been overshadowed in the critical literature by the success of the initial scenes. Again, the text displays an acute reading of the Vulgate: Cain's celebrated response, "Am I my brother's keeper?", seems reflected in a sardonic, mocking, brutal, and evasive personality. Cain's ironies are completely lost on the earnest and innocent Abel. Once again, the stage setting uses clear directional symbolism: Cain's altar is to stand at the left hand of God, Abel's at the right. Again the stage business is ingenious. Abel is to conceal a pot in his costume; when Cain strikes it the breaking sound accentuates the force of the blow.

Perhaps least accessible to a modern audience is the final section of the play, the *Ordo prophetarum*. The procession of prophets predicting the Nativity seems to have been inspired by a widely popular polemical work, the *Sermo contra Judaeos, paganos et Arianos* (Sermon against the Jews, Pagans and Arians), wrongly ascribed to St. Augustine. While the pagans and Arians for the most part receded rapidly into the classical past, the Jews remained familiar figures, inhabitants of most Western European communities. It is chiefly as a *Sermo contra Judaeos* that the work appears in the liturgy of Advent. Young praises it for its literary energy, which helped to make it a popular feature of the Christmas liturgy across Europe. He notes that the vehement quality of the attacks on the Jews makes it especially effective. The series of prophecies in the *Sermo* lent itself to dramatic presentations in which the prophets themselves appeared in appropriate costumes to announce their visions. Some of the livelier prophecies were developed into dramatized vignettes. Sepet's hypothesis that the later cycle plays developed out of the *Ordo prophetarum* has been rather discounted by recent scholars: few plays other than those centered on Daniel show much correspondence to the series of prophets in the *Sermo*. Still, the serial presentation of these biblical and classical figures and the explicit connections in the *Ordo prophetarum* between Old and New Testaments do correspond in notable ways with the structure of the mystery cycles. Many of the same ways of thinking about the Bible and about history appear in both contexts.[21]

In the case of the *Ordo representacionis Adae,* the list of prophets differs in some respects from that of the much earlier *Sermo*. Abraham, Moses, Aaron, David, Solomon, Balaam, Daniel, Habakkuk, Jeremiah, Isaiah, and Nebuchadnezzar appear in succession: of these, Abraham, Aaron, Solomon, and Balaam do not appear in the original *Sermo contra Judaeos*. All of the prophets are appropriately costumed, often bearing their iconographic attributes. Moses carries a rod and the tablets of the Law, Aaron a rod sprouting fruit and flowers. David and Solomon are dressed as kings, and Aaron as a bishop. Others wear wide robes that must have fallen into sculptural folds. They each step forward with dignity from the hidden place where they have been assuming their costumes. Several of them take their seats on a bench before they recite their prophecies, though Balaam appears riding his ass. Habakkuk is instructed to raise his hands toward the church in a stylized gesture of wonder and fear. After each prophet has announced his prediction of Christ in the Latin of the Vulgate and provided a traditional Christian explication in French verse, the devils reappear and lead him to hell. In the most dramatic moment of the series, Isaiah is challenged by a Jew: "*tunc exurget quidam de synagoga, disputans cum Isaia*" (Then somebody from the synagogue will rise up, disputing with Isaiah) (Bevington, *Medieval Drama,* 119). Beginning in a bantering tone, the Jew resorts to name-calling, treating the prophet as a fortune-teller but finally declaring that "this generation will listen to your teaching." As in Hilarius's *Suscitatio Lazari,* so here the stage Jew of the twelfth century is depicted as a skeptical materialist, an unbeliever. Isaiah's responses veer between the damning "You have the disease of evil / You will never be healed in all your life" and his vaguely positive conclusion: "This will all truly come to pass / In this you ought to place your hope" (Bevington, *Medieval Drama,* 121).

The identification *quidam de synagoga* is a trifle puzzling. Does it simply mean "a member of the synagogue," that is, a Jew? This would be the simplest solution, since no location is assigned to "the synagogue" in any other reference to the stage setting. Whence, then, does this Jew enter? Is the actor planted in the audience? Or should *quidam de synagoga* be interpreted more lavishly, to suggest some collective Jewish presence as an audience for the *Sermo* addressed so energetically to them? This mystery of Isaiah's Jew and his sudden appearance should perhaps be connected to the larger question of the audience of the *Sermo contra Judaeos* and its descendant, the *Ordo prophetarum* of which this section of the *Ordo representacionis Adae* is a variant. Did its author envision Jews in the audience? Many English urban centers contained visible Jewish communities up to 1290, when Edward I expelled the Jews from England. Compelling the members of these communities to attend sermons in church was certainly an established practice later in history. In the absence of actual Jews, a group of actors in distinctive Jewish costume, placed among the spectators, might have provided a visible target for the polemics of the prophets as well as a plausible spot from which Isaiah's *Judaeus* could spring.

Theologically, of course, this may be a needlessly literal interpretation of the text. Since late antiquity ecclesiastical thinkers had considered Christians to be the true Israel (*verus Israel*) for whom the Bible must have been intended all along. At certain points in the church calendar the reenactment of sacred events might place the Christian community in the position of the synagogue, awaiting the birth of Jesus or His resurrection. In addressing the Jews, the *Ordo prophetarum* also addresses the followers of Jesus who wait, again, to be convinced of His coming. This attitude looks forward to the most dramatic moments of the later cycle plays, when a shocked English Christian audience will momentarily find itself laughing at the grim jokes of Jesus' tormentors, sinful humanity participating in the death of its redeemer. Addressed consistently as Jews throughout the speeches of the prophets, the audience finds themselves at once arraigned for a "Jewish" lack of faith in the coming of Jesus, and invited to share in the crescendo of excitement as the prophets point with increasing clarity toward the narrative of the Nativity.

The social consequences of this entirely standard ecclesiastical characterization of the Jews, disseminated with increasing effectiveness through vernacular literature and performance, also deserve some mention here. The series of celebrated anti-Semitic events that shook England in the twelfth and thirteenth centuries included a riot at the coronation of Richard I in 1189 and the infamous massacre of York, 16–17 March 1190. The stage Jew of the medieval religious drama, by way of later medieval Latin and vernacular plays, naturally becomes a direct ancestor of Shylock and the Jew of Malta. The drama that translated the Latin theology of the church fathers into the language of rulers and their people contributed to polarizing Jewish and Christian communities in later medieval Europe, abruptly breaking off an early medieval period of coexistence. The *Ordo representacionis Adae* is a forerunner of later plays in this darker vein, as well as in the many charms of its language and staging.

It is possible that the *Ordo representacionis Adae* would have gone on to present New Testament scenes. The text is tied together by continued references to Adam's imprisonment in hell and to the coming of Jesus that will release him from bondage. The idea of Christ as the new Adam occurs powerfully in the writings of Paul and was widely current by the later twelfth century. The combination of varied performing techniques—interweaving liturgical responsories chanted by the choir, the adept versification of the French script, and sequences in pantomime—enriches the event enormously.

The stage directions for *La seinte Resureccion* are written in Anglo-Norman verse, and seem intended for presentation. They designate twelve "places" and "mansions," acting stations representing significant locations in the scene or positions for groups of characters. *La seinte Resureccion* begins with a conversation between Joseph of Arimathea and Pilate; it ends tantalizingly just as four Roman soldiers swear solemnly before Caiaphas to guard Jesus' tomb. Characterizations are developed through deftly handled dialogue and action, embellishing the scriptural narrative. The diplomatic Joseph, the somewhat timorous Nicodemus who assists him, and a suave Pilatus who places his faith in Hercules are perhaps the most striking. Longinus, the blind soldier who is told to pierce the crucified Jesus' side with a spear and who miraculously regains his sight, also plays a key role in the fragment. After the healing of Longinus, the deposition of Jesus from the Cross is the emotional high point of the play as it stands and is clearly intended to lead up to the lost resurrection scene. It allows Joseph and Nicodemus to review the events of the Passion, lamenting Jesus' suffering and betrayal. As with the *Ordo representacionis Adae,* we are confronted with a mutilated text. The loss of the ending makes both plays difficult to evaluate conclusively.[22]

Also associated with this period are the Middle English Shrewsbury fragments, which have been connected with records of performances at Lichfield Cathedral, possibly going back to the late twelfth century. One is a section of a shepherds' play, *Representacio pastorum,* for Christmas night. The other two are scraps of Easter scripts, part of a Resurrection scene for Easter morning, and part of a scene between the risen Christ and the pilgrims for Easter Monday. The texts themselves have affinities with the later York cycle plays. The manuscript reproduces a single actor's part, with cue words indicating when he is to speak. These early fragments are too short to allow much reconstruction of the plays from which they came.[23]

In examining this group of vernacular plays one must remain acutely conscious that with the exception of the Shrewsbury fragments these specific texts may not have been performed in Britain at all. They do seem to correspond roughly to the types of drama, the Old Testament plays excepted, represented in the surviving English records for the twelfth and thirteenth centuries. Easter and Christmas plays and saints' plays all seem to have taken root in England during this period, at monastic centers, cathedrals, and churches. If these particular texts were not in fact performed in England, others like them undoubtedly were. A reconstruction of the English church drama of the period can only remain approximate, given the state of the evidence. It would be a mistake to assume too much about the state of British drama based on these examples: it would be a far greater mistake to disregard them entirely.

COURT PAGEANTRY OF THE TWELFTH AND THIRTEENTH CENTURIES

Peter Dronke and Richard Axton have discussed as a form of drama the elegant role-playing dancing games and love games that were developing at the European courts of the twelfth century. We have less evidence of this pastime for the British Isles than we do for the Continent. They do seem to have become a ubiquitous form of entertainment at the courts of the later Middle Ages. Lists of games that we think of as children's party entertainment before the advent of television were in fact the adult entertainment of our ancestors. They might be rowdy, rough-and-tumble events ("Hot cockles"), opportunities to ask embarrassing personal questions (*Le roi qui ne ment*), or displays of literary prowess (*"Bouts rimés"*). They might involve a circle dance in which a soloist placed in the center portrays a character. Perhaps in the Middle English lyric "Maiden in the mor lay" we have an instance of such a dance. At least part of their social function seems to have been to provide an opportunity for elegant flirtations in a society where marriages were customarily arranged for children by their parents for political and economic reasons. The revolutionary development, in twelfth-century Provence, of a code of romantic love between individuals challenged the structure of Western society. Dancing games in which participants chose roles and partners may well have allowed the players to indulge fantasies of passion and individual choice that could have few alternative outlets. Dancing certainly came to be considered as much an aristocratic accomplishment as prowess in combat. At the same time, testimony from a variety of sources shows that dances provided opportunities for flirtation and seduction in every echelon of society. It is hardly surprising that the church campaigned to eject village dances from the churchyards of England during this period.[24]

Toward the end of the twelfth century certain records suggest that the courtly dance is becoming an occasion for dramatic entertainment of a different kind, one that looks forward to courtly "disguisings" and eventually the more familiar masques. A ring dance during the wedding celebrations of King Alexander of Scotland at Jedburgh Abbey in 1285 seems to have been interrupted by the appearance of a figure disguised as a corpse. This startling memento mori hints at the "dance of death" popular in fifteenth-century art, and perhaps at a pageant intended either to lend a serious note to the celebration or simply to enliven the proceedings further (Lancashire, 321).

In the twelfth century pageantry and athletic performance gradually became allies in the rise and elaboration of the tournament. War games and practice or ritual combats were a perennial form of amusement in warlike societies. The Romans had theirs, as did their Germanic opponents. Professor Wickham cites the gladiatorial and military games of the Roman amphitheater as precursors of the medieval tournament. This tournament seems to have coalesced in the eleventh century; by the twelfth century English knights like William Marshal were making a living on the professional tournament circuit. Early tournaments have been compared by one eminent medievalist to modern motorcycle rallies. A group of armed knights would meet at an agreed location, usually someone else's field, to test their skill in a mass battle, a melée. Few details distinguished these early tournaments from actual war: casualties were frequent, and as in war a captured knight would be held to ransom. The church naturally disapproved of this dangerous and destructive sport, as did many rulers. They were frequently banned, and those who died in them were denied Christian burial. Nevertheless, the enthusiastic support of its aristocratic participants ensured the survival of the tournament, and the game was gradually provided with rules to limit, if never entirely to check, its peril.

The idealized tournaments of the late twelfth-century romances have been credited with inspiring innovations in the real-life tournaments held by readers and hearers of those romances. Individual "jousts" between pairs of knights became popular displays of prowess, which distinguished their participants from the scrimmage of the melée. The presence of female spectators connected these more elegant tournaments with the love games of the aristocracy. A final touch of romance would be provided by a surprising variety of pageants in which knights, ladies, and entertainers might all take part, both during the tournament and at the associated banquets. In July 1288 at Boston in Lincolnshire the combatants in a tournament amused themselves by dressing as monks or regular canons. In 1309 one Giles Argentine appeared at a tournament at Stepney in Middlesex costumed as the "king of the greenwood" (Lancashire, 86, 268). From the later thirteenth through the seventeenth centuries tournaments became occasions for the most elaborate forms of aristocratic pageantry and allegorical drama. The stagecraft necessary for these presentations and the structure of the tournaments themselves proved key influences on drama and theaters in Britain. By the fifteenth century Sir Thomas Malory could speak of a knight performing in a tournament as "playing his pageant." As Professor Benson points out, these events were regarded by their participants and spectators as serious emulations of the most admired chivalric deeds of the past, a most elevated form of performance. It is the skeptical modern critic who too often dismisses them as decadent forms of escapism.[25]

Edward I's evident fondness for entertainment and pageantry is an important factor at the close of the period. Indeed, he should perhaps be regarded as the first English monarch to use pageantry to underline his political goals. Earlier rulers were known to employ entertainers: William the Conqueror's minstrel Taillefer and Henry I's fool Rahere were both well-known historical characters. Records of a royal chapel choir begin as early as 1135. It remains possible that Walter Map wrote the Latin comedy *Babio* at the court of Henry II. With Edward I, though, references to court entertainments and pageants become more than sporadic. A former crusader popular among his subjects for his military athleticism, he pursued an aggressive English expansionist policy in Scotland and Wales, where many of his castles still stand. The financial records of his court reveal a distinct a continuing interest in varying forms of entertainment. The extensive list of minstrels who appeared there in 1306 has been memorably studied by Constance Bullock-Davis in her *Menestrallorum Multitudo: Minstrels at a Royal Feast;* it is also reproduced in Chambers's *The Medieval Stage.* This chapter has already mentioned the saint's play of St. Magnus that the London Fishmongers presented in a procession honoring Edward, and the miracle plays that Edward's queen, Margaret of France, witnessed in the north.

Perhaps most striking in the records of Edward I's court are the references to reenactments of incidents from poular romances of his day. In 1299 a tournament in honor of Edward's marriage to Margaret was embellished by the appearance of participants disguised as characters from King Arthur's Round Table. Evidence from the Continent earlier in the thirteenth century indicates that such pageants had become fashionable at French tournaments as well. The "vows of the swan" that Edward is said to have enacted in 1306 as a prelude to his war with the Scots parallel chivalric oaths taken on a peacock in Jean de Longuyon's Alexander romance, *Les voeux du paon* (*The Vows of the Peacock*). The same romance lists for the first time the Nine Worthies, a list of the nine greatest chivalric heroes of world history that would become a staple of the chivalric mythology of the later Middle Ages and Renaissance. Maurice Keen discusses the importance of this "chivalric mythology" in the development of the knight's sense of his role in history. By linking himself to the great British worthy, Arthur, and to the world of the chivalric romances, Edward lent himself and his court an ambiance of lengendary glamour and authority. Such pageants were also an immensely attractive form of play for the knights and ladies who took part in them, a chance to enact love and war games in the guise of their favorite fictional characters. It is hardly surprising that Edward's pageants anticipate to the proliferation of such aristocratic performances in Britain over the next four centuries.[26]

CONCLUSION

The drama of the British Isles throughout the early periods under discussion is the drama of a sophisticated culture shaped by its international contacts, whether imperial Rome, the papacy, or closer influences of Gaul and later the Frankish Empire. Invariably British communities became multilingual, whether they combined Celtic languages and Latin or English, Latin, and Anglo-Norman. Their entertainments reflect this linguistic diversity. The links between drama and religion are patent, connecting Roman paganism and the theaters, village fertility cults and their dramatic ceremonials, or early medieval Christianity and its reenactments of the central events of church history. Drama remains an act of worship for these diverse believers. It makes their faith visible. At the same time the continuing role of drama as entertainment should not be minimized. This dual character of drama, as play and as the most solemn ritual, is certainly one of its strengths. It also triggers the ambivalent or hostile feelings of the austere moralists of every historical era. The most reverent dramatization can be accused of mixing levity with the most serious forms of human activity. While St. Thomas Aquinas recognized play as necessary to human life, other thinkers were not so positive.

Over this early period drama moved away from the Roman system, when public performances were funded by municipalities and local magnates as a political and religious responsibility. Private performances continued to attract patrons and audiences from all levels of society, though the character of performance and performers varied drastically. Examples of short dramatic works suitable for performance at feasts may be found in *Dame Sirith* and the *Interludium de clerico et puella*. The dismal social status of performing artists in the days of the Roman Empire did not prevent certain powerful figures from expressing their fascination with the drama, either by performing most indecorously themselves or by marrying their favorite performers. Similarly, medieval evidence shows that members of every social class might indulge themselves by taking part in dramatic activities—village rituals, aristocratic games, or monastic plays. The role of major monastic centers in the development of a rich ecclesiastical drama in the tenth century needs to be stressed here. As key cultural centers they seem to have led the church into the exploration of drama as an aid to devotion. Finally, the court plays a role by fostering new types of theater in which professional entertainers and aristocratic patrons collaborate. The roots of the seventeenth-century court masques run as deep as the age of Edward I.

The fact that we have so few texts of plays from the British Isles for this period and that the texts we do have tend to be fragmentary may tell us something about the status of drama as literature and the status of literature itself. For drama in particular the period 100–1300 may have been largely an age of oral composition, beginning with early improvisations and Roman mimes. The work of Brian Stock reminds us that literacy occurs in a wide range of intermediate forms. Then again, we may simply have lost the key sources. The student of the period can never be quite sure.[27]

CHAPTER III

BRITISH DRAMA IN THE FOURTEENTH AND FIFTEENTH CENTURIES

Between 1335 and 1350 British drama entered a new phase, perhaps reflecting a sense of confidence sparked in England by the personal rule of a young and charismatic Edward III. The Hundred Years' War, the Black Death of 1349 and succeeding years, the Peasants' Revolt of 1381, and the Lollard followers of John Wyclif in the later years of the fourteenth century all tested the Britons of this era. The later fourteenth century ranks among the most exciting in the history of English literature, one the writers of the age of Elizabeth looked back to for inspiration. Geoffrey Chaucer, John Gower, William Langland, the poet of "Pearl" and "Sir Gawain and the Green Knight" were all approximate contemporaries. None of them were playwrights, but all remarked on the drama of their age. Early in the fifteenth century the poet John Lydgate would write "mummings" for performance. English musicians of the late fourteenth and fifteenth centuries developed a distinctive style of polyphony that would alter musical thinking across Europe. English philosophers and mathematicians—John Duns Scotus and William of Ockham, Swineshead and Bradwardine—were also influential. The rise of "individualized" piety among laymen is notable throughout this period. It manifests itself in the production of personal books of hours for wealthy patrons, but also in the surprising spiritual autobiographies and adventures of such disparate characters as Duke Henry of Lancaster and Margery Kempe of Lynn.

This was unquestionably an opulent age, an age of display, of conspicuous consumption and glaring discrepancies between rich and poor. The "materialism" of the later middle ages has alienated a number of twentieth-century critics, perhaps because of their distaste for its apparent parallels today. But this was also an age of refined and sophisticated artistry. Yes, the men and women of the later Middle Ages loved beautiful things. They also made them.

Many of the earlier modes of performance described in chapter 1 continued throughout the British Isles. Village festivals and "clerk's plays" flourished; the London clerks maintained their tradition of scriptural plays at Clerkenwell, and their audiences may have continued to trample local property. Dramatic liturgical ceremonies also persisted from the fourteenth into the sixteenth century.

For most students of drama, though, the fourteenth and fifteenth centuries are notable for the rise of the two most familiar varieties of medieval play, the Corpus Christi cycles associated with civil guilds across England, and morality plays like *Everyman* and *The Castle of Perseverance*. This chapter begins with the cycle plays and the pageantry of fourteenth- and fifteenth-century towns. It then proceeds to discuss the morality plays and saints' plays, with their differing modes of performance and performers; court festivals; and finally the popular genre of the Robin Hood play.[1]

THE CORPUS CHRISTI CYCLES
AND CIVIC PAGEANTRY

The development of a distinctive Corpus Christi drama depended initially on the institution of the ecclesiastical feast of Corpus Christi, projected in the thirteenth century as a special celebration of the Real Presence of Christ in the Eucharist, which had become official church doctrine at the Fourth Lateran Council of 1215. The feast was officially instituted in 1311 by Clement V. In England, records of its celebration are widespread from 1318 on (Lancashire, xv). Tied to the movable feast of Easter, it might take place as early as 21 May or as late as 24 June, at midsummer. The festival's chief official event was a procession carrying the Host, starting at the main local church and proceeding across the town with intermediate stops at other churches (Wickham, *Medieval Theatre*, 66). The town's mercantile community quickly became involved in this procession; members of the trade guilds, in costume, carrying their banners, figured prominently in it. In many cases Corpus

Christi provided a new occasion for single religious plays, some still enacted by companies of clerks. Lancashire cites examples of individual scriptural plays on the feast of Corpus Christi from King's Lynn (1384–85), Bury St. Edmunds (1389), and Tamworth (1530s) (xvii–xv).

The church and individual members of the clergy remained involved, most often as writers, in the plays sponsored by the trade guilds. The evolutionary fallacy, accepted by Young and Chambers, that the Corpus Christi cycles represent an increasing "secularization" of church drama has been forcefully rejected by most recent scholars. It is also a mistake to ascribe any literary genre too strictly to a single class, either as authors or as an audience. Members of the aristocracy and their merchant contemporaries shared many of the same tastes in art and literature, as the careers of Chaucer and William Caxton both demonstrate. The church was embarrassed by the knowledge that less refined members of the clergy might relish the same entertainment as their more raucous parishioners. In the case of the mystery cycles, the experience of production was shared by clerical writers, civic authorities and mercantile sponsors, and professional and amateur performers and craftspeople. The performances might be witnessed by anyone from king to peasant.[2]

A review of technical vocabulary is important here. In the latest work on these Corpus Christi performances, the familiar critical terms *mystery cycles* or *cycle plays* continue in active use. They are also often replaced by the terms used in the original texts. To their audiences these comprehensive dramatic works, often lasting a day or spread over several days, were perhaps best known as "Corpus Christi plays." Individual guild "pageants" might be either the wagons that carried scenery and performers on their prescribed route through the city, or the biblical episode they presented. The dramatic form envisioned by the playwrights, an extended play composed of a series of pageants drawn from biblical history, seems unfamiliar to modern readers. Each pageant should be considered more as a scene than as a complete play. The failure of critics to consider the cycle of pageants as an artistic unit contributes to the persistent and depressing undervaluation of medieval drama (Stevens, 3–16).

In the absence of specific evidence, we need to resist the happy assumption that every town of any size had a play cycle. Four substantial cycles survive: one from York (1376–1580), one from Chester (1421–1575), the N-town or Hegge cycle formerly ascribed to Coventry, and one from Wakefield in Yorkshire (the Towneley plays). Besides these four major texts, records uncovered to date indicate that cycles were being performed in Coventry (1392–?), Ipswich (ca. 1400–?), Exeter (ca. 1413–?), Durham (1403), Worcester (1424–?), Newcastle (1426–1521 or 1589), Aberdeen, Scotland (1440), Dundee, Scotland (ca. 1450), Dublin, Ireland (1498–1569) and Kilkenny, Ireland (to 1639) (Lancashire, xvii–xviii). Other biblical cycles also were performed, apparently unconnected with either the feast of Corpus Christi or the trade guilds. At London companies of clerks continued their older tradition of biblical performances in August through the later fourteenth century. In Cornwall from around 1375 into the sixteenth century the cycle of biblical plays known as the *Ordinalia* was acted in circular playing places (Lancashire, xvii).

Debate continues regarding the plays' staging. "True processional staging" of cycle plays in England has been associated with York and Chester in particular. According to the generally accepted reconstruction of this method, a group of guild "pageant wagons" would line up early in the morning on the feast of Corpus Christi, each mounted with scenery. Every wagon would stop in its turn at each of the locations on the official list to present its pageant. Alan Nelson's challenge to this basic approach has generated controversy among specialists. Would this "true processional staging" be possible at all, or is it as much a fiction as Chaucer's presentation of the *Canterbury Tales* by a group of riders? The local evidence indicates that the answer is complicated. Practices clearly differed in different locations, sometimes changing from year to year. Some cycles, like N-town, are obviously designed for "place and scaffold" staging rather than processional presentation. As the discussion that follows will demonstrate, the intended method of staging can alter the character of the drama itself.[3]

Corpus Christi plays continued to be performed through the later sixteenth century. The last recorded performance of the York cycle occurred in 1569. As a boy growing up in Stratford-on-Avon, Shakespeare might have been taken to see the Coventry cycle. Most of the records that document the cycles' production come from sixteenth-century manuscripts.

THE CORNISH *ORDINALIA*. The earliest recorded Cornish "playing place" (*plain an gwarry*), at Castilly in Cornwall, was a prehistoric henge. Around 1275–1325 it was remodeled as a circular arena that would accommodate two thousand spectators, reminiscent of the Roman amphitheaters (Lancashire, xv). In 1375 the earliest suggestions of the performance of plays in similar "playing places" appear; performances went on into the sixteenth century. The trilogy of biblical plays known as the Cornish *Ordinalia* is associated with Penryn. It seems to have been written by a cleric at Glasney and produced with town support. The three plays, performed on successive days, are the *Origo mundi* (*The Origin of the World*), *Passio Domini nostri* (*The Passion of Our Lord*), and *Resurrexio Domini nostri* (*The Resurrection of Our Lord*). The distribution of biblical subject matter recalls the twelfth-century Adam and Resurrection plays discussed in chapter 7. Instructions for staging the plays are written in Latin, suggesting an active clerical role in the production.

The staging diagrams that accompany the play texts fascinate stage historians. Much of the literature on the plays concerns staging. Within the circle of the surrounding banks where the spectators were seated, actors performed at ground level on the central space or on eight raised scaffold stages distributed around the edge of the space to represent important locations in the play. Eighteenth-century descriptions of "Cornish rounds" are also useful to the student of medieval drama. Richard Southern's provocative description of *The Medieval Theatre in the Round* is based in part on the Cornish evidence and in part on the enigmatic staging diagram for the morality *The Castle of Perseverance*.

A saint's play in Cornish, *The Life of Saint Meriasek,* is linked with Camborne, whose patron saint Meriasek was. All of these plays are receiving greater critical attention today than in the past, illuminating their relationship to the Corpus Christi cycles and their merits as drama. They represent an important phase of medieval British drama: cycle drama seen from a Celtic perspective.[4]

THE YORK CYCLE, 1376–1580. A year after the first record of the Cornish *Ordinalia* comes the first documented performance of the York cycle of Corpus Christi plays. The earliest known record of drama at York mentions a Christmas night performance of the shepherds and Epiphany pageant of the three kings. This fourteenth-century document stems from the period of York's greatest prosperity, in the second half of the fourteenth century. The international wool trade, especially its clothmaking industry, helped to make York the largest city in England after London and to ensure its prominence as an intellectual and cultural center. Richard II recognized the importance of York in 1396 by elevating the city to the status of a county. Martin Stevens emphasizes the corporate character of the York cycle, the involvement of the town government and the entire community in the production. Initially the product of a successful, self-confident city, the York cycle also reflects in its history the economic decline that set in around the middle of the fifteenth century. At the height of its success in the fourteenth century York had a population approaching fifteen thousand. By 1550 this number had fallen by nearly fifty percent. In the face of this economic erosion, the city struggled to maintain the expensive dramatic tradition that symbolized its civic identity.

Much of our information on the York cycle and its performance history is drawn from documents edited and analyzed by Alexandra F. Johnston and Margaret Rogerson (REED volume) and from the manuscript containing the text of the plays, edited by Lucy Toulmin Smith (1885) and reedited in 1982 by Richard Beadle. This manuscript (now British Library Additional MS 35290) was evidently an official register of the plays. Most recently it has been dated between 1463–77, but with later annotations.[5]

The number of pageants and the guilds assigned to perform them varied from year to year. Fifty-nine pageants were listed in the second of two pageant lists of 1415 (Lancashire, 294), beginning with the creation of heaven and earth, originally the pageant of the Tanners and later the play of the Barkers, a related guild. The second through eleventh pageants presented events from the books of Genesis and Exodus: the five days of Creation (Plasterers), the creation of Adam and Eve (Cardmakers), the prohibition of the Tree of Knowledge (Fullers), the Fall of Man (Coopers), the expulsion from the Garden of Eden (Armorers), Cain and Abel (Glovers), Noah's building of the ark (Shipwrights), the Flood (Fishmongers and Mariners), Abraham's sacrifice of Isaac (Parchment Makers; Bookbinders in the text), and Pharaoh, Moses, and the Exodus (Hosiers).

The twelfth pageant began the account of the life of Jesus with the Spicers' play of the Annunciation, followed by Joseph's trouble about Mary (Founders; Pewterers in the text), a Nativity scene at Bethlehem (Tile Thatchers), the shepherds (Chandlers), Herod's interrogation of the three kings (Goldsmiths; later Masons and still later Minstrels), the three kings in Bethlehem (Goldsmiths), the presentation of Jesus in the temple (St. Leonard's Hospital; later Masons with Hatmakers and Laborers), the flight into Egypt (Marshals), the slaughter of the innocents (Girdlers; Nailers in the text), Jesus in the temple among the scholars (Spurriers and Lorimers), John's baptism of Jesus (Barbers), the marriage at Cana (Taverners—text lost), Jesus' temptation in the desert (Smiths), the Transfiguration (Curriers), the feast at Simon's house (Ironmongers—text lost), the woman taken in adultery (listed in 1415 as a separate pageant of Plumbers; connected to next pageant in the text), and the raising of Lazarus (Capmakers).

The entry into Jerusalem (Skinners) commenced a series of eighteen pageants that culminated in the Passion. The Cutlers next performed Judas' selling of Jesus, succeeded by the Last Supper (Bakers; Baxters in the text), the washing of the apostles' feet (Waterleaders—text lost), the agony in the garden and the capture of Jesus (Cordwainers), Jesus before Caiaphas (Bowyers and Fletchers), Jesus before Pilate (Tapissers; text also has Couchers; this play includes Pilate's wife's dream), Jesus before Herod (Dyers; Litsters in text), followed by a composite play of the second trial before Pilate, Judas' repentance, and the purchase of the Field of Blood (Cooks and Waterleaders in text; not listed in 1415), Judas' contrition (Cooks—text lost or perhaps an earlier version of the previous pageant), Judas' hanging (Saucemakers—text lost), Jesus condemned by Pilate (Tilemakers), the scourging and crowning with thorns (Turners and Bowlmakers—text lost), Jesus led to Calvary (Shearers), the division of Jesus' garments (Millers—text lost), the nailing of Jesus to the Cross (Painters; later Pinners), the raising of the Cross (Latteners—text lost). The Passion series ended with the death of Jesus (Butchers).

Seven pageants record events associated with the Resurrection: the Saddlers' Harrowing of Hell based on the apocryphal Gospel of Nicodemus, a pageant of the Resurrection by the Carpenters, Jesus' appearance to Mary Magdalene (Winedrawers), Jesus' appearance to the travelers to

Emmaus (Woolpackers; Sledmen in the text), Jesus' appearance to Thomas (Scriveners), and finally the Ascension (Tailors).

Seven final scenes connected the Resurrection with the apocalypse: a Pentecost play (Potters), the death of Mary (Drapers), Mary's appearance to Thomas (not in lists; Weavers in the text), the carrying of the body of Mary, or Fergus play (Masons; later Linenweavers—text lost), the Assumption (Woolenweavers—the text combines this with the next play), the coronation of Mary (the Mayor; later Innholders), and finally the Last Judgment (Mercers). Pageants were assigned with some sense of appropriateness to the craft, often through visual symbols within the narrative. In some cases the reasoning is obvious. The Armorers provide the angel with the sword in the expulsion from the Garden of Eden, Shipwrights build Noah's ark, the Fishmongers and Mariners present the Flood, and the Butchers dramatize the death of Jesus. In other cases symbolism is less obvious or even impossible to detect.

The preceding separation of the pageants into groups should not obscure the fact that in the offical lists and the text there are no such categories; the pageants appear in an unbroken series, beginning to end. The list by itself indicates the magnitude of the undertaking; it is, in its way, a document of economic and social history as well as of dramatic history. Guilds change their identities, merge and cooperate: pageants are combined, discontinued, and reworked.

The York Corpus Christi play is conceived on a larger scale than any other surviving English Corpus Christi play. More stations were permitted, and more pageants included, than at any other location. Alan Nelson questions whether a "true processional performance" would be possible at York, given the size of the cycle. The York performance seems to have occupied the entire day, from four-thirty in the morning, when the actors were required to line up with their pageants, ready to proceed through the city. Guilds were required to provide torches to accompany the procession. A sense of the exigencies of time also reveals itself in some pageant texts. In play 40, the Sledmen's pageant of the travellers to Emmaus, the pilgrims halt their preaching: "Here may we notte melle [of] more at this tyde, / For prossesse of plaies that precis in plight" (Smith, lines 191–92). We can imagine a Creation at daybreak and a Doomsday well after dark, with the entire course of providential world history between them.

The York register records revisions dating from the fifteenth through the sixteenth century. In spite of alterations and changes of direction, as it exists today the York Corpus Christi play remains a single great play composed of forty-eight pageants. The documents allow us to reconstruct earlier phases of the York performance as far back as 1376. Alexandra Johnston's analyses of technical materials allow us to visualize this most elaborate of surviving English Corpus Christi plays as it was performed in the mid-fifteenth or the early sixteenth century.

The production of such a major dramatic event was clearly a communal effort. According to an ordinance of 1476, preparations were to begin in Lent when the mayor would appoint four of the more experienced local players "to serche, here, and examen all the plaiers and plaies and pagentes thrughoute all the artificers belonging to Corpus Xt^i Plaie." Those found sufficiently skilled "to the honour of the Citie and worship of the saide Craftes" were to be allowed to participate, while "all other insuffient personnes, either in connyng, voice or personne" were to be ejected (REED; Smith, xxxvii). There follows a puzzling regulation forbidding any player from engaging himself to perform more than twice on the feast of Corpus Christi. This stricture has been interpreted as a curb on the practice of "doubling," in which a single actor might perform more than one part in the same play. The regulation is also capable of other interpretations—either as a suggestion that the pageants were not in fact supposed to be performed at more than two of the stations, or even as a check on ambitious or popular actors who might be tempted to perform with more than one guild, creating a logistical nightmare. The temptation might be strengthened by the reappearance of popular characters in several successive pageants. An actor who achieved the definitive Pilate might be courted by the Cutlers, the Tapiters and Couchers, the Cooks and Waterleaders (Smith, xxxvii).

Each craft guild appointed a "pageant master" to supervise the guild's preparations, the performance, and, of course, the expense account. Every guild had its pageant wagon and properties in storage; the expense of renting storage space occurs regularly in the records. Properties and costumes needed to be inventoried, inspected, and perhaps refurbished. The guild also paid for refreshments for rehearsal or

A modern re-creation of a medieval pageant wagon, here representing
Noah's ark in a Poculi Ludique Societas production, University of Toronto.
Reproduced by permission of the photographer, Professor Harry Roe.

workmen's breakfasts. Musicians were hired as needed in the script: in
1561 the new Musicians' guild enforced a monopoly by local musicians. York is one of the few Corpus Christi cycles for which music
survives, in this case six songs apparently composed for the Weavers'
pageant (no. 46), "The Appearance of Our Lady to Thomas" (see
JoAnn Dutka, *Music in the English Mystery Plays*, 8–9, 15, 65–66, 73–
74, 136 note 45).

The city established the series of stations that marked the path of
the Corpus Christi pageants through York. An ordinance of 1417
specified that these profitable locations should be rented out, and by
1554 the number had increased from twelve to sixteen. In a June 1417
list the pageants were to begin "at the gates of the priory of the Holy

Trinity in Mikel-gate" and finish "on the Pavement." The chief municipal officials witnessed the pageants as a group. In 1397 Richard II seems to have been seated at the gates of Holy Trinity, the first station, to witness the plays, perhaps from a specially constructed scaffold (Smith, xxxii–xxxiii).

A proclamation of the performance on the eve of Corpus Christi forbade the bearing of arms, to prevent breaches of the peace. Knights and "squires of worship" might have their swords carried behind them. Participants were reminded to play only at the assigned locations, marked with banners bearing the arms of the city (Smith, xxxvi). Guild torchbearers and players were cautioned to be ready and on their best behavior. A fine of one hundred shillings would be assessed against any craft that failed to bring forth its pageant "in order and course by good players, well arayed and openly spekyng" (Smith, xxxiv). The pageant master and the senior members of the guild were to accompany their wagon along its route.

The exact nature of these pageant wagons has been a matter of debate. The surviving guild documents record materials and properties belonging to some of the guilds. The play texts reveal lively action and a wide variety of special effects: divine beings ascend and descend on clouds, souls rise from sepulchres, Noah's ark takes shape before the audience's eyes, the risen Jesus appears and vanishes. Machinery mounted on the wagons made many of these scenes possible.

The York Corpus Christi play opened with the Tanners' or Barkers' "Creation and Fall of Lucifer," with an expository speech by "Deus," God the Father. The initial plays of the other surviving mystery cycles, on the same subject, each offer a parallel opening speech. As at York, this announcement juxtaposes God's eternity and the inception of universal history. The dramatic rhythm of the York cycle next becomes apparent as the two virtuous angels praise their divine creator, while their narcissistic chief, Lucifer, praises only himself: "And I so semely in syghte my selfe now I se" (Smith, p. 3, line 51). Finally he proposes to ascend to the highest place, making himself equal to God. Bevington and Sheingorn discuss the dramatic structure of the York Last Judgment pageant as a series of highly charged symbolic vertical and horizontal movements. In the Last Judgment, precisely choreographed movements to the left, right, up, and down all convey strong theological messages: salvation and damnation are plotted in opposing vectors on the grid that allots specified spaces to heaven, earth, and hell. The saved travel to the right and upward; the damned move inexorably to the left and down. From the start of the York Corpus Christi play these directionals are firmly established. In this initial pageant, Lucifer's tentative climb in the wrong direction is immediately and forcibly countered by the most explosive event of the scene, as he and his followers are violently expelled and descend into hell, in fact in mid-line. (The French *Mistère du Viel Testament* gives the stage direction at this point: "Adoncques doivent trebucher Lucifer et ses Anges le plus soudainement qu'il sera possible" [Then Lucifer and his Angels should fall as suddenly as possible] [Patrick Collins, *The N-Town Plays and Medieval Picture Cycles,* 45 note 54].) Lucifer and his fallen angel emerge pitch-black. The action clearly expects a lower playing area to represent hell, possibly in front of the pageant wagon; it also expects a radical and extremely rapid change of appearance, perhaps produced with the aid of a bag of soot. Lucifer and his follower express their change of status additionally through changed language, as they roar, lament, and trade accusations. Meanwhile in heaven, the remaining cherub reiterates his praise of God and asks what happened. God replies pithily, "Those foles for thaire fayre-hede in fantasyes fell" (Smith, p. 6, line 129). He turns to the next order of business, his plan for creating the world and mankind to replace the fallen angels. He orders the angel to restore light to earth and separate day from night, both appropriate to a dawn performance. The Barkers' pageant ends with a blessing, a signal of dismissal familiar from the liturgy, repeated as appropriate in many of the following plays.

The total effect of the first York pageant remains strongly visual, employing vertical symbolic motion, stations, and the special effect of the fallen angels' transformation. At the same time, the playwright distinguishes characters through language, differentiating effectively among the majestic speech of God, the perverted self-praise of Lucifer, and the exclamatory fallen dialect of the devils. The resources of rhyme, alliteration, stanzaic design, Latin tags, and variations in line length are all deployed. So is the angelic music JoAnn Dutka has discussed as a key dramatic tool in the English cycle plays. The angels respond to God's initial speech establishing the nine orders of angels by singing the *Te Deum;* after God proceeds to create the world and appoint Lucifer his deputy, they sing *Sanctus sanctus sanctus, dominus deus sabaoth.* As Dutka notes, both selections are drawn from the liturgy: the *Te Deum* occurs as a hymn at the end of matins, whereas *Sanctus, sanctus, sanctus* might refer either to a chant in the Ordinary of the Mass or to a repeated line from the *Te Deum* (Dutka, 37, 49, 69). Music is used here to manifest the heavenly concord that Lucifer is about to disrupt. (Groups of singing angels reappear in the York cycle in the pageants of the Ascension, the death of Mary, and the appearance of Mary to Thomas. Two angels sing at the moment of Christ's baptism, and a single singing angel celebrates the Resurrection (Dutka, 73–74].) All of these elements—visual, literary, and musical—combine to enrich the pageant. The pageant's variety of effects, from ecclesiastical Latin and liturgical music to graphic action, are calculated to fascinate its varied audience, which, as we have seen, might span the entire spectrum of English society.

This initial pageant reveals some of the primary challenges that the form of the Corpus Christi play offered to its dramatists and illuminates the conventions and the opportunities of the genre. Clearly the division of the play into a series of relatively brief pageants, to be performed by different companies and necessarily separated by variable intervals, enforced discontinuity. (It has also led to incomprehension by later readers.) The playwright needed to regain audience attention at the beginning of each new pageant. The standard opening tactic, still familiar to Elizabethan and Jacobean audiences, was to present an authoritative character who would address the distracted audience directly, summoning them to reenter the stream of biblical history. In the York Creation and Last Judgment pageants this figure is appropriately Deus, God Himself. In many of the medial plays an earthly ruler, often a most ungodly tyrant, occupies this key position. Pharaoh, Herod, Pilate, and Caiaphas each take their turns. This initial prominence and the practical need for a forceful, visually awesome, audible presence to reestablish audience attention helps to account for the way such characters became proverbial figures, rooted in the memory of their viewers, as in Chaucer's "Pilates voys" and the phrase "out-Herod Herod."

If the Corpus Christi play was to work as a single dramatic entity and not to disintegrate into a series of disconnected spectacles, it was also vital to stress the connections among the pageants. At key points in the play these initial speeches are used to review the action, reminding the audience of past and impending events. Pageants 1, 8, 12, and 46 in the York cycle (the Creation, the building of the ark, the Annunciation, and the appearance of Mary to Thomas) all begin with major recapitulatory speeches. But to a lesser degree recapitulation connects each pageant to its predecessor, stressing that the York Corpus Christi play is a single unit running from creation to doom. Bevington and Sheingorn discuss recapitulation as a fundamental linking technique in the mystery cycles (*Homo, Memento Finis,* 134–37). This recapitulatory initial speech functions as a kind of prologue, but one that moves without a break into the main action of the pageant. Patrick Collins also emphasizes visual elements as thematic links, paralleling their use in contemporary picture cycles like the *Holkham Bible Picture Book.* Recurrent visual motifs like the symbolic fruit, Eve's apple, Noah's dove, and the dove of the Holy Spirit all help to make iconographic connections (Collins, *The N-Town Plays and Medieval Picture Cycles;* Davidson, *York Art*).

Similar exigencies governed the endings of the York pageants. The York Corpus Christi play operated under strict time constraints. Players needed to make a quick, emphatic break in order to move on and make room for the next performance. In some cases, the characters simply say their farewells and leave. Very often a pageant ends with a blessing, prayer, or song of praise, testimony of God's benificent order. The opposite tactic, a concluding curse, is used strikingly in Cain and Abel, Jesus before Caiaphas, Jesus before Herod, the second trial before Pilate, and Jesus condemned by Pilate. The Fall of Man ends with Adam's cry or song of distress. In all cases the playwright provides an explicit exit line for the pageant. Just as the shift from divine rule to human tyranny signals a deterioration in relations between man and God, so the change from concluding blessings to curses intensifies the downward movement in biblical history. These conventional transitions underline the cohesive structure of the play as a whole, its authors' comprehensive vision of unity.

In the past, criticism looking toward the "secularization" of the

sixteenth-century theater and the advent of Shakespeare had a tendency to overstress the role of "bourgeois domestic comedy" in the
Corpus Christi plays. Since well before the time of Sir Walter Scott, in
fact, the idea of a comic element in biblical drama (or, indeed, in the
Bible itself) has scandalized serious-minded readers. This prejudice
has led to a popular misconception of the English mystery plays
mounted by the medieval craft guilds as universally abounding in
blasphemously raucous and inappropriate humor, requiring some anthropological excuse or apology. In fact, varying levels of comedy
play different roles in different Corpus Christi plays, as each playwright and community found appropriate. In every case, the use of
comedy in the mystery cycles bears witness to the intimate relationship between the biblical narrative and the later medieval believer, not
to crass popularization or any form of disrespect. At the same time, it
should be said that this question of irreverence was debated vigorously
by medieval opponents and supporters of religious drama.

In fact the York cycle deploys comic effects with notable restraint
and understatement, as Martin W. Walsh's study of the York "Troubles"
pageant indicates. The Creation pageant discussed above exemplifies
this caution. It juxtaposes the balance and poise of God with the lively
consternation and fury of the devils at their physical transmogrification
in an effective comedy of reversal and contrast. The creation and fall of
Lucifer also offers the subtler entertainment of Lucifer's self-worship,
which directly parodies and inverts the other angels' concurrent song of
praise. The effect is one of a verbal black comedy of contrast and disso-
nance, exploding into the broad physical comedy of the expulsion and
transformation. If anything, these comic effects underline the shocking
nature of the pageant's events. Lucifer is portrayed as both perverse and
ludicrous, as he gets everything backwards.

The York cycle does inject comedy into the biblical drama at many
of the traditional medieval occasions. Noah is here, as elsewhere, a
benevolent but oppressed ancient struggling to stuff his masterful wife
aboard the ark. Similarly in later medieval tradition, Joseph is famil-
iarly characterized as the aged Jewish bachelor carpenter who discon-
certingly finds himself married to the radiant, young, pregnant Virgin
Mary. Walsh's study of Joseph demonstrates how the York playwright, in contrast to many English and continental contemporaries,

evades low farce to create a more subtle figure. The York Joseph is still old and suspicious, but he is also a sympathetic, reverent husband, funny but not ridiculous. The psychological realism of the York Joseph's dithering mental agony is nowhere else so attractively handled in the English cycle tradition, even in the strong Towneley Annunciation play so much admired by A. W. Pollard.

The Corpus Christi play throughout England remained strongly connected to other forms of civic pagantry. This relationship is hardly surprising, since the participants in plays, royal entries, processions, and other local pageants were often the same group of people, frequently recycling the same resources. The York entry into Jerusalem (no. 25) exploits this shared experience as the burgesses of Jerusalem celebrate Jesus' arrival as a "royal entry."

Perhaps its impressive scale makes it most difficult for modern readers to appreciate the York cycle as a unified dramatic work. Overall, the York Corpus Christi play is notable for its sustained control, the steadfastness of its corporate purpose. Martin Stevens discusses the York Corpus Christi play as an expression of corporate life in the tradition of carnival drama studied by Bakhtin. In Stevens's view, the York cycle both affirms the communal experience and indirectly criticizes the civic power structure. The range and variety of the cycle's theatrical effects, understated power, and cumulative impact cannot be overestimated. At the same time its language is economical, measured, and restrained. Its influence is evident in the Towneley cycle, five of whose plays seem to have been borrowed from York. Truly drama written for performance, its greatness is best appreciated by witnesses and participants in modern re-creations of all or part of the cycle, like that mounted at the University of Toronto in 1983.

Over and above this monumental Corpus Christi performance, York evidently had a Pater Noster play produced by the Pater Noster guild, a Creed play, and a procession and play of St. George. They were performed by religious guilds, social and devotional societies, rather than by the local trade guilds. Lucy Toulmin Smith and Lancashire both note that the manuscripts containing these plays seem to have been the property of local clergymen, the guilds' chaplains. These, too, became objectionable to the religious authorities of the mid-sixteenth century, and have disappeared. Smith quotes a letter of

1568 from Dr. Matthew Hutton, dean of York, recommending against the performance of the Creed play: "ffor thoghe it was plawsible to yeares agoe, and wold now also of the ignorant sort be well liked, yet now in this happie time of the gospell I know the learned will mislike it" (Smith, xvi). Lancashire conjectures that the York Pater Noster play, depicting the vices and virtues, may well have resembled the *Castle of Perseverance*.

THE CHESTER CYCLE (PERFORMED CA. 1421–1575). To the southwest of York, the ancient city of Chester also had its civic cycle. The history of drama at Chester goes back to the Romans. An amphitheater for eight thousand was in use at its Roman predecessor, the town of Deva, from around 70 to 350 C.E. The minstrels of Chester also had an impressive history and ceremonials of their own, which are described in the REED volume on Chester.

Records from 1422 through 1474 (and perhaps through 1521) document the Chester Corpus Christi play. The earliest describe a short cycle, eleven plays long, mainly focusing on New Testament subjects. From before 1521 until 1575 a cycle of biblical plays, perhaps an augmented version of the original cycle, was enacted during three days at Whitsun, having been transferred to that date from the feast of Corpus Christi.

Eight manuscripts contain varying amounts of textual material from the town of Chester. The earliest fragment of the cycle is preserved on a single leaf of around 1500. The Peniarth manuscript of the Chester *Play of Antichrist* probably dates from the end of the fifteenth century, with sixteenth-century annotations. Still, the principal sources for the Chester cycle remain the youngest. Huntington MS 2 (formerly the Devonshire MS) has been most recently edited by R. M. Lumiansky and David Mills. It bears the date 1591. Another group of manuscripts—British Library Additional MS 10305, Harley MS 2013, and the Chester Coopers' Guild MS—were all written between 1592 and 1600 by George Bellin, the scribe of the Chester Coopers' Guild. Harley MS 2124 (of 1607) and Bodley MS 175 (of 1604) were also executed well after the final performances of the Chester pageants, perhaps for nostalgic local antiquaries. Although the cycle manuscripts are contemporary with Shakespeare, it is appropriate to discuss them here. Discussing the cycle here not only allows for convenient comparison with the other related Corpus Christi and Whitsun plays, but it also maintains the accepted chronological distortion that sees British religious drama as an extinct medieval form, unknown to the age of Elizabeth.[6]

Chronologically, the performance data for Chester take precedence over the play texts. At Chester in 1539–40, twenty-five Whitsun pageants were presented on wheeled carts over three days. A period of rehearsals preceded the play; one general rehearsal of the entire series of pageants is documented. Banns were also proclaimed to announce the performance. The first pageant, the fall of Lucifer, was the Barkers' or Tanners' play. Then came the creation of Adam and Eve combined with Cain and Abel (Drapers and Hosiers), Noah's ark (Waterleaders and Drawers of the river Dee), Abraham and Isaac (Barbers, Wax Chandlers, and Surgeons), and Moses and the prophecy of Balaam (Cappers, Wiredrawers, and Pinners). At this point, the pageants turned to the New Testament for the Annunciation and the Nativity (Wrights, Slaters, Tilers, Daubers, and Thatchers), the shepherds (Painters, Embroiderers, and Glaziers), Herod and the three kings (Vintners and Merchants), the offering of the three kings (Mercers and Spicers), the slaughter of the innocents (Goldsmiths and Masons), the purification (Blacksmiths, Furbishers, and Pewterers), the temptation and the woman taken in adultery (Butchers), the raising of Lazarus (Glovers and Parchmentmakers), Jesus at Jerusalem (Corvisers), the Last Supper (Bakers and Milners), the trial and flagellation (Fletchers, Bowyers, Coopers, Stringers, and Turners), the Crucifixion (Ironmongers and Ropers), the Harrowing of Hell (Cooks, Tapsters, Hostilers, and Innkeepers), the Resurrection (Skinners, Cardmakers, Hatters, Pointers, and Girdlers), Jesus on the road to Emmaus (Saddlers and Fusters), the Ascension (Tailors), Pentecost (Fishmongers or Fleshmongers), the prophets of Antichrist (Clothworkers or Shearmen), Antichrist (Dyers and Bellfounders), and Doomsday (Websters and Walkers). The final performance seems to have taken place at midsummer in the year 1575 (Lancashire, 109).

Martin Stevens regards the existing texts of the Chester cycle as later sixteenth-century products, responding in many respects to Reformation strictures about the improprieties of this Catholic dramatic genre. For a reader of the other three English mystery cycles, the Chester cycle immediately differentiates itself by its circumspection, its concern to make its meaning crystal clear, particularly to the "unlearned" auditor. The sixteenth-century revisers of the pageants were evidently sensitive to their Reformation critics on a number of fronts. It is particularly interesting for students of the history of British drama to examine the impact of sixteenth-century criticism on the Chester cycle, already the product of two centuries of performance.

This discussion is based on the Early English Text Society (EETS) edition of the Huntington MS. As Lumiansky and Mills note in their introduction, eight major differences separate a group of four manuscripts that includes Huntington MS 2, British Library Additional MS 10305, Harley 2013, and Bodley MS 175 (from the rather divergent Harley 2124). Among the most striking of these differences are the omission of the key scene in which Noah frees the raven and dove from the ark and variations in the handling of the transition from the Old to New Testaments. These two combine to alter the series of pageants sufficiently to make each of them a somewhat different version of the Chester cycle. Lumiansky and Mills give the twenty-four pageants of the Huntington MS, with major omissions and key items from other manuscripts in their appendices: these items include the raven and dove scene absent in the "group manuscript" version of the Noah pageant and the Peniarth manuscript's text of the Chester *Play of Antichrist*.

For those interested in the effects of sixteenth-century revision on the English mystery plays, a key element of the Chester cycle is the occasionally intrusive "Doctor" or "Expositor" who appears to explain or apologize in a number of the Chester pageants. When he rides up in the midst of the Barbers' play of Abraham, he explains that his commentary is introduced here so "the unlearned standinge herebye / maye knowe what this may be" (62). The Doctor makes a strong effort to direct audience interpretation of the pageants into approved channels, rather like an animated marginal gloss. He conveys a sense of the revisor's distrust, either of the plays' potential ambiguity or of the audience's interpretive capabilities. His role might be compared profitably with that of Contemplacio in the N-town cycle, which also employs explanatory interludes. Some standard iconographic references have vanished in the Chester cycle. The play of Moses concerns neither the Burning Bush as a symbol of the conception of Christ nor the Exodus from Egypt. Instead, it is unevenly divided between the giving of the Ten Commandments and Balaam as a prophet of Christ. The Doctor who appears here anticipates critical objections to the play's omissions of biblical events: "But all that storye for to fonge / to playe this moneth yt were to longe" (81). Does this line suggest that the Chester playwrights had begun to encounter increasing numbers of combative readers of the English Bible in their audience? A changing historical attitude may also have led to a reworking of the character of Octavian in the Wright's play *De Salutatione et Nativitate Salvatoris Jesu Christi*. Octavian first appears as an alliterative tyrant as he proclaims his universal empire and commands a census to "send about and see / how many heades I have" (106). By his second appearance, though, he bears a far greater resemblance to the Caesar Augustus of the humanistic schoolroom, rejecting his subjects' proposal to worship him as a god in response to the Sibyl's prophecy of the birth of Jesus. The Doctor's citation of Roman architectural evidence for the miraculous events of the plays may also reflect new challenges to the historicity of long-accepted extrabiblical Christian legends. The church of "St. Mary Ara Caeli" "that yett lastes untyll this daye, / as men knowe that there have binne" (124) bears witness to the story of Octavian and the Sibyl.

Sixteenth-century Chester remained susceptible to misogynist humor. The Chester cycle retains Adam's tirades against Eve and her "woman's counsel," as well as Noah's rebellious wife and a brief sketch of Joseph's concern about his cuckoldry. The dramatization of the events in Eden is singular for its vivid description of the serpent, with its wings, adder's "feet," and maiden's face, a striking instance of the medieval iconographical motif of the woman-headed snake studied by Nona Flores in her University of Illinois dissertation. Adam is almost totally exonerated of blame in the Chester version of his fall, which manages to suggest that he has no notion where Eve found the apple she directs him to eat. The devil initially targets Eve for temptation, since "wemen they be full licourouse," and at the end of the play Adam warns all his descendants to beware the rampant desires and enticements of the female sex, since "my lycourouse wyfe hath bynne

86

my foe." The devil represents wrath and woman gluttony; neither of them should be trusted more than the other (27).

The sequence of pageants from the Cappers' *De Moyses et de lege sibi data* (*Of Moses and the Law Given to Him*) through the Wrights' *De Salutatione et Nativitate Salvatoris Jesu Christi* (*Of the Salutation and the Nativity of Our Savior Jesus Christ*) and the Painters' *De Pastoribus* (*The Shepherds*) to the Vintners' *Trium regum orientalium* (*The Three Eastern Kings*) reveals some of the "group manuscript" version's style and tactics for maintaining the play's continuity. The cycle's fifth pageant, that of Moses, begins with Moses hearing God recite the Ten Commandments on Mount Sinai. For purposes of dramatic economy the same mountain also serves as the vantage point from which Balaam is called upon to curse the children of Israel later in the pageant. The children of Israel themselves never appear; the audience itself seems to stand in their place. The pageant's major incidents are separated by the comments of the Doctor. Here his comments intensify our sense of disjunction. Despite their use of the same setting, the two halves of this peculiarly organized pageant differ radically in character. Moses hears the Ten Commandments and speaks to the people. The Doctor then appears to explain that much biblical material has unavoidably been omitted and narrates the breaking of the tablets of the law. We then return to Moses, as God directs him to make new tablets and write on them. Following a second speech in which Moses stresses the sanctity of the Sabbath, he descends from the mountain, and King Balak immediately rides up. We find ourselves in the second phase of the pageant, the sole dramatization of the story of Balaam and his ass to appear in an English cycle. Where the initial section alternated reverential tableaux with preaching, the second division of the pageant offers vigorous comic characterization and action. Balak rants typically. Balaam complains frankly to God that his obedience is costing him money. The talking ass and the angel chasten the furious prophet effectively. Balaam's blessing of the Israelites infuriates Balak, who thinks Balaam is doing it only to annoy him. In spite of his status as the vehicle of the divine word, the Chester cycle's Balaam remains a sleazy character; he earns his fee at last by suggesting that Balak send a troupe of beautiful women to seduce the Israelites so they will displease God. At the end of the Balaam episode the Doctor reappears to describe additional events from the Book of Numbers that have also been omitted, and to invite the audience to return the next day for the birth of Christ. Clearly the Doctor is performing a vital role as a controller of the action. This essentially composite pageant itself functions as the final play of the Old Testament and as a *processus prophetarum,* with Balaam's linking prophecy of Christ augmented by the Doctor's linking Balak with the Magi, his descendants.

The second day of the Chester cycle opens directly with Gabriel's greeting to Mary. She responds, "How may this be, thow beast so bright? / In synne know I no worldly wight." This pageant's combination of events, like that of the preceding pageant, suggests consolidation. Chester runs together the Annunciation, Mary's meeting with Elizabeth, and Joseph's troubles in a tightly packed series of encounters. A messenger (Nuntius) then calls for room to allow Octavian to "come in and playe." Does this instruction refer to the advent of a new pageant wagon, or is it merely a verbal scene division? Joseph reacts by complaining that he uses his tools to get his living "as a symple carpenter." An especially happy touch here is Joseph's reaction to Octavian's tax, when he summons up the courage to ask the emperor's herald if the poor must pay as well as the rich: "that were a wonders wronge." The Nativity scene includes the two midwives, who also appear in the N-town cycle. In the Chester version of their story Tebell merely marvels that she has never encountered anything like this in all her years of practice, but Salome insists on feeling whether Mary is a virgin or not, and her hands wither. The Expositor appears to cite evidence for this and other miracles attendant upon the Nativity, drawing on the wonders of Roman pagan antiquity. In the final scene, the Sibyl returns to the emperor to announce Christ's birth. Inspired, Octavian experiences a vision of Mary and the Christ child. He commands them to be worshiped with incense. The Expositor has the final word: "unbeleeffe is a fowle sinne, / as you have seene within this playe" (124).

The Chester shepherds' pageant, assigned to the Painters' guild, deserves special mention. Overshadowed in the critical literature by its better known cousins, the Wakefield first and second shepherds' plays, the Chester pageant offers an elegant solution to the same problems. In its plot outline it bears clear resemblances to the Wakefield plays. The three senior shepherds, Hankeyn, Harvey, and the deaf and henpecked Tudd, gather with much comic shop talk about herbs and veterinary medicine. They lay out their supper, eat, drink, and sing. They then summon their shepherd boy Trowle, who wrestles with all three in succession and throws them. Following this exertion, they sleep, to be awakened by a blazing light and the song of the angel. After a review of the relevant prophecies and a rather extended comic discussion of the angel's song—"hit was 'glorus, glarus, glorius' "—they try to imitate it, apparently calling on the audience to join in (145). On the angel's instructions, the group proceeds, singing, to Bethlehem, where they admire Mary and the child "lapped in haye," and puzzle over the presence of Joseph: "Whatever this ould man that here ys?" . . . "His beard is like a buske of bryers / with a pound of heare about his mouth and more" (147). The pageant concludes with the shepherds' offerings, reflecting their poverty: a bell, a flacket with a spoon hanging from it, a cap, "a pair of my wyves ould hose." After the four shepherds have offered, four boys imitate their masters, bringing a bottle without a stopper, a hood, a shepherd's pipe, and a nuthook "to pull downe apples, payres, and ploomes." Finally, the shepherds bid farewell to one another, proposing to leave their craft and become wandering preachers or hermits. The Chester pageant elaborates attractively on the basic narrative. Its realistic comic shepherds with their appropriate properties and interests, its precise balance of physical horseplay and reverential tableaux, all make it memorable. The friction between the shepherds and young Trowle is submerged in their common experience of the Nativity. The final action of the pageant is their exchange of a kiss of peace. As an essay in domestic realism, an effective genre picture consistently and thoughtfully worked out to the last detail, it merits further attention.

In the Vintners' pageant of the three eastern kings the outrages of King Herod are deliberately restricted by the script. The play opens not with the expected tyrannical tirade, but with a reminiscence of the Cappers' pageant: the three kings, descendants of King Balak, visit the mountain and witness the star of the Nativity, borne by an angel who summons them to follow. They then propose to ride their dromedaries in search of the prophesied Christ child. When they ask Herod's messenger for directions, he warns them that any mention of a rival king will cause Herod to go wild "and flye out of his skynne." Only at this point do we encounter Herod, who uses his staff and sword, which he throws on the floor and ultimately breaks, to punctuate a characteristic tirade on his personal greatness: "I maister the moone. Take this in mynd" (164). Herod demands that the Doctor search the prophets to confirm the three kings' tidings. This action provides an opportunity to insert and dramatize additional material from the procession of prophets tradition. The Doctor recites the passage in Latin and then explicates it in English verse; one particularly effective touch is the furious Herod's own mock prophecy using the same format: "*Effundam super parvulum istum furorem meum*" (I shall pour out my wrath upon this little one). The kings are sent out with instructions to report on the location of the Nativity: their homage to the infant Jesus is the subject of the Mercers and Spicers' succeeding pageant. Meanwhile, Herod continues to plot the slaughter of the innocents, dramatized in 1539–40 by the Goldsmiths and Masons (170). The Vintners' pageant ends with a hint to the audience as Herod calls for a drink; his anger at the news of Jesus' birth has given him a raging thirst. "This boye doth mee so greatly anoye / that I wax dull and pure drye. / Have done and fill the wyne in hye; / I dye but I have drinke!" (174). Taken altogether, this segment of the Chester series of pageants contributes some attractive variations on familiar themes.

Among the many distinctive features of the Chester cycle should be mentioned its Antichrist play, which is also unique among the extant English cycles. It precedes a Last Judgment pageant that interestingly parallels the late medieval dance of Death in its identification of saved and damned souls according to their social status.

The Chester cycle includes many pageants that focus closely on a single biblical event: instances of this familiar dramatic unit include the fall of Lucifer, Noah and the Flood, the shepherds, the Passion, the Resurrection, Doomsday. Many other Chester pageants combine related multiple events. The Creation, the Fall, and the murder of Abel are united in the Chester pageant of the Drapers and Hosiers. The Wrights' Nativity pageant draws together the Annunciation, the visit to Elizabeth, Joseph's troubles, the Emperor Octavian and the Sibyl, and the Nativity with the episode of the two midwives. In this feature as well Chester comes closest to the N-town cycle with its complex units that suggest minicycles within the larger compilation of biblical history. The effect of the variation in scale from pageant to pageant is an interesting one.

From the point of view of stagecraft the Chester documents offer some parallels and some surprises. The texts frequently refer to the arrivals of mounted characters, and even specify that the three kings select dromedaries as their mounts as the fastest means of locomotion: "One I have, ye shall see." Unfortunately the stage directions vary a great deal in their completeness: some merely indicate "staff," "sword," or "cast up." The actor no doubt knew exactly what they meant, but the modern reader is often left wondering.

Its overt displays of the "new learning" and of anxiety over Reformation theological politics reflect the Chester cycle's special historical position. It preserves a sixteenth-century English civic cycle text in its final revised form, one last attempt to "rescue" this threatened species of religious art. Besides this chronological importance the Chester cycle also offers its own striking approaches to major dramatic problems.

THE N-TOWN CYCLE (ca. 1451–75). This cycle text has proven difficult to place geographically. Edited as *Ludus Coventriae; or, The Plaie called Corpus Christi,* it has also been described as "the Hegge plays," after the first known owner of the manuscript.[7] The modern usage "the N-town cycle" comes from the proclamation that begins the manuscript, in which three "vexillators," standard-bearing messengers, describe a series of forty pageants to be performed "a sunday next . . . In N. town" (Block, 16). "N" could stand for the Latin *nomen,* "name," suggesting that the name of a different town might be used to fill in the blank when the performance changed its location. In the past, the N-town cycle has been assigned to Coventry and Lincoln. Currently its students are arguing for Norwich, or possibly Bury St. Edmunds. The manuscript, British Library MS Cotton Vespasian D viii, is currently being reedited for the Early English Text Society by Stephen Spector. K. Block was its previous editor for EETS. The N-town cycle is a late fifteenth-century compilation, bringing together plays that seem to have been performed separately. The manuscript evidence suggests that the compiler of the N-town manuscript combined parts of existing cycles and unrelated single plays.

Forty-one pageants are included in the manuscript, which runs from the creation of heaven and the fall of Lucifer to Doomsday. The initial proclamation summarizes the events to be presented: "Ffor we purpose us pertly stylle in this prese / the pepyl to plese with pleys ful glad" (2). These messengers promise to thrill their audience with grue-some scenes, like the slaughter of the innocents: "the knythtys do sle hem euyn at A swap / this is a rewly syth" (7). Doomsday, the final pageant, will be terrifying: "who se that pagent may be agast." More than once the vexillators stress that the material of the pageants is all biblical: "Of holy wrytte this game xal bene / and of no fablys be no way" (15). The performance is "game" but serious and deeply mov-ing. Correspondences between the proclamation and the pageants it introduces suggest that this tail-rhyme piece was specially composed, presumably by the compiler of the manuscript himself, to introduce a series of plays. Discrepancies hint that the compiler may have changed his mind as he went along and neglected to alter the proclamation as much as necessary (Block, xxxiii). Similar discrepancies occur be-tween the "banns" of the *Castle of Perseverance* and the play itself.

Among the N-town manuscript's many distinctive features is its sequence of pageants centered on Mary. Pageants of the conception of Mary, Mary in the temple, the betrothal of Mary, the parliament in heaven, the salutation and conception, Joseph's return, Mary's visit to Elizabeth, and the trial of Joseph and Mary all precede the Nativity. Of this series, the conception of Mary, Mary in the temple, the betrothal of Mary, and the trial of Joseph and Mary are without parallel in any other surviving English cycle. The presence of Contemplacio (contem-plation), who introduces the plays and appears in the parliament in heaven, also marks this group of plays as a separate unit, possibly from the same source. The compiler of the N-town manuscript may have been attempting to salvage an older Marian cycle of pageants by inserting it into a comprehensive biblical history (Lancashire, 9–11). The interest in Mary is not confined to this section of the compilation. The explicit action of N-town *Passion Play I* ends not with the capture of Jesus but with Mary Magdalene bringing the news to the Virgin and with the Virgin's lament (269). *Pasison Play II* provides dialogue among the Virgin, John, and Jesus on the Cross. The Virgin embraces the Cross and, as Jesus dies, falls as if dead before it. In *Drama and Art*

Clifford Davidson discusses the tableau of the Virgin cradling the crucified Christ that climaxes the deposition (103–4). This image, familiar in medieval and Renaissance art as the pietà, is much less visible in English religious drama. But it does occur here. The risen Jesus greets Mary first. Pageant 41 is an elaborate Assumption that perhaps parallels the lost York *Fergus* play. All of these elements underline the emotional heightening of this cycle and its focus on Mary as a central figure.

Of this important cluster of pageants, the trial of Joseph and Mary is one of the most original, though it would be unfair to call it representative. The Chaucerian social comedy provided by the Summoner, who acts as both introducer and character within the pageant, certainly differentiates it from the surrounding scenes. One of the most unpopular professions of later medieval England certainly demanded dramatization. (Chaucerian Pardoners receive dramatic treatment in a number of later medieval moral interludes, notably in John Bale's *Kyng Johan* of 1538–60.) The Summoner opens the trial of Joseph and Mary with a Rabelaisian or Skeltonian list of the whores of the diocese who come under his supervision, calling them into the bishop's court to be fined for their vices; he hints broadly that, like Chaucer's Summoner, he is eminently bribable: "Megge mery wedyr and Sabyn sprynge / Tyffany Twynkelere ffayle ffor no thynge / The courte sal be þis day." As an introduction it recalls Leporello's list of Don Giovanni's conquests. The Detractors who report on Mary's suspicious pregnancy to the Bishop receive equally effective satirical treatment. Their lascivious gossip about Mary's pregnancy and the man responsible attracts Bishop Abizachar's reproof. Mary is his kinswoman. Finally, "Sym samonore" is sent out to summon Joseph and Mary, both of whom he browbeats. Mary and Joseph maintain Mary's continued virginity and Joseph's chastity before the Bishop and his dubious Doctors of Law. The pageant climaxes in an ordeal in which the parties drink a mystical beverage guaranteed to strike down the guilty, and they walk seven times round the altar. The dramatic tension of the ordeal builds, as first Joseph and then the pregnant Mary drink and then circle the altar to establish their innocence, accompanied by the jeers of the Summoner and the Detractors. When both emerge unharmed, the first Detractor accuses the baffled Bishop of changing the drink to save his relative. The Bishop orders him to drink himself; he does, and falls down in agony. The scene ends with all begging the vindicated Mary's forgiveness, as she and Joseph praise God. The sharp contrast between the sordid catalogue of whores and cuckolds, into which the Summoner and the Detractors attempt to fit the holy family, and the exemplary figure of Mary herself makes the scene work. It has the same verbal and visual interplay as a later medieval Netherlandish Nativity, in which the Madonna shines out of her graphically detailed, crudely rustic surroundings. The ordeal itself confronts cynical rationality with the paradox of the virgin birth, and faith emerges triumphant. These unworthy doubts squelched as thoroughly as possible, the audience can proceed to the Nativity.

The Marian pageants form a subunit within the larger compilation of the N-town manuscript. Another major subunit that cries out for detailed examination is the N-town passion sequence, which divides after the betrayal to form two blocs of material, *Passion Play I* and *Passion Play II*. Again, this suggests the collection of texts from different sources. *Passion Play I* begins with a speech by Lucifer himself: "I am ȝour lord Lucifer þat out of helle com / Prynce of þis werld and gret duke of helle" (225). He courts his followers among the audience: Lucifer's "Gyff me ȝour love" startlingly parallels Jesus' appeals to humanity, "Love me ageyn I aske no more" (201). Lucifer directs his male and female followers to adopt specific fashions, no doubt to the discomfort of any fashionable members of the audience. Men are to wear long pointed shoes and long hair "to herborwe qweke bestys þat tekele men onyth." In female costume Lucifer recommends décolletage. The men are to swear and fight in gangs, the women to engage in lechery. All are to employ semantic evasions to disguise their sin: "ȝe xal kalle pride oneste and 'naterall kend' lechory" (229). Again parodying Jesus, he reminds his followers that he is always with them. This astonishing prologue is the first signal of the division between the passion sequence and the earlier pageants. It is not explicitly connected with the pageants that follow it, however. The council of the Jews has its own prologue, in which John the Baptist offers a sermon praising the middle way, "the patthe of hope and drede" (229). His recommendation of penance and the inheritance of heaven stands in the manuscript as a refutation of Lucifer's speech. These two opposing exhortations demonstrate the conflicting moral exhortations that would challenge an audience of this composite cycle.

Passion Play I runs in continuous action from the council of the Jews and the entry of Jesus into Jerusalem, through the Last Supper and the agony in the garden, to the betrayal scene, which concludes with Mary's lament. At this point two Doctors appear. As the first explains, he functions as a teacher of "þe pepyl not lernyd" and as "a gostly precher" to the educated (269). He then begins a description of a procession of the apostles, Paul, and John the Baptist. The manuscript breaks off at this point, without a clear conclusion.

Passion Play II takes up the action with Jesus' appearance before Herod. Herod, Pilate, Annas, and Caiaphas all appear in procession and mount their scaffolds. An "exposytour in doctorys wede," identified in the manuscript as our old friend Contemplacio, reviews the narrative from Jesus' entry into Jerusalem through His betrayal and capture. Interestingly, Contemplacio says that the players now intend to go on with the material they omitted last year, or perhaps, to start at the place where they stopped last year. He begs the audience to pay attention, for the good of their souls: "Besekyng ȝou for mede of ȝour soulys to take good hede þer Atte (271). This introductory speech certainly presents the Passion as broken into two extended plays for performance in successive years. *Passion Play II* carries the account through the trials before Herod and Pilate and through the Crucifixion as far as Pentecost, without a major break until a Doctor appears to introduce the Assumption.

This distinctive structure has the effect of splitting one great play into two more manageable units. The first Passion play effectively ends with the powerful mob scene in which Jesus is betrayed, captured, and carried off in triumph, while Mary mourns. The action of the second Passion play begins with the news of Christ's capture, brought by a messenger running and shouting through the central playing "place," "Tydynges, tydynges . . . Jhesus of Nazareth is take, Jhesus of Nazareth is take!" It is more difficult to determine where the action would have ended. A case could be made for continuous action through the Assumption, or for earlier conclusions at the Ascension or at Pentecost. Effective use is made of simultaneous action in both plays. The multiple scaffolds enable *Passion Play I* to present the conspiracy of Judas and the Jews concurrently with the Last Supper; in the second Passion play the soul of Christ, *anima Christi,* descends to hell gate while the dead Jesus is taken down from the Cross and entombed.

Aside from its individual features of organization, the N-town Passion play is notable for its visual and emotional force. The drama focuses attention on scenes of intense feeling. The relationships among the apostles, between Mary Magdalene and Jesus, and between Jesus and His mother are all underlined. The first Passion play stresses the Communion both in the Last Supper and in the agony in the garden, when an angel comforts Jesus with a host and chalice from heaven. As Block notes, the N-town passion narrative differentiates interestingly between the Jewish nobles and prelates who conspire against Jesus and the common people who support him. As at York and Wakefield, these Jews accept the blood of Jesus for themselves and their descendants: "þe blod of hym mut ben on vs / and on oure chyldyr aftyr vs" (290: Matthew 27:25). This approach effectively rationalizes the ostracism if not the persecution of all subsequent Jews, a state of affairs familiar to the fourteenth- and sixteenth-century English audience by report rather than by extensive personal experience. The 1990 Oberammergau Passion play retained this ominous line.

The settings for these two Passion plays, or perhaps for this extended Passion play in two "acts," betray noticeable similarities. In the first play Annas and Caiaphas appear on separate scaffolds; a central council house in the center may also be raised, with some type of curtain or screen that allows it to be concealed and revealed. The house of Simon opens similarly to disclose the Last Supper: "þan xal þe place þer cryst is in xal sodeynly vnclose round Abowtyn." A "place lych to A parke" is also provided; it must be supplied with suitable equipment so that an angel can descend from heaven to offer Jesus a chalice and host, and "ascend again suddenly." Action in the space before and between these specialized scenes includes processions between scaffolds and the vivid crowd scene in which Jesus is arrested. *Passion Play II* has separate scaffolds for Herod and Pilate, while Annas and Caiaphas appear to share one. The necessary locations for the Cross, the sepulchre, and hell gate are not clearly defined.

The N-town cycle has been described as the most theatrical of the four major Corpus Christi cycles (Block, lvii). It offers the most detailed stage directions and also some of the most graphic theatrical effects. The manuscript's references to the placement of different characters suggests strongly that the N-town pageants, unlike those of Chester and probably York and Wakefield, were intended for stationary rather than processional staging. *Passion Play I* requires separate raised scaffolds above a playing "place" for Annas, Caiaphas, and their retinues. Their council takes place in a central location that can be opened and closed to reveal the actors, thus giving the effect of an interior scene. The same effect is used to reveal the scene of the Last Supper. This staging might refer to some type of raised booth stage with curtains like those that appear in European paintings of this approximate period. It will be worth recalling these settings later in this volume, in connection with the long and lively debate over the presentation of interiors on the Elizabethan stage. Its stationary presentation connects the N-town cycle with known evidence for the staging of European cycle plays, as well as with British works like *The Castle of Perseverance. The Castle,* a play with similar East Anglian antecedents, also uses a group of scaffolds for different characters, with processions between them across the *platea,* the playing place.

The cycle is strongly clerical in the sources it employs, among them Bonaventure's *Meditationes vitae Christi* by way of Nicholas Love's English translation, *The Mirrour of the Blessed Lyf of Jesus Christ,* and the *Golden Legend* (xxiv). The N-town plays also tend to be more technical in their theological interests; Block compares the detailed discussion of the Incarnation between Christ and the Doctors in the N-town pageant with the less complex conversations in the other English versions of this scene (liii). Its direct recourse to didactic language and tendency to insert sermons at appropriate moments also differentiate the N-town cycle from the civic Corpus Christi and Whitsun cycles of York, Wakefield, and Chester. Moses, John the Baptist, Peter, and Christ all preach directly to the N-town audience, often as the culmination of a pageant. The late medieval pulpit here takes to the stage; preaching and play are fused, much as they frequently are in the moral plays. The exemplary value of biblical events for the living audience is underlined frequently in the course of the pageants themselves.

As we have seen, a number of features link the N-town cycle with contemporary moral interludes. The introduction of personified abstractions as characters, as in the parliament of heaven, the commentator Contemplatio, and the character of Mors (Death) in the death of Herod is an unmistakable link to the moralities. Indeed, a parallel parliament in heaven, where the four daughters of God—Truth, Mercy, Justice, and Peace—debate the destiny of the human soul, is a climactic event in *The Castle of Perseverance*.

The N-town cycle also displays its independence in unique scenes. The death of Cain occurs here unexpectedly as an interlude in the pageant of Noah. The pageant of the birth of Jesus includes an abbreviated episode paralleling the "cherry tree carol." The N-town cycle is also independent in the way it visualizes key events. The procession of prophets in the N-town cycle combines kings of the line of David and prophetic commentators as an animated version of the Tree of Jesse that so often appears in medieval art. Overall, the outstanding visual imagination displayed throughout the cycle of pageants suggests that the compiler of the N-town manuscript selected them with this feature in mind.

The language of the pageants is unquestionably uneven. There is attractive (if not distinguished) poetry in the initial Creation pageant and elsewhere. On the other hand, many passages, notably the proclamations, are pedestrian. The cycle compensates with a flair for spectacular dramatic effects. Block cites the flight of the adulterous lover in play of the woman taken in adultery as an example of the superior dramatic effect of the N-town presentation. Whereas the York pageant drags in the woman, the N-town pageant entraps the guilty couple in the woman's house and produces her lover, who flees clutching his unfastened breeches and menacing the terrified authorities with his knife. The visual specificity of the stage directions extends on many occasions to the actors' costumes, gestures, and tone of voice. In the following pageant, an emotive raising of Lazarus, a series of graphic actions also help to project the heightened pathos of the events. The dying Lazarus asks his sisters to put him to bed. After his burial Mary Magdalene kisses Lazarus' tomb. When Lazarus is praised, Jesus weeps—"*Hic ihesus fingit se lacrimari*" (221). The heaviness of the stone enclosing the tomb is stressed as the four "consolers" struggle to move it aside. Jesus raises his eyes to heaven and summons Lazarus in a great voice: the unseen Lazarus replies from the grave. The climactic effect is Lazarus' final appearance "with his hands and feet bound up like those of a corpse prepared for burial" (*"ligatis manibus et pedibus ad modum sepultus"*; 224). The note of rejoicing, as the consolers hail Jesus as divine, shifts effectively to foreboding when Jesus predicts his own imminent death: "Toward my passyon I wyl me dyght. . . . Vpon a cros I xal be slayn" (225). This change in key provides an elegant transition, theologically and dramatically, from the pageants presenting Jesus' life to those of his passion and resurrection. It should be added that gesture alone does not carry this pageant; the raising of Lazarus is also notable for its development of charcterizations suggested by the scriptural narrative. Martha and Mary Magdalene are beautifully differentiated. It is the pragmatic Martha who asks her brother, "What wele ȝee ete, what wele ȝe drynk" (whereupon Lazarus promptly dies). She also suggests intelligently that the stench from Lazarus' tomb may be infectious. Her sister Mary rejects the platitudes of her consolers: "I thank ȝow frendes ffor your good chere / Myn hed doth ake as it xulde brest" (221). They suspect she is mad with grief. The consolers, with their recommendations of positive thinking as a remedy for Lazarus, and their reminders of the inevitability of death and the futility of grief, are perhaps more sympathetic figures here than in other versions of the scene. The slight touches of humor generated by their inappropriate efforts help to balance the pageant emotionally by staving off unrelieved gloom.

The difficulty of finding a home for the N-town plays raises certain questions about the material. Should N-town be read as a civic cycle at all? It is unquestionably a cycle, but is it civic? In spite of its affinities with York, Chester, and Towneley, the N-town cycle betrays clear differences. Its consistent use of larger units, its extensive Marian material, its lack of interest in trade guilds all differ in significant ways from the other major surviving cycles. Do these differences mean that the N-town cycle was not civic in origin or sponsorship at all? Perhaps it should be read as a rare example of the rival "clerk's play" or of the plays of devotional guilds rather than craft guilds. This conjecture does not diminish the importance of uncovering the cycle's true origins. Perhaps the components of the cycle originally belonged to very different groups of performers. Perhaps all these eccentric features simply bear witness to natural variations in taste from one medieval

English town to the next. Do critics still expect more homogeneity between the cycles than they should?

THE TOWNELEY CYCLE AND THE WAKEFIELD MASTER (CA. 1450–1576?). The most celebrated and most thoroughly studied Corpus Christi play is that associated with the market town of Wakefield in Yorkshire and with the anonymous author who has been designated "the Wakefield Master." The *Second Shepherds' Play* is unquestionably the most famous of this unquestionably outstanding cycle. The manuscript in which these pageants survive, Huntington MS HM 1, is currently being reedited by Martin Stevens and A. C. Cawley. It took the name "Towneley" from the Towneley family of Towneley Hall in Lancashire, whose library housed the manuscript. Marginal references in the manuscript and local allusions within the pageants both connect the cycle with the town of Wakefield, one of the upstart communities that in the mid-fifteenth century attracted the cloth trade away from York. The rise of Wakefield seems to be tied to York's decline as an economic center; the Wakefield cycle's borrowing of plays from York is entirely consistent with the smaller town's mode of operation in the socioeconomic sphere. It should be noted that recent scrutiny of the manuscript references to Wakefield has cast doubt on their authenticity—this pageant's locale will require reassessment.

The manuscript contains thirty-two pageants, many not assigned to craft guilds (a number are better known by their Latin titles): the Creation (Barkers), the killing of Abel (*Mactacio Abel;* Glovers), Noah (*Processus Noe cum filiis*), Abraham, Isaac, Jacob, and the prophets (*Processus prophetorum*), Pharaoh (*Pharao;* Litsters), Caesar Augustus, the Annunciation (*Annunciacio*), the salutation of Elizabeth (*Salutacio Elizabeth*), the *First Shepherds' Play* (*Pagina pastorum* or *Prima pastorum*), the *Second Shepherds' Play* (MS *Alia eorundum,* "another of the same thing," or *Secunda pastorum*), the offering of the magi (*Oblacio magorum*), the flight of Joseph and Mary into Egypt (*Fugacio Josep & Marie in Egyptum*), Herod (*Magnus Herodes*), the purification of Mary (*Purificacio Marie*), the play of the doctors (*Pagina doctorum*), John the Baptist, (*Johannes Baptista*), the conspiracy, the buffeting (*Coliphizacio*), the scourging (*Flagellacio*), the Crucifixion (*Processus Crucis*), the talents (*Processus talentorum*), the deliverance of souls (*Extraccio animarum*), the

Resurrection (*Resurreccio Domini*), the pilgrims (*Peregrini;* Fishers), Thomas of India (*Thomas Indie*), the Ascension (*Ascenio Domini*), the Last Judgment (*Iudicium*), and two items out of sequence—the Lazarus pageant and a monologue spoken by Judas, possibly the opening of an incomplete pageant of the hanging of Judas (*suspencio Iude*). Of these plays, six have traditionally been identified as the work of the Wakefield Master: The *Mactacio Abel,* the *Processus Noe cum filiis,* the two shepherds' plays, *Magnus Herodes,* and the *Coliphizacio.* All but the *Mactacio Abel* are written in a distinctive nine-line alliterative stanza with internal rhyme that has been identified as the Wakefield Master's work. Additional passages in this same nine-line stanza have been noted in the *Flagellatio,* the *Processus talentorum,* and the *Iudicium* and in *Lazarus.* Five of the other pageants are closely related to their counterparts at York: *Pharao* (York 11), the *Pagina doctorum* (York 22), the *Extraccio animarum* (York 37), the *Resurreccio Domini* (York 38), and the *Iudicium* (York 48). What seems to survive, according to A. W. Pollard, is a three-stage collection: an initial group of religious pageants, later supplemented by borrowings from York, and finally reworked by the Wakefield Master. Martin Stevens has mounted a vigorous and persuasive attack on this long-accepted model of composition. In his view the Wakefield Master, operating in the final third of the fifteenth century, compiled the cycle from a variety of outside sources, and himself tied them together in a new drama appropriate to his own setting. The nine-line stanza becomes an editorial artifact. "The Wakefield Master is not a mere redactor, he is a playwright-poet of extraordinary genius" (Stevens, 125).

The styles of the cycle's varied sources combine with the highly individual work of the Wakefield Master to give this cycle a startling degree of contrast, as the stylistic approaches of the component pageants diverge. The *Processus prophetarum* takes its viewers back to the series of single lecturers of the *Ordo representacionis Adae,* without the diversion of devils dragging the prophets to hell. *Johannes Baptista* depicts the baptism of Christ in an appropriately stately, even rather static, highly iconographic and didactic manner. Indeed, Jesus presents John with a lamb, his pictorial attribute, so that he can finish the play in a pose familiar from contemporary religious art. The pageants selected from the York cycle contribute their dignity and economy of style to this new context, wherein a number of unusual elements also appear. The successive pageants of Jacob's deception of Isaac and his later spiritual experiences are both unparalleled in the other English cycles, mostly because some effectively different characterizations enliven the Wakefield Cycle, as when, rather than meekly surrendering to his sacrificial fate, the Wakefield Isaac pleads and struggles with Abraham. Pollard praised the Pre-Raphaelite charm of the Annunciation pageant. Doubting Thomas, the main character of the twenty-eighth pageant, *Thomas Indie* (Thomas of India), is vividly portrayed as a tough-talking, fashionably dressed materialist. If he had been present when the risen Christ appeared, he would have insisted on putting his finger in a nail hole. When Jesus reappears, Thomas manifests his repentance graphically by casting off most of his elegant costume, while he pleads for Jesus' forgiveness.

Meanwhile the native Wakefield playwright inserts his own pointed social commentaries and trenchant language at points he considers apt. Examining the Towneley cycle as a whole reveals the full extent of the Wakefield Master's activities as revisor and author. It also sheds light on the role of the individual playwright as he shapes his own distinctive civic cycle. Pollard regrets "that a writer of such real power had no other scope for his abilities than that offered by the cyclical mystery play" (xxx). If we rashly assume that the Wakefield Master was given a free hand to compile and revise the cycle, the elements that he chose to compose afresh might be seen as a kind of critical commentary, revealing the playwright's view of the limitations of his material. The Wakefield Master's voice is especially apparent in rustic characters and scenes, in domestic strife, torturers, tyrants, and devils. The risen Lazarus' graveside meditation on the horrors of decomposition also employs his talent for telling alliterative detail to powerful effect.

The Wakefield audience would have first encountered the characteristic voice of the Wakefield Master in the second pageant, the Glovers' *Mactacio Abel*. Here the familiar depiction of Cain as a sullen and stingy farmer goes well beyond anything attempted in the other extant cycles. The pageant begins with Cain's boy, Pikeharnes, a new character in this version, calling for quiet. Cain is the central figure of the drama; he appears next, ploughing. His verbal abuse of his pert boy and of the unfortunate oxen prepares effectively for his confrontation with the pious Abel. The extended comic business in which Cain fusses as he selects the worst possible sheaves as his tithe, his irreverent reaction to God's rebuke "Whi, who is that hob-over-the-wall?"—"God is out of hys wit" (17)—all build inexorably toward the murder. Cain threatens the audience; he is then overtaken by fear. His responses to God's questioning reveal his guilt to an embarrassing extent. Abel must be in hell, "or somewhere fallen on slepyng. / Whan was he in my kepyng?" The play ends with a final exchange between Cain and his boy that also parodies a contemporary legal proclamation of immunity: Cain threatens the boy and skulks off to hide. As it is developed here, the virtuoso role of Cain provides a magnificent opportunity for the pageant's chief actor. The playwright confronts the audience with a central figure who is a familiar, completely understandable contemporary, by turns hilarious and menacing. The chasm between the Barkers' more stylized pageant of the Creation and Fall and the rich colloquial realism of the *Mactacio Abel* emphasizes the estrangement of fallen creation from its divine maker. The cycle exploits these radical differences in language to express a dramatic change in atmosphere and in theological status.

The third pageant, the Wakefield Master's *Processus Noe cum Filiis,* begins with a long recapitulatory speech by Noah that denounces the seven deadly sins, endemic since the Fall: "And now I wax old, / Seke, sory, and cold, / as muk apon mold / I widder away." God responds with an equally long speech: "Man must luf me paramoure." We are then introduced to Noah's unnamed wife, *vxor* (Latin "wife"); Noah declares that he's afraid of her, and indeed the two of them come to blows. Noah talks to himself as he builds the ark, complaining again of his age. The domestic tension escalates as Noah's wife expresses her suspicion of the ark—she has never been in any such thing. She sits and spins while she and Noah provoke one another as they offer competing marital advice to the audience. According to Noah's wife, many women out there wish their husbands were dead. This Chaucerian debate naturally degenerates into another fight, while Noah's children, looking on, reproach their parents. Once Noah manages to drag his recalcitrant wife on board, the narrative of the flood resumes its normal course with Noah's sounding for land, his sending out the dove and raven, and his final prayer. Noah's wife, now reasonably amicable, discusses the birds with him. The orchestration of the debate over marital supremacy to coincide with the anger of the elements is a traditional feature of the English Noah play, employed effectively at both York and Chester. The Wakefield exemplar stresses the popular late-medieval theme of the war between the sexes, with its universal applicability, perhaps more than the York and Chester plays do. In terms of characterization, this elderly Noah looks forward to Joseph and several Wakefield shepherds, while the wife is a direct ancestress of Gill in the *Second Shepherds' Play*.

If we are detecting the presence of the Wakefield Master by means of his distinctive stanzaic form, the fourth through the eleventh pageants, running from Abraham to the salutation, yield no apparent contributions. At one notable moment in *Pharao,* though, Pharaoh complains of the plagues: "We! lo, ther is no man that has / half as mych harme as I." His first knight corrects him: "Yis, sir, poore folk haue mekyll wo / to see thare catell thus out cast" (74). This concern for the suffering of the poor, and the brutal insensitivity of their over-lord, certainly fits in with the consistent attitude of the Wakefield Master. The character of the comic messenger, Lightfoot, in the other-wise unremarkable *Caesar Augustus* pageant also suggests his work. But with the two shepherds' plays of the Nativity sequence the Wake-field Master returns with éclat.

The Wakefield Master's shepherds' plays are generally presumed to be interchangeable in practice, if not in content. Both depict the an-gel's announcement of Jesus' birth to the shepherds and their visit and offerings to the Christ Child. It is reasonable to assume that the pro-ducers of the pageants might choose to present one or the other of the two plays in a given year but would not mount both of them. Perhaps this practice was simply a matter of artistic caution. Depending on their taste or on local public opinion, they might prefer the attractive *First Shepherds' Play* to the longer, more brilliant, and much more controversial *Second Shepherds' Play*.

The first play resembles the Chester Painters' play on the same subject, enlivened by the Wakefield playwright's inimitable verbal fire-works. The play begins with Gyb, the first shepherd, complaining in a rather lugubrious voice about the insecurity of the world; he has lost all his sheep and is going to buy more. His comrade John Horne objects to thieves, boasters, braggers, and bullies with daggers who lord it over others. The two quarrel in vivid terms over where Gyb will pasture his hypothetical flock. The third shepherd, Slow-pace, turns up as they are coming to blows, and reminds them both that the sheep as yet do not exist: "Ye fyssh before the nett." The boy, Jack, compares them to the fools of Gotham. More or less pacified, they share a wildly imaginative communal meal and drink and sing. The remnants are given to the poor. They sleep, to be awakened by the angel's song of good tidings. The shepherds admire the angel's vocal technique, "wonder curious with small noytys emang." Their review of the prophecies of a miraculous birth terminates with Gyb quoting in Latin from Virgil's *Fourth Eclogue,* much to John Horne's disgust. "Tell vs no clergye / I hold you of the freres." After an attempt to imitate the angel's song, they go east to Bethlehem, where they experience an attack of timidity outside the stable. Finally Gyb, the eldest, is shoved in first. The three rustic speeches they address to the infant Jesus project much of the same affectionate intimacy as their more famous counterparts in the *Second Shepherds' Play.* Mary responds suitably, and the shepherds go off with a song.

The shepherds—Gyb, John Horne, and Slow-pace, with their boy Jack—are all distinctive in their individual concerns. Their feast has been analyzed as foreshadowing the Communion ceremony. Certainly the plot stresses the conflict between the shepherds and its resolution, the "love feast" and the gift to the poor as instances of "good will among men," building toward the divine revelation of the angel. The strategic use of contrasting musical styles is clearly important to the play, in the shepherds' drinking song and the angel's complex Latin vocalization, the shepherds' attempt to imitate the angel and their final song (Dutka, 9–10, 80–81, 109–111). Indeed, as Dutka stresses, in both Wakefield shepherds' plays the supernatural impact of the angel's appearance at the center of the pageant is enforced by its stylistic contrast with the play's rural background. This use of music for dramatic purposes is, according to Dutka, unique in the cycles (111). The shepherds' world is imagined in acutely observed detail as the nearby Yorkshire countryside. In it the shepherds appear to their fifteenth-century Wakefield audience as familiar local characters.

The *Second Shepherds' Play* explodes the established pattern of the *First Shepherds' Play* still further. As in the first play, the shepherds

begin with characterizing monologues expressing their personal difficulties. The first shepherd objects to the oppressions of the upper
classes and their retainers, specifically to the "livery and maintenance"
that was one of the abuses of the age. The second grumbles about the
weather and his marital difficulties. Finally, their boy Daw arrives,
lamenting the floods, the general uncertainty of the world, and the
problems of servants like himself. His remark that men who walk at
night looking after their livestock "see sudden sights when other men
sleep" anticipates the angel's appearance. The shepherds sing, apparently one of the "three-men's songs" (also known as "Freemen's
songs"), with the melody in the tenor, that were so popular in the
fifteenth and sixteenth centuries (Dutka, 80–81).

Up to this point the *Second Shepherds' Play* might be a simplifica-
tion of the first, with the dramatic conflict between the shepherds
downplayed to permit expansion of the shepherds' social commentary. Then a fourth character, Mak, turns up, and with him what has
been (perhaps unfortunately) described as the first instance of a major
nonbiblical comic subplot in an English mystery pageant. Mak is also
given an initial complaint, in which he objects to the size of his family.
He addresses the shepherds in a faked southern accent, pretending to
be the king's yeoman. The shepherds recognize him immediately as an
unsavory local character, reputed to be a sheep thief. When the group
lie down to sleep, they place Mak between them. In spite of this
precaution, he awakens, casts a spell to prevent the shepherds' wak-
ing, and catches a sheep. Here the staging requires a "house" for Mak
and his equally ingenious wife Gill. Does this double as the stable
where the Nativity will later appear, or is it a separate "mansion"?
When Mak brings in the sheep, it is Gill who thinks up the jest of
hiding it in the cradle. She echoes the Wife of Bath in her praise of
women's counsel: "Yit a woman avyse / helpys at the last." Mak
returns and takes up his place among the shepherds. When they
awaken, he tells them that he has dreamed his wife gave birth to
another child: "Wo is he that has many barnes / And therto lytyll
brede!" The shepherds go to count their flocks, while Mak returns
home to Gill. The Wakefield Master gives her a complaint of her own
concerning the innumerable duties of the housewife. "Ful wofull is the
householde / That wantys a woman." She tells Mak to sing a lullaby,

which he does, very badly. When the shepherds arrive seeking their lost lamb, Mak and Gill act their parts convincingly, even vowing to eat the "child" in the cradle if they have stolen the sheep. The startling parallel already apparent between the "lamb of God" and Mak's stolen sheep in the cradle is reinforced by this allusion to the sacrament of Communion. The shepherds leave; outside, the first shepherd asks if they gave the child anything. This charitable impulse, the mirror image of the shepherds' later offerings to the Christ child, unmasks the deception as the shepherds peek into the cradle and discover their sheep. Mak and Gill continue to insist, first that it's a lovely baby, and then that it must be a changeling. The shepherds talk of hanging but, again generous, toss Mak in a canvas as punishment. Exhausted, the three shepherds fall asleep, and awaken to the angel's song. From this point, the *Second Shepherds' Play* again parallels the first, as the shepherds discuss the angel's music and the prophets, imitate the angel's song, and make their simple but highly symbolic offerings of "a bob of cherys," bird, and ball at the manger. Like the *First Shepherds' Play*, the second ends with the shepherds' three-part song.

At one time the innovative audacity of the *Second Shepherds' Play* shocked its scholarly readers. The direct parallel it drew between the Mak episode and the Nativity was regarded as blasphemous. Today the Wakefield Master's introduction of a comic anti-Nativity is generally seen as a stroke of genius. The play is not in the least irreverent, though it is lively and high-spirited. Mak and Gill remain two of the most notable comic roles in medieval English drama; the moment of revelation when Daw unveils the sheep's nose is superbly hilarious. Still, the Wakefield playwright resists burlesquing the shepherds' gifts, a temptation that seems to overcome the Chester playwright when he brings on "a pair of my wife's old hose" as an offering. On the most serious level, the stolen sheep in the manger is a type of the Lamb of God. Mak's act of trickery foreshadows the act of substitution, divine being for mere human, by which the devil will be deceived and mankind saved. Unlike many later comic subplots that have little structural meaning, Mak's escapade is theologically and dramatically essential. Using a single schematic building for Mak's house and the stable would emphasize the parallel between the two scenes.

The *Second Shepherds' Play* uses music much as does the first, with

the significant addition of Mak and Gill's discordant lullaby. The playwright adds this raucous attempt as a reflection of their sinful state and
thus widens further the spectrum of musical styles, concord and dis-
cord, at work in the play (Dutka, 6). Finally, the *Second Shepherds' Play*
sharpens its analysis of the shepherds' role in society, presenting it in
specific terms a fifteenth-century audience would recognize immediately. The poverty of the shepherds and of Mak's household is underlined to good effect. The search of Mak's house turns up only two
empty platters. After the angel's song, the shepherds marvel at their
selection as witnesses "To so pore as we ar / that he wold appere." The
entire piece is a beautifully balanced work of art, deeply satisfying to
the reader, the performer, and the spectator.

For a long time it has been customary to place the Wakefield Master in a class of his own, as the outstanding playwright of the English
Middle Ages. Martin Stevens's analysis tends to support this viewpoint. A second, probably related commonplace of criticism is to
identify the Wakefield Master's talent as essentially comic or farcical;
regrettably, he is too often seen as the author of a single anomalous
masterpiece, the *Second Shepherds' Play,* while the full extent of his
work throughout the Wakefield cycle remains unappreciated. The su-
periority of the Wakefield Master seems at first glance to be connected
to the longstanding critical preoccupation with the "progressive secularization" of English drama.

More recent developments in research have led scholars to reevaluate both the Wakefield playwright's position and the nature of his
genius. The product of that genius, the Wakefield cycle, is by comparison to its counterparts the most varied in its stylistic range and startling comic effects, in many cases tending toward black comedy. It is
perhaps the most socially conscious of the surviving cycles, though
they all express notable concern for contemporary abuses. The York
play is the more level and cohesive work; the N-town compilation
offers large spectacular scenes and operatic emotion, which reflect late
Gothic sensibility in art, as well as more sermons. Its rejection of
misogyny in favor of Marian interests make it in many respects a
women's cycle. When we look beyond the mystery cycles toward the
moral play, the unknown author of the monumental *Castle of Persever-*

ance can make a good claim to be ranked beside the Wakefield Master. The author of the *Second Shepherds' Play* is one of the greatest playwrights of medieval England, but not the only great playwright of his time.

THE COVENTRY CYCLE (1392–1580): REMNANTS AND RECORDS. A distinguished list of royal visitors, including Marguerite d'Anjou, Richard III, and Henry VII (who was there twice) witnessed the Coventry Corpus Christi plays in the course of the fifteenth century. Records indicate that this Corpus Christi drama was performed at from 1392 until 1580. Interesting performance records survive, including lists of properties, but disappointingly few texts. Eleven pageants appear in the guild documents. Surviving are a play running from the Annunciation to the slaughter of the innocents, presented by the Shearmen and Tailors; a version of the Weavers' pageant, which immediately followed it; the presentation in the temple; and Jesus' debate with the elders. The Smiths evidently presented the betrayal, trial and Crucifixion, the Cappers were responsible for the descent from the Cross, the Resurrection, the Harrowing of Hell, and the meeting with the Marys, and the Drapers presented Doomsday. Records also mention that the Whittawers and Butchers, the Pinners, the Tilers and Wrights, the Girdlers, the Mercers, the Tanners, and the Painters all offered pageants at one time or another in the history of the Coventry Corpus Christi drama. It is regrettable that the loss of many texts makes it difficult to evaluate the total effect of this celebrated English cycle.[9]

DRAMA AT LONDON: PAGEANTRY AND PROFESSIONAL PLAYERS. Finally, some attention should be paid to the differing situation at London, where the craft guilds evidently did not produce their own plays. Instead, clerks' plays seem to have continued on the outskirts of the city; on occasion in Southwark, "ther many a shrew is inne," according to Chaucer. At Clerkenwell large-scale scriptural cycles were still mounted by companies of clerks through the reigns of Richard II and Henry IV. The texts do not survive; reports from 1384 through 1411 describe plays "of the Passion of our Lord and the Creation of the World," "showing how God created Heaven and Earth out of nothing and how he created Adam and on to the Day of Judgment." The cycle may have varied in length from three to seven days. The audience, sometimes including the royal family, were in one case seated on a scaffold (Lancashire, 113, 361).

The gravitation of dramatic performances to the rowdier outskirts of the late medieval metropolis paved the way for the Elizabethan public theaters in many of the same or similar locations. During the fifteenth century the king's court and many of the London trade guilds hired traveling companies to entertain them. These might be the troupes maintained by a nobleman, town players from elsewhere, or unattached professional actors (Lancashire, xx). Jack Travaill and his London-based troupe performed interludes twice before child-king Henry VI at Christmas in 1426 and 1427. The appearance of the REED volumes for London and its vicinity should provide important evidence for the study of these issues. At the moment it is possible to note the presence of an active commercial theater tradition in the London area, served by semiprofessional and professional companies.[10]

Isolated biblical plays survive from other locations, further extending this dramatic tradition. There are performance records of the Newcastle upon Tyne Noah play from 1427–1589. Plays on the sacrifice of Isaac are associated with Brome Hall in Suffolk (ca. 1454–99) and with Northampton in 1461. Biblical cycles appear in Scotland and Ireland, where one instance, at Kilkenny, extends the history of the cycle into the mid-seventeenth century. While any notion of finding a cycle in every small town in Britain should be strenuously discouraged, it is clear that the practice of performing biblical plays like those of the major cycles was widespread. These may have been detached pageants from larger cycles, smaller cycles of pageants, or plays intended for individual performance from the start. At the moment the range and development of devotional drama in fourteenth- and fifteenth-century Britain is only beginning to be appreciated by specialists in the field.[11]

Critics like Peter Happé have characterized the English Corpus Christi cycles as very much alike, an essentially fixed, homogeneous, conservative tradition. By contrast, he presents the morality play or moral interlude as the progressive dramatic genre, pointing the way toward the Elizabethan theater. David Bevington's classic discussion in *From Mankind to Marlowe* lends weight to this interpretation, which in fact dates back at least to the days of Sir Walter Scott. These attempts to contrast the cycles and the moralities tend to minimize the many points of contact between these medieval theatrical genres. The descriptions of the cycles above have pointed up many parallels in dramatic conception and technique. Martin Stevens's study reasserts the individual character of the four major cycles. My own view is that that these attempts to stress oppositions between these major genres, or to denigrate the cycles at the expense of the moral plays, have proven unfortunate as well as unnecessary. Both of these key medieval forms are powerful in their dramatic effect as well as in their influence.

It should be noted at the same time that such comparisons are in line both with earlier historians of the drama and with the debate over the theological propriety of religious theater that developed force in England from the fifteenth into the seventeenth century, fueled by the Reformation. This introduction to the English Corpus Christi cycles cannot neglect the comments offered by their vocal contemporary critics and supporters. The debate is particularly valuable for the light it sheds on the theory of late medieval biblical drama and on the attitudes of producers and audiences. The most important critical text remains the Middle English Wycliffite *Treatise of Miraclis Pleyinge*. It appears in British Library Additional MS 24202, fols. 14–21. Apparently written in the early fifteenth century, perhaps in the central midlands, by an anonymous adherent of John Wyclif, the *Treatise* indicts the biblical plays and plays depicting nonscriptural miracles as hypocritical and disrespectful "pleying" with the highly serious miracles performed in earnest by God for man's salvation.[12] It objects particularly to the participation of priests in any such activities. Two elements of this discussion have impressed modern readers. The first is the encapsulated defense of the cycles that the writer includes in order to refute it. Here the supporters of the biblical dramas defend their activity by insisting that the plays are serious acts of worship and that they deeply impress or convert many members of their audiences. Such performances are permitted to Christians for entertainment, they argue, just as paintings of the same scenes in church are permissible. Indeed, plays are more efficacious, "for this is a deed bok, the tother a qu[i]ck" (p. 40, lines 218–19). The author retorts that such plays "ben made more to deliten men bodily than to ben bokis to lewid men" (45). The second notable feature of the *Treatise* is its stress on the idea of play itself as intimately connected to the "miraclis." "Miraclis pleying" is a pejorative term as the author uses it here. Play itself, of children or of adults, is invariably associated with sin, with mockery, and with the delights of the flesh. It is the pleasure that performers and audience derive from the act of performance that discredits them most thoroughly to the Wicliffite critic, "as they in greet likyng ben don and to grete liking ben cast biforn. . . . And sithen miraclis pleyinge is of the lustis of the fleyssh and mirthe of the body" (37, 38). It is less sinful to perform "rebaudye"—a secular farce like *Dame Sirith,* perhaps— than to perform plays based on biblical history. In its line of argument and in its suspicion of corporeal pleasure, laughter, and the representation of the bible in "play," the *Treatise* looks forward to the Puritan opponents of the theater. At the same time, as Clifford Davidson notes in his introduction, it continues a long Christian antitheatrical tradition that reaches back at least as far as Tertullian.

As the *Treatise* itself indicates, the Corpus Christi cycles also had vigorous contemporary defenders. Reginald Peacock's *Repressor of Overmuch Blaming of the Clergy* and *Dives and Pauper* both defend the drama as a form of devotion.

The account of the suppression of the Corpus Christi plays in Britain under the combined stresses of Reformation theology and an altered national economy will appear in Chapters Three and Four.

Other forms of pageantry beyond the biblical cycles also engaged the attention and the funding of fourteenth- and fifteenth-century townspeople. Royal entries elicited magnificent semidramatic or dramatic pageants, as they still would in the sixteenth and seventeenth centuries. A conspicuous display of wealth was a statement of the town's prosperity and importance, as well as a flattering gesture to a powerful visitor. Often, the two dramatic forms would be combined: a special performance of the local Corpus Christi cycle or some key segment of it might be mounted for a very important visitor. Usually the royal entries reversed the concept of processional staging. Rather than move a series of performances past a stationary audience, in many civic pageants it was the visitor who proceeded past a series of fixed points where different scenes were enacted and speeches or songs performed. The civil audience could witness both the royal procession and the stationary entertainments. Such pageants frequently represented figures from chivalric mythology like the Nine Worthies. Often the visitor would be presented with valuable gifts or symbols of the city's homage. Such occasions could carry a powerful political charge. On 21 August 1392 Richard II and Queen Anne entered London in a procession sealing the city's "reconciliation" with its imperious monarch after a particularly stormy contest of wills. Among the scenes they encountered were a castle from which two young angels descended with crowns for the royal couple, an appearance of God surrounded by angels at St. Paul's, and a forest full of wild animals at Temple Bar as a setting for John the Baptist, one of Richard II's patron saints: an angel descended from the forest bearing tablets, symbols of biblical law and of the new accord between Richard and his capital (Lancashire, 176–77). Again, the REED volumes, Professor Lancashire's *Dramatic Texts and Records of Britain,* and specialized studies like Withington's pioneering work on English pageantry all demonstrate the range and spectacular qualities of this tradition.[13]

THE MORALITY PLAY AND ITS PERFORMERS

This vernacular drama was of a different variety, written and performed by a different cast of characters under entirely different circumstances. Sir Walter Scott speculated early in the nineteenth century that the "morality play" was developed as a kind of reaction against the blasphemy of the Corpus Christi cycles, "in which passages from Scripture were profanely and indecently mingled with human inventions of a very rude, and sometimes an indecorous character" (*Essay on Drama,* 320–21). The much disputed evolutionary notion of the "progressive secularization" of drama from the Middle Ages to Shakespeare retains some of the same assumptions. In fact, the moral play and the Corpus Christi cycle are contemporaries throughout their histories.

It was clear to early historians of British drama that the moral play belonged to a different species than the Corpus Christi cycles. Where the cycle plays dramatized the events of biblical history, the morality plays dealt with allegorical figures in conflict. Their characters were abstractions: a hero—Mankind, Everyman, or Humanum Genus—

would encounter equally symbolic figures, normally vices and virtues, that typified the spiritual struggles of life itself. When we think of English morality plays, we think principally of *Everyman*, the most famous example of the genre. Plays like *The Castle of Perseverance*, *Wisdom*, and *Mankind* are also moralities, and in the sixteenth century literary innovators like John Skelton and Sir David Lindsay would extend the genre to overtly political subject matter. The genre was at least equally popular on the Continent: the most famous English example of the moral play, *Everyman* is in all probability a translation from the Dutch of ca. 1500. In French there are an immense number of moral plays, long and short, from the fifteenth and sixteenth centuries—*Mestier et marchandise*, *La condemnacion de Banquet*, to name only a few. A Welsh example survives from the sixteenth century.

The term *morality play* has proven as dampening to later readers as the epithet "Moral" that Geoffrey Chaucer applied to his friend and rival John Gower. Some modern scholars now prefer "moral play," but both terms still persist in critical literature on the subject. The "moral interlude" that has attracted much critical attention in the early Tudor period is a compressed form of the morality, designed for performance indoors at a banquet.

David Bevington, in *From Mankind to Marlowe*, traces the shaping influence of the morality plays and their performance tradition on the Elizabethan stage. As in the case of the Corpus Christi cycles, the history of the moral play continues vigorously throughout the sixteenth century.[14]

THE CASTLE OF PERSEVERANCE. Ian Lancashire suggests that *The Castle of Perseverance*, by far the most ambitious moral play to survive from the English Middle Ages, was in fact a Pater Noster play performed originally by a troupe of clerks at Lincoln from 1397–?. The York Pater Noster play, performed between 1385 and 1575 and supposed to reprove vices and encourage virtues, may have been conceived in a similar style. This large-scale depiction of the experiences of Humanum Genus (Man) portrays life on earth as a battleground of personified forces warring for the human soul. Happé questions whether such an epic drama would have been suited for performance by a small troupe of traveling players: the play itself seems to require twenty-two performers, all or most visible to the audience at the same time. It is difficult to see how more than one part could be assigned to a single actor, as they often are in the later moralities analyzed by David Bevington (see chapter 3).

The Castle of Perseverance is accompanied in its manuscript by a rather cryptic diagram that suggests possibilities for the play's staging. The proper interpretation of this unique image has generated much debate among students of medieval drama. It depicts a circular space, in the center of which appears the "castle" of the title. Five scaffolds are placed around the outer rim of the circle, each assigned its point of the compass: "Sowth: Caro skafold"; "South: Flesh's scaffold." The adversaries of man—the World, the Flesh, Belial the devil, and Avarice, the principal vice—occupy four of the scaffolds with their supporters, while the fifth is reserved for God the Father on his throne and the four daughters of God, Mercy, Truth, Justice, and Peace. A particularly mysterious feature of the diagram is the provision for "water abowte the place, if any dyche may be mad ther it schal be pleyed." Was this moat intended to separate players and spectators? Or was it supposed to divide paying customers from other casual onlookers, as Richard Southern argues? Did it circle the perimeter of an arena or merely mark off the performing space, or was it a smaller moat defending the central castle itself, as Happé suggests? The diagram is difficult to interpret on this point. Certainly if the moat encircles the castle it can become an important dramatic factor in the play's battle of the vices and virtues. It would also presumably be smaller and easier to dig. The manuscript does specify a number of interesting features of performance: the Soul, perhaps a small boy, is directed to lie concealed under "Man's" bed at the base of the castle until his moment to enter the play. The devil Belial goes into battle equipped with pipes filled with burning gunpowder in his hands, ears, and "arse."

In The Castle of Perseverance the basic morality pattern of temptation, fall, repentance, and divine mercy is expanded. The representative of the human race undergoes two temptations, not just one. He opens the play as a naked, newborn child, ages in the course of the action, and dies, whereupon the fate of his soul is debated by the four daughters of God, and he is finally pardoned and permitted to ascend God's scaffold in a powerful concluding image of salvation. From the opening of the action, man is enmeshed in a web of opposing forces.

He first appears wavering between his good and evil angels, meditating on the unknown purpose of his life: "Wher-to I was to this werld browth / I ne wot." Ensnared by the physical attractions of the World, Man mounts his scaffold to enter his service. Throughout the play the multiple stations are used to signal the main character's spiritual state, his location within the geography of salvation. From the World's scaffold Man passes across the playing space to Avarice's scaffold, where he consorts enthusiastically with the seven deadly sins. The rejected good angel appeals to Confession and Penitence to rescue Man. Penitence responds by striking Man with a lance, "the prick of conscience" made visible. Following confession and absolution, Man enters the Castle of Perseverance, where he is guarded by the seven virtues, all feminine personifications. This arrival sets the scene for the lively and inventive battle of vices and virtues that stands at the center of the drama, an allegorized siege that the virtues finally win when they shower roses on the vices. The scene recalls contemporary visual depictions of sieges of castles of love, and the drama of the later medieval tournament. The vices are routed, all except for Avarice, who reclaims Man by persuasively evoking the timeless fears of old age: "If thou be pore and nedy in elde / Thou schalt oftyn evyl fare."

The final sections of the play turn at last to the pattern made familiar to modern readers in *Everyman*. They dramatize the arrival of Death, Man's appeal to the World, and his discovery of the World's fickleness. Particularly powerful as drama is the confrontation scene between Man and the Boy, "I-wot-nevere-Whoo," sent by World to inherit Man's possessions. When Man dies his soul is carried off by the evil angel, but after a thorough debate among the four daughters of God, God pardons the Soul, and the daughters retrieve it from Belial's scaffold, bringing it finally to God. The Banns that preface the play in the manuscript suggest that in an earlier version of the play, the Virgin Mary might have intervened to rescue the Soul.

The Castle of Perseverance seems atypical of the British morality tradition in its scale, though its action reproduces many characteristic dramatic patterns and allegorical elements. Its closest affinities appear to be with Sir David Lindsay's monumental *Ane Satire of the Thrie Estaitis*. However, students of the problem should not conclude too hastily that the long form of the morality play is aberrant and the shorter forms adopted by small troupes of professional actors is the standard. Instead, it may be possible that the shorter moralities condense an originally large-scale genre to make it portable. At least *The Castle of Perseverance* presents a substantial moral play as a sophisticated and compelling form of drama. The visual clarity of its presentation, the often alliterative splendor of its poetry, and the intensity of its conflicts all appeal to modern audiences and readers who have discovered this often neglected masterpiece of the medieval English stage.

MANKIND. One of the companion pieces to the *Castle of Perseverance* in the Macro manuscript is *Mankind* (ca. 1464–70), a slightly later moral play also in the East Midland dialect. For the purposes of this discussion it provides a useful and attractive contrast with *The Castle of Perseverance,* suggesting the range of scale and approach current in fifteenth-century English morality drama. Perhaps a college play performed by a road troupe of students in the Cambridgeshire area, *Mankind* is by far the rowdiest of the English moralities. The main character is, again, the generic human being, in this case Mankind. The brisk plot shows Mankind aided by the personified divine attribute Mercy and bedeviled by a lively gang of vices— Mischief, New Guise, Nowadays, and Nought—in the employ of the devil Titivillus. Mankind's temptation, fall, despair, and redemption succeed one another in short order. This playwright makes effective use of language as a mode of characterization. Mercy is unmistakably aureate in his dignified disquisitions on the virtuous life, and the audience sympathizes with the vices' mockery of his "English Latin." Later they may find themselves cozened into participation in a song that turns out to be scatological, as in the Toronto Poculi Ludique Societas production of 1983 at Kalamazoo, Michigan. Like Mankind himself, viewers are enticed by the slapstick comedy of these inventive rascals. For Mankind the wages of sin are very nearly death.

Some aspects of the play's staging can be inferred from the text. The playwright envisioned an indoor performance, in some type of hall; the text incorporates a collection, which occurs, as in minstrel performances, at a climactic moment. The audience must cough up a contribution in order to glimpse the "man whose head is of great omnipotence," Titivillus. Doubling would allow performance by a troupe of five actors. A few properties, like Mankind's spade, rosary, and bag of seed, might easily be borrowed locally, allowing the actors to travel very light indeed. They might equally well be mimed. The most portable of the moralities, *Mankind* illustrates the classic pattern of temptation, fall, and redemption in capsule form. Its own character-istic verve, impudence, and economy speed up the pace of the moral drama astonishingly. If it was indeed a student performance, this en-gaging play suggests that university drama was alive and well by the mid-fifteenth century.

SAINTS' PLAYS IN THE FOURTEENTH AND FIFTEENTH CENTURIES

The previous chapter discussed early examples of saints' plays associ-ated with England and the records of performances testifying to their presence from the beginning of the twelfth century forward. St. Kath-erine, St. Nicholas, and St. Magnus all had their representations in the early period of English drama; these dramas are lost today. Their association with the Catholic cult of the saints made them particular targets of the Reformation, and this prejudice may account for the scarcity of their dramatic records. We know that the polemical Protes-tant playwright John Bale attacked the cult of St. Thomas Becket at Canterbury in a lost book as well as in a performance of 1539 before Archbishop Cranmer. Performance records of pageants of St. Thomas at Canterbury suggest varying dramatic representations of the martyr-dom on and off between 1504 and 1555, and these were presumably Bale's target.

Texts for fourteenth- and fifteenth-century English saints' plays are considerably scarcer than the records of their performances. We have the 1480–1520 text of *Mary Magdalen* from East Anglia, perhaps from King's Lynn (then Bishop's Lynn) and the 1495–1501 *Life of Saint Meriasek* associated with Cambourne. *The Conversion of Saint Paul* from East Anglia or Cambridgeshire might also qualify; it is contem-porary with *Mary Magdalen*. Norwich had a St. George procession and some type of play. (Remarkably, the dragon, Snap, continued to ap-pear in mayoral processions, and survives in the Norwich Castle Museum.) A special case that does not exactly fit any of the categories is the anomalous Croxton *Play of the Sacrament,* which Bevington classifies as a miracle play. The fragmentary "Dux Moraud" also seems to be a miracle play.[15]

MARY MAGDALENE. *Mary Magdalene* (late fifteenth century), the most substantial English saint's play, survives in Bodleian MS Digby 133, along with the compact *Conversion of Saint Paul.* The longer play combines biblical and legendary elements to produce a life of Mary that ranges from Palestine to Marseilles, heaven to hell. The play's characters demonstrate its composite character still further. Biblical figures recalling the scriptural cycles consort with allegorical figures that might have stepped out of *The Castle of Perseverance.* The World, the Flesh, good and evil angels, and the seven deadly sins all reappear in *Mary Magdalene*'s cosmic drama. The central character, the tempted, fallen, and penitent Mary, is at once a saint, a human being whose pattern of fall and redemption mirrors that of Humanum Genus, and a romantic heroine. In its staging *Mary Magdalene* may well have resembled *The Castle of Perseverance* closely: Professor Bevington suggests that the saint's play might also take place on a circular playing area, surrounded by eleven stations, with Mary's father's castle at the center of the space (*Medieval Drama,* 688).

THE CROXTON *PLAY OF THE SACRAMENT.* Its banns locate the performance of this play at Croxton, Suffolk, ca. 1462, and suggest that it could have been a touring production. The "vexillators" who announce the play present it as the representation of an actual miracle, an event that happened in Aragon and was confirmed in Rome as recently as 1461. In fact the plot presents a late thirteenth-century libel in which Jews obtain and torture a host. From the Continent examples occur in French drama. The appearance of this and other thirteenth-century legends affirming the true presence of Christ in the Eucharist may have been related to the definition of the doctrine of transubstantiation by Innocent III's Fourth Lateran Council of 1215. (The same council required Jews to wear some type of distinguishing garment.) In the English play the Jews' actions echo the events of the Passion, from the buffeting and flagellation of Jesus through the Crucifixion, entombment, and Resurrection. The Christian merchant Aristorius, mirroring Judas' betrayal, sells a host to his Jewish colleague Jonathas. When the Jews stab the host it bleeds; when Jonathas throws it in a boiling pot it sticks to his hand. The scene degenerates (or builds) into a comic chase and tug-of-war as they nail the host to a pillar and try to pull Jonathas away. As in the lost York *Fergus* episode, the hand of the desecrator comes off. Here the main action of the play is interrupted by the appearance of Colle and the quack doctor he serves, Master Brundiche of Brabant, who lives near Babwell Mill. Master Brundiche comes very close to the comic doctor who performs the resurrection of the dead champion in many surviving mummers' plays. Here, after some devastating banter with the audience, the doctor offers his services to the Jews and is driven away. The stage is now set for the final appearance of Christ, the healing of Jonathas, the conversion of the Jews, and the restoration of the host to the church.

The Jews' torture of the host is presented as a demonstration of the fallacy of Christian belief, but in fact the Jews' actions presuppose a perverse belief in the true presence of Christ and a demonic desire to torture and kill Him again. In reality, as the vexillators indicate, the play aims at resolving the Christian audience's doubts of transubstantiation, perhaps fomented by the followers of Wyclif. How can they doubt, when even Jews believe? David Mills's analysis of the Croxton *Play of the Sacrament* focuses on the play's combination of dramatic elements from the Mass itself and from the folk play tradition in the puzzling scene of the doctor. Mills suggests the dramatic structure directs the mood of the audience from the literal-minded comedy of the initial scenes through the folk play to the serious drama of miracle, conversion, and worship.

A major challenge to all of these types of religious drama was provided by the Lollard movement, inspired by the teachings of John Wyclif. Attacks on scriptural plays, focused especially on clergymen who participate in performances, can be found in works ascribed to Wyclif himself and to his followers. The "Treatise of Miraclis Pleying" of 1380–1410 is the most famous. Revisions to some of the play manuscripts, notably *The Castle of Perseverance* and the N-town cycle, suggest to Professor Lancashire that the clergy were sensitive to these criticisms and were amending their performances accordingly (xviii).

LATE MEDIEVAL COURT PAGEANTRY: AN OVERVIEW

This chapter could hardly close without a brief survey of developments in court pageantry. Earlier sections of the chapter have suggested the pervasive role of display in later medieval life. Pageantry was clearly important to towns and trade guilds as a manifestation of their identity and success. It was also of vital importance to the court and the aristocracy, as the accounts of expenses for tournaments and banquets during this period indicate. Modern students of the later Middle Ages and the Renaissance are sometimes consoled by recalling the economic role that this type of expenditure, shocking to us, must have played in its own day. These pageants employed skilled craftspeople on a regular basis; indeed, they were one of the few means of economic stimulation that an aristocrat, forbidden to engage in trade, might carry out. Of course economic need was not their principal reason for existence, as far as the fourteenth-century ruler was concerned. Pageants were important means of establishing the personal and collective prestige of monarchs and great princes. The royal courts of England and Scotland are most important here, but subsidiary courts might also become loci for court pageantry, not just as the ruler's satellites, but as his rivals. Each court, indeed each individual developed his or her own style, reflecting individual tastes and philosophies of royalty.

This survey can only indicate the basic types of pageant associated with the court and their connections with the history of drama. The Jacobean court masque of the early seventeenth century is most familiar to us as a distinct dramatic genre, but earlier courts also made use of their own styles of dramatic entertainment. Civil pageants for royal entries have already been discussed earlier. They really belong with the Corpus Christi cycles, since both were the productions of the towns rather than of the court itself—though it is important to note the way court and city interact in them. The royal audience plays an important role in shaping the performance and functions dynamically as both auditor and performer. The court itself employed professional entertainers and temporarily entertained others. It produced its own pageants for tournaments, major banquets, and holiday celebrations.

Tournaments in the fourteenth and fifteenth centuries became increasingly dramatic as participants took on a surprising variety of roles drawn from folk plays and chivalric romance. The tournament has indeed been cited as an influence on the structure of the morality play, as in the siege of *The Castle of Perseverance*. Banquets could not be complete without some form of interlude between courses. The Christmas festivities in particular became an occasion for masking, "mummings" or "disguisings" and misrule; later a Lord of Misrule would take charge of the season's entertainment, reflecting the social reversal of the Feast of Fools and that of the boy bishop. Normally a mumming would involve the ceremonial visit of a group of masked performers to present a gift to an important personage and perhaps to dance before unmasking. Cavendish's *Life of Wolsey* depicts Henry VIII taking part in such a disguising. The mummings ascribed to the poet and monk John Lydgate in the reign of Henry VI present us with all these elements: a descriptive text, costumed performers, a dumb show or dance among the performers or with audience. It is clear from the surviving documents that fourteenth- and fifteenth-century British courts were influenced by developments in pageantry across Europe, and in fact a lively competition to produce the most impressive spectacles went on between the major and minor courts.[16]

Stagecraft at tournaments and banquets could be elaborate and influential. That masterpiece of Middle English romance, *Sir Gawain and the Green Knight,* portrays Christmastide revels at the court of King Arthur and at a nobleman's household in the country, presumably drawing on personal observation of later fourteenth-century practice. This is a fictional work, not properly a document of theater history, but it helps modern students of the subject to appreciate the atmosphere of festivity that might permeate the holiday season at a major English court of this period. *Sir Gawain* is particularly valuable for its illustration of the variety of entertainments that might be combined: musical performances, dances and courting games in which kisses are forfeited, hunts, tournaments, and banquets. Indeed, the plot of the romance is presented as a series of "Christmas games," and the entry of the magnificent and terrifying Green Knight with his challenge to Arthur and his court in fact takes the form of an interlude before a banquet. An elegant love debate between a knight and a lady, like that between Sir Gawain and his host's wife, might equally well be seen as another courtly "Christmas game." (This traditional form of challenge in Arthurian romances may well owe something to early medieval performance practices; it certainly returns to later medieval performance in banqueting entertainments modeled on those of the romances.) The romance gains immensely from its sophisticated play with questions of game and illusion, with the "disguisings" popular at the Christmas season, with visual symbolism and performance. Without being a play itself, *Sir Gawain* is permeated with allusions to the courtly entertainments of contemporary life.

Properly this chapter's account of court pageantry should begin with Edward III. At the end of the Introduction I discussed Edward I's experiments with pageantry as courtly entertainment and as a political statement. Although his unfortunate son Edward II was accused of consorting with low companions and players, we know little about pageantry at his court; but Edward I's pageants may well have served as models for Edward III. The records of revels at court suggest that his fifty-year reign was a lively period. Edward III's active interest in chivalric pageantry and Arthurian revivals like those of his grandfather's court led to his founding of the Order of the Garter. The list of tournaments includes a notable appearance of Edward III's mistress Alice Perrers as the Lady of the Sun. Some overlap between dramatic traditions seems to have taken place: at a 1362 tournament at Cheapside, the challengers were costumed as the seven deadly sins.

Richard II, Edward's grandson, entertained a different image of himself as king than had his grandfather, and consciously presented a differing image of kingship. He was a gourmet and an art patron, the inventor of the handkerchief, in this and other respects well ahead of his time. His portrait in the Wilton Dyptych shows the young, clean-shaven, sharp-featured king supported by John the Baptist. His deep affection for his first wife, Anne of Bohemia, may have found expression in courtly games that echo in Chaucer's poetry. The especially notable and expensive series of pageants reconciling the City of London with Richard involved Anne herself in the role of intercessor. Richard, physically frail, only once performed in a tournament. Geoffrey Chaucer, as clerk of the King's Works under Richard II, was responsible for the physical arrangements.

Long before Henry earl of Derby, Richard's athletic and musical cousin, entertained a thought of challenging Richard for the throne, he seems to have been well aware of the importance of chivalric pageantry in the development of a personal image. Indeed, it could be argued that much of Henry's immense popularity, among the Londoners in particular, stemmed from his success as a performer and from his astute selection of the role he chose to perform. Unlike his unpopular father, John of Gaunt, Henry displayed his chivalric prowess in jousts, as well as in his "crusade" with the Teutonic knights in Prussia and in his pilgrimage to Jerusalem, which also became a European chivalric tour. Henry continued his interest in tournaments after his rise to power in 1399; the tradition of receiving Christmas mummers at court was made the occasion of an early plot by the followers of Richard to assassinate him. (A similar plot was later devised against Henry V.) He is of special importance for the history of English music; as earl of Derby he took a six-man band on his tour of Prussia. There are documents indicating that he was a musician himself, and the Old Hall manuscript is associated with his household chapel and those of his sons. It may be important for the student of British drama to note that the sophisticated English composers of the late fourteenth and early fifteenth century were setting the pace for musical developments across Europe. Leonel Power and John Dunstable in particular inaugurated a distinct shift in style that was to affect the major Burgundian composers of the fifteenth century, Dufay and Binchois.

Henry V continued his father's interest in music and mummings, though the principal concern of his reign remained the war with France. Among the dramatic records of his son Henry VI are surviving pageants for the child king's coronation at Paris and his return to London, with some texts no longer ascribed to John Lydgate, as well as pageants for Henry VI's most unsuitable marriage to Marguerite d'Anjou. Marguerite evidently enjoyed dramatic entertainment. She held Christmas disguisings in 1452–53 and witnessed the Coventry Corpus Christi play in 1457 (Lancashire, xviii, xxi). By contrast, John Blacman reported that her saintly husband objected to a Christmas pageant at court on account of bare-breasted women.

Edward IV's reign, punctuated by resumptions of the Wars of the Roses, is remarkable for Bristol's appropriate civic pageant of William the Conqueror. Tournaments like the 1467 Joust of Lord Scales (Anthony Woodville) and the Bastard of Burgundy at Smithfield were occasions for diplomacy and international contact, emulating the fashionable international style of the opulent Burgundian court. The record of this joust is particularly interesting for the scene that prompted the challenge, described in Anthony Woodville's letter to his opponent. Woodville creates a new version of the chivalric *Impresa del braccioletta,* already current in France and Spain. Kneeling before his sister the queen, Woodville is surrounded by ladies who affix a "collar" adorned with "flowers of souvenaunce" to his thigh. Woodville is charged to wear this badge until he has performed a feat of arms, in this case challenging the Bastard of Burgundy to a duel. In this attractive scene we see Caxton's future patron and the ladies of Edward's court dramatizing an episode from courtly romance. Woodville would reveal his dramatic proclivities again later in Edward's reign when he appeared at a 1477 tournament in the costume of a white hermit. Lancashire regrets that there seem to be no records of drama at the court of Edward IV. Among the nobles, a different situation occurred, with a number of Edward's contemporaries employing household troupes of players. Still, the activities of Anthony Woodville at least suggest that court pageantry had its admirers under Edward IV (Lancashire, xxi).

Richard III, as duke of Gloucester, seems to have maintained a troupe of players. There is little evidence for revels at his court, though William Caxton around 1484 suggested hopefully that Richard might like to sponsor some type of national tournament in the interests of military preparedness. Richard did see the Coventry Corpus Christi cycle performed in the summer of 1485, prior to his defeat by Henry VII.

With Henry VII's victory over Richard III at the Battle of Bosworth Field in August 1485, we enter the realm of Sydney Anglo's masterful study *Spectacle, Pageantry, and Early Tudor Policy.* Much of his material relating to Henry VIII and Edward VI belongs in a discussion of sixteenth-century drama (chapter 3).

In Scotland, fifteenth-century records of royal pageants are rich and suggestive, as are suggestions that interludes and school plays were taking place across the British Isles.

POPULAR ENTERTAINMENTS: ROBIN HOOD PLAYS

The question of whether the man Robin Hood really existed is still as debatable as the existence and identity of a historical King Arthur. References to popular Robin Hood plays may go back as far as thirteenth-century Scotland. By William Langland's time, at the end of the fourteenth century, the name of the legendary outlaw was a byword throughout Britain. By the end of the fifteenth century Robin Hood, his merry men, and Maid Marian had all become entangled in the traditional spring festivities of the English villages. Is this development due to conflation with the Robin and Marion who figure in the French pastoral tradition, as in Adam de la Halle's *Robin et Marion* (and Robert Henryson's pastoral debate poem "Robyn and Makyn")? Earlier May games seem to have centered around the selection of a May king and queen, a young man and woman who symbolized the renewed fertility of the natural world. Their Lincoln green costumes and their traditional associations with the greenwood and with social reversal made Robin and Marian especially appropriate for the season of Maying and its revelry. At the end of the sixteenth century Ben Jonson's *Sad Shepherd* borrowed from this well-established native tradition. It is clear that Robin Hood continued to be a popular dramatic character into the seventeenth century.

The earliest ballad of Robin Hood, "Robin Hood and the Monk," goes back to the mid-fifteenth century. The earliest extant text of a Robin Hood play seems to be the fragmentary "Robin Hood and the Sheriff of Nottingham" associated with Norwich and dated around 1475. It begins with a series of physical contests between Robin and Sir Guy of Gisborne. Robin and his opponent shoot, cast the stone, and wrestle, before they finally duel to the death with swords. A fight with the Sheriff's men leads to the capture of the outlaws; the ballad tradition suggests that the play ends with Robin's rescue of his men. This is a play centered on combat, like the surviving mummer's plays. Its presence among the Paston papers associates it with Sir John Paston's delinquent servant, W. Wood, who is mentioned in one of his master's letters, perhaps sarcastically, as a performer of Robin Hood and Saint George plays. In this early version, village tests of strength and the tension between knight and yeoman are given schematic dramatic expression.[17] Sixteenth-century texts of Robin Hood plays show Robin defeated by Friar Tuck and a potter, injecting additional comedy and dramatic reversal into the action.

CONCLUSION

The historian of fourteenth- and fifteenth-century British drama must be aware of the dangers of focusing exclusively on Corpus Christi cycles and morality plays while neglecting to recognize other less visible but perhaps more pervasive forms of drama like courtly pageantry or folk plays. He or she also needs to avoid misplacing these dramatic genres chronologically. The Chester cycle text in particular, treated for convenience in this chapter, is a sixteenth-century document. Many performance records date likewise from the sixteenth century. Forgetting this chronology can generate false images both of medieval drama and of the Tudor stage. It is true that much of the future of drama in Britain rests with the dramatic forms summarized briefly at the end of this chapter, with the courtly revels and secular drama of the May games. Still, it is equally damaging to undervalue the impact of the religious drama of medieval Britain on the secular drama of the sixteenth and seventeenth centuries. Critics are becoming increasingly aware of their pervasive shaping influence on later dramatic conventions. In themselves, the moralities, saint's plays and Corpus Christi cycles are major achievements in the history of British dramaturgy. They deserve all the recognition they have so far received, and more.

CHAPTER IV

THE SIXTEENTH CENTURY

The sixteenth and early seventeenth centuries still stand at the heart of any study of British drama. For a long time it was supposed that British drama began with the sixteenth century, the age of Shakespeare, just as British literature was imagined as beginning with Chaucer. It is also important to recognize the last decade of the sixteenth century as the age of Marlowe and of Shakespeare's many active colleagues and competitors in the theater. Equally, the sixteenth century is the age of the great bulk of evidence for performance and later repression of the Corpus Christi cycles and of the major moral plays *Magnyfycence* and Lindsay's *Satire of the Three Estates*. Besides all this activity, the sixteenth century is the era of humanist drama in schools, universities, and the inns of court, of opulent court and civic pageantry. Edmund Creeth has hailed the "emergence of drama as a secular art under Henry VII," perhaps a shade belatedly for the medieval specialist.[1] Drama overshadows nondramatic literature for the first time. The multiple roles of drama in sixteenth-century British society must be scrutinized if one is to arrive at a just estimate of drama's importance.

Attempting to trace the history of British drama in the sixteenth century by way of recent criticism can have a disorienting effect. It often seems as though two or three distinct histories are going on at the same time, in the same place, completely oblivious of one another. The history of "medieval" drama, bolstered by massive collections of records relating to performances, stagecraft, and play texts, continues unchecked into the 1570s and 1580s if not the 1600s. Often quite independently the history of Renaissance drama, covering the same period, focuses on the new learning of the humanists, the rediscovery of classical literature and literary theory, and the appearance of the Elizabethan drama modeled on Greek and Roman plays. When the two topics are further isolated in separate volumes, readers can hardly help supposing that they cannot have much to do with one another. The most formidable challenge for the historian of drama remains to combine these two histories, following in the footsteps of scholars like David Bevington. Until "medieval" and "Renaissance" can be reconciled, the study of sixteenth-century British drama will continue to suffer from a split personality.

To see the sixteenth-century experience of drama in Britain as a totality it is necessary to collect, examine, and arrange a group of disparate, conflicting elements in some kind of rational order. Foreign and native ingredients are equally important. The traditional Renaissance-oriented view of sixteenth-century dramatic history stresses the stimulus of new, foreign influences. It focuses on the appearance of tragedy and comedy based on classical and contemporary Italian models in the wake of humanist education. Seneca, Plautus, and Terence, read and performed at English schools and universities, inspired the plays of Shakespeare and his contemporaries. At the same time new critical attention to the principles of Aristotle led to a changing view of dramatic construction. Columbus and Copernicus, Luther and Henry VIII all radically altered British attitudes to produce the drama of Shakespeare.

By contrast, histories of drama from the medieval perspective focus on a powerful popular dramatic tradition that continued to shape British drama and stage practice into the seventeenth century. They point to the obstinate persistence of medieval dramatic patterns, especially the cosmic geographic and temporal scope of the cycle plays and the plot design of the moralities. The unclassically British mixture of tragedy and comedy, a stubborn resistance to the introduction of neo-Aristotelian unities of time, place, and action all suggest to these observers that Elizabethan playwrights, players, and audiences remained surprisingly medieval. Only the advent of an exclusive theater inspired by models from the Continent with the restoration of Charles II in 1660 ended this native British dramatic tradition.

Both of these views are correct, in different ways. The student of the drama needs to value their rival contributions to construct a balanced picture of sixteenth- and seventeenth-century British drama. It is, after all, this complex, hybrid inheritance that gives the Elizabethan stage its special resources of stagecraft and literary range. These elements merit our respect as key phases of dramatic history in their own right, not merely as precursors of Shakespeare and his contemporaries.

RELIGIOUS DRAMA AND THE REFORMATION

Lavish productions of the Corpus Christi cycles preoccupied provincial corporations into the final quarter of the sixteenth century. All of the major cycles seem to have been performed in the sixteenth century; at Wakefield our evidence for performance derives solely from this period. Moralities proved popular with the most elegant sixteenth-century audiences. Several of the most impressive deserve discussion here: John Skelton's *Magnyfycence,* John Bale's *King Johan,* and Sir David Lindsay's *Ane Satire of the Thrie Estaitis* rank among the masterpieces of morality drama. Religious drama flourished on the European mainland throughout the century, in both new and traditional forms. Reports of the spectacular Jesuit school plays of the sixteenth and seventeenth centuries and the Spanish *autos sacramentales* of Lope de Vega (1562–1635) and Calderòn (1600–81) may well have put British dramatists on their mettle.

The history of the religious drama in sixteenth-century Britain is, necessarily, the history of the Reformation. In the course of the century the population of the British Isles altered their religious identity radically on more than one occasion. England and Scotland both began the century under Henry VII and James IV as staunch allies of the Pope. It was after all Henry VII who determined to marry his son Arthur—and after Arthur's death his second son, Henry—to Catherine of Aragon, daughter of those most Catholic monarchs Ferdinand and Isabella. At the time of this fateful alliance, as Stephen Ozment observes, a Spain forcibly unified in religion by the expulsion of the Jews in 1592 and the Moors in 1502 was becoming the European stronghold of Catholic resistance to the Reformation. The magnificent Henry VIII began his reign in 1509 as an active supporter of the Pope, orthodox in his piety. Frustrated by the Pope's refusal to permit him to divorce Catherine in order to obtain a male heir, in 1534 Henry VIII declared himself head of the Church of England. Those English Catholics who objected, most prominently Thomas More and John Fisher, were executed. Among the economic benefits of his decision for Henry and his supporters was the acquisition of church property through the dissolution of the monasteries and diversion of church revenues to the crown. Images of saints, relics, and manuscripts were destroyed in waves of Protestant iconoclasm. Despite these actions, Henry remained conservative in his attitude toward changes in religious doctrine, in particular discouraging the use of vernacular bibles. Reciprocally, as England became Protestant, Scotland drew closer to Catholic France, even after Scottish Protestantism began to gain ground following James V's death in 1542.

Under Henry's son Edward VI Protestant ideas became more advanced in England. Cranmer's *Book of Common Prayer* in 1549 gave English churches a new format for devotion. The Sunday sermon replaced the Mass. Clergymen were permitted to marry, though their parishioners remained dubious about the merits of this development. But when Catherine of Aragon's daughter Mary succeeded Edward VI in 1553 she took immediate steps to reconcile England with Rome. English Protestants were faced with the choice of flight to Protestant Switzerland or Germany, conversion, or martyrdom. Mary's marriage to Philip II of Spain in July of 1554 was intended to return the English conclusively to the Catholic fold. Then with Elizabeth I in 1558, an English Protestant monarch again controlled the religious destiny of Britain. English Catholics and Catholic doctrine once more became targets of official repression. Even in Scotland the Catholic Mary Queen of Scots found herself surrounded by a Protestant aristocracy.[2]

The ferment of religious debate, publicized through the medium of the printing press, polarized British society. All ranks of society were called upon to take sides, making spiritual decisions that could have fatal consequences. The execution of prominent members of the opposition as heretics and traitors was hardly a new tactic. Executions had been a horrific form of public drama at least since the days of the Romans. Under Henry IV in 1401 Parliament had passed the statute *De heretico comburendo* (*Concerning the Burning of Heretics*), which established procedures for the arrest, incarceration, and in obstinate cases public burning of heretics. The measure was aimed particularly at the followers of Wyclif, the Lollards (Jacob, *The Fifteenth Century*, 94–96). The fascination of execution and sixteenth-century religious martyrdom can be traced on the stage as well as in nondramatic works like John Foxe's *Book of Martyrs.*

THE MORAL PLAY IN THE SIXTEENTH CENTURY. Many sixteenth-century dramatic works are moral plays or moral interludes; in sixteenth-century practice the terms are interchangeable. Bevington's *From Mankind to Marlowe* discusses a wide range of plays, short and long, for popular or elite audiences, all conceived in the tradition of *The Castle of Perseverance* and *Mankind*. Titles like *Mundus et infans* (*The World and the Child;* ca. 1500–22), *The Interlude of Youth* (ca. 1513–29), *Impatient Poverty* (ca. 1547–53), *The Marriage of Wit and Wisdom* (before 1570), and *New Custom* (1558–68) reveal their allegorical approach immediately. They carry the dramatic conventions of the moral play into the reign of Elizabeth. Many other surviving play texts, printed and in manuscript, indicate the popularity of abstract characters and the plot conventions discussed in chapter 2. A large number of these plays were the property of small, itinerant professional troupes of actors, often no more than four performers, or Bevington's "four men and a boy." Doubling allowed plays with large casts to be performed by small acting companies. This tactic had dramatic consequences, already suggested by the doubling of Mercy and Titivillus in *Mankind*. Bevington documents the replacement of abstractions by social stereotypes in the "intermediate morality" of the 1560s and 1570s. At the same time the morality's basic plot structure, the war between vice and virtue, remains a cornerstone of the Elizabethan drama.[3]

Faced with the large volume of moral plays produced in the sixteenth century, this chapter can describe only the most prominent examples.

Everyman may be the best-known English moral play. The original Dutch version, *Elckerlijk,* was printed around 1495. It appears in four English editions printed between 1508 and 1537. No British performance history has as yet been discovered, and some scholars question whether the play ever was acted in England. The printed copy describes itself as "a Treatise . . . in Maner of a Morall Playe," not precisely as a play. Still, *Everyman's* dramatic force convinces later readers and producers. Of all the moral plays in English, this is the one most often revived.

A product of the same fifteenth-century Netherlandish spirituality that led to Thomas à Kempis's *Imitation of Christ, Everyman* focuses on the main character at the ultimate moment of crisis, his summoning by Death, God's messenger. As Everyman calls successively upon his friends, relatives, and riches, he experiences a series of betrayals. The shift from cordiality to rejection in each discussion is vividly dramatized. Only his Good Deeds, piping up from the ground underfoot, offers to accompany him, and calls Knowledge to her assistance. Everyman is prepared for death according to orthodox church doctrine, through the penitential sequence of confession, contrition, absolution, and satisfaction. In this respect *Everyman* seems more didactic than the moralities discussed earlier. After Everyman's penitence Good Deeds can rise and accompany him, along with Discretion, Strength, Beauty, and his five wits. In the play's closing moments Everyman's helpers lead him to the grave, and they, too, leave him. Only Good Deeds descends with Everyman into the earth to be welcomed by an angel. The pattern of this shorter play recalls *The Castle of Perseverance* in its double series of rejections, divided by the demonstration of confession and penitence. Again, the drama ends in the salvation of humanity. In this case it also ends in an epilogue, spoken by a Doctor, to stress the applicability of the plot to the audience at large.

Magnyfycence remains the principal dramatic work of the Tudor poet John Skelton (1460?–1529). Both Oxford and Cambridge honored the young Skelton as poet laureate, and his rhetorical skill was admired by William Caxton in his 1490 preface to *Eneydos*. Skelton was the future Henry VIII's tutor in the 1490s, when he wrote a *Speculum Principis* for that prince's edification. As a poet Skelton is remembered for his verbal and metrical virtuosity, his often baffling political satires, and a range of mood that carries him from the Rabelaisian *The Tunning of Elinor Rummyng* to the delicate characterization of *Philip Sparrow*. Besides *Magnyfycence*, Skelton is rumored to have written other plays. References to two additional moralities, a comedy, and an interlude performed at Woodstock are all questionable. A more conventional morality, *Good Order*, may in fact be his.

Magnyfycence seems to have been written between 1515 and 1523; it was printed around 1533 by John Rastell. The idea that the play was intended as a satire of Cardinal Wolsey has been questioned. *Magnyfycence* employs classic morality structure in the service of court satire and royal instruction. The prince, Magnyfycence, begins the play with a well-ordered court, where the princely virtues of Lyberte and Felycyte are governed by Measure. This harmonious structure is infiltrated almost immediately by a group of courtly vices, fools, flatterers, and thieves, who entice the king into dismissing his virtuous advisors and adopting a career of lechery and self-indulgence. The main section of the play is devoted to the flamboyant crowd of tempters that surround Magnyfycence, all masquerading as virtues: the court fools Foly and Fansy, and their sinister friends Courtly Abusion, Cloaked Collusion, Crafty Conveyance, and Counterfeit Countenance. Schooled by these suave counselors, Magnyfycence becomes conceited. Courtly Abusion instructs him in lechery and court finance, before absconding with his wealth. It is left to the fool, Fansy, to reveal the true identities of Magnyfycence's counselors. At this point the morality plot accelerates abruptly, as Adversyte appears onstage. Happé compares the advent of Adversyte to the appearance of Death in *Everyman* and *The Castle of Perseverance*. Like Death, Adversyte is a powerful messenger of God, sent to punish folly but also to test the virtuous. He strikes down Magnyfycence, leaving him to Poverty and to the crude mockery of his former servants. Rather than repenting appropriately, Magnyfycence falls into a state of self-pity. Dyspare and Myschefe urge Magnyfycence to suicide: "The worlde waxyth wery of the; thou lyvest to longe" (Happé, 301). At the critical moment, Good Hope appears to rescue and rehabilitate the king. The end of the play supplies Magnyfycence with a new group of virtuous advisors, who stress the deceptive nature of the world and the importance of the right use of wealth.

Bevington is particularly interested in *Magnyfycence* because of its effective use of doubling; five actors are called upon to play eighteen characters. No more than four are ever onstage at the same time. Occasionally, a single character addresses the audience in an extended monologue while the others change costumes offstage. As in *Mankind,* the use of the same actors in different guises to play their own moral opposites gives this already complex play an additional degree of complexity in performance. *Magnyfycence* is even more effective on stage than on the printed page, as the Poculi Ludique Societas of the University of Toronto demonstrated in its 1975 production. The audience is caught up in the fascination of watching Skelton's collection of courtly villains manipulate the passionate and vulnerable king. Skelton's analysis of the psychology of the abuse of power remains astute. Most of all, in production the versatility and power of the morality plot structure become clear. The shocking reversals of the king's fall, despair, and reprieve make for compelling drama.

Catholic moral plays provoked rival Protestant playwrights. Of these the most notable remains John Bale (1495–1563), whose extensive autobiographical writings allow us to know him better than almost any other playwright of the sixteenth century. Bale's career parallels those of many Protestant reformers of his day. A disillusioned Carmelite, educated at Jesus College, Cambridge, he rose to be prior of Doncaster before turning to Protestantism around 1534. A friend of the king's antiquary John Leland and a protégé of Thomas Cromwell, Bale was one of many humanist writers marshalled in the 1530s to support the king's claim of 1534. After Cromwell's fall in 1540, he and his wife fled to the Continent. He returned after 1548, to be made bishop of Ossory in Ireland in 1552, just before Mary's accession to the throne, which necessitated a second period of European exile. Bale evidently returned to England with the advent of Elizabeth and ended his career as a canon of Canterbury.

King Johan is Bale's most celebrated work, possibly performed before Thomas Cranmer, archbishop of Canterbury, as a Christmas entertainment in 1539. "Bale and his ffelowes" were paid thirty shillings for playing before the archbishop. Bale's manuscript survives; it is still regarded as a major step in the direction of the Elizabethan history play and has been the basis for several editions. *King Johan* presents the historical King John as a proto-Protestant martyr. His contest with the pope for control of the Church of England parallels that of Henry VIII. Historical figures mingle with abstract characters. Sometimes their identities merge, as when Sedicyon, the play's major agent of evil, becomes the historical archbishop Stephen Langton, or Dissymulacyon turns into the poisoner Simon of Swynsett. This attractive combination of allegorical and historical figures recalls *Mary Magdalene*. Bale's design breaks with the traditional morality pattern in the fact that, unlike Magnyfycence, King Johan remains virtuous throughout the play. It is the three estates of England—Nobylyte, Clergye, and Cyvyle Order—who succumb to the machinations of the Pope and the vices. This entrapment and destruction of an innocent prince has been considered a new development in the direction of tragedy. Bale ended his revision of *King Johan* in the reign of Elizabeth with a female figure, Imperial Magesty, restoring order to England.

Bale's other surviving dramatic works are *The Chefe Promyses of God, Johan Baptystes Preachynge in the Wyldernesse,* and *The Temptacyon of Our Lorde,* all performed in Ireland, and *Thre Lawes, or Nature, Moses, and Christ.* Creeth classifies the first three as Protestant approaches to the mystery play, whereas *Thre Lawes* is more like a morality (xxii–xxv). Bale deployed his polemical theater to challenge both church and state in Ireland, notably in his Kilkenny productions defying the proclamation of Mary as queen in 1553. In the same way he had confronted the religious establishment at Canterbury by presenting his (now lost) play *De imposturis Thomae Becketi* as a frontal attack on the cult of the martyred St. Thomas à Becket. Bale also seems to have written an English version of the German Protestant playwright Thomas Kirchmayer's Latin *Pammachius* of 1538 (Creeth, xxiii).

Ane Pleasant Satyre of the Thrie Estaitis was first produced at the Palace of Linlithgow in 1540 as an interlude for the feast of the Epiphany. Its author, Sir David Lindsay (or Lyndsay; 1490–1555) was prominent as a herald and poet at the court of James V. Political comment and free advice to the rulers of Scotland play prominent roles in Lindsay's surviving nondramatic poems, as they do in his play. The only surviving moral play from Scotland, *Ane Satire of the Thrie Estaitis,* remains the major contribution of Middle Scots to dramatic literature and theater history. For Bevington, Lindsay's play seems old-fashioned, with its large cast and expansive staging requirements. In these respects it recalls *The Castle of Perseverance* rather than *Magnyfycence.* Major alterations in the play's text relate to known performances. The 1540 version of the play was expanded for two additional presentations, the first at Cupar in 1552 before James V and the second, again revised and extended, at Edinburgh in 1554. *Ane Satire of the Thrie Estaitis* shifted from a hall in the palace to a succession of open-air playing places. In the process the play grew; the Edinburgh performance lasted from nine in the morning to six at night (Happé, 57–61).

Lindsay's monumental moral play is not only much longer but much less tightly organized than Bale's or Skelton's political moralities had been. Anticlerical satire, comic interludes reminiscent of folk plays, and detailed programs of political reform all find their places here. Initially the play focuses on Rex Humanitas, his seduction by Sensuality and his recovery by Correction. This initial section most closely resembles the classic morality. It is tempting to speculate that this first part of the script might represent the 1540 play. After a comic interlude Lindsay suggests reforms of the three estates, Spirituality, Temporality, and the Merchants. The play ends with a Parliament to punish abuses. The vices are unmasked, Flattery betrays his fellows Dissait and Falset to the gallows, and John the Commonwealth joins the Parliament. At the last moment Flattery escapes and the play ends with Folie's mock-sermon on the text *Stultorum numerus est infinitus* (Eccles. 1:15, "That which is wanting cannot be numbered"; Folie's Latin translates as "The number of fools is countless"). For Lindsay, the world continues to resist complete reformation. *Ane Satire of the Thrie Estaitis* began its dramatic existence as a courtly interlude; in its final stage it is a communal event that marshals all the estates of Scotland to witness its moral concern.

ANTITHEATRICAL LITERATURE OF THE SIXTEENTH CENTURY. Not every reformer joined Skelton, Bale, and Lindsay in their approval of the drama as a potential tool of political and religious reformation. Many humanist clergymen and educators, echoing the strictures of Tertullian and other classical authorities, were dubious about the role of drama in a properly conducted social order. With the rise of professional drama in London, antitheatrical authors in the extreme Protestant wing sprang up in the footsteps of the Lollards. The initial association of theater with the old religion and with image worship parallels the line of thought of the *Treatise of Miraclis pleying*.

Stephen Gosson (1554–1624), probably the most celebrated of the sixteenth-century critics of the stage, was a playwright whose works are no longer extant, presumably not by accident. Converted to the Puritan camp, Gosson commenced his attacks on both plays and poets in his *The Schoole of Abuse, Containing a pleasaunt inuectiue against Poets, Pipers, Plaiers, Iesters and such like Caterpillers of a Commonwelth . . .* (1579), which he dedicated to Sir Philip Sidney without permission. He followed up his argument with *Ephimerides of Phialo* (1579), and *Playes confuted in Fiue Actions* (1582). Many of Gosson's shots are aimed at the lewd behavior of members of the audience. "In our assemblies at plays in London, you shall see suche heauing, and shoouing, suche ytching and shouldring, too sitte by the women" (Chambers, *Elizabethan Stage,* 4:203). The players are to blame for corrupting the imagination, providing occasions for sexual immorality, Sabbath-breaking, and idleness in general. Of course the players responded: Thomas Nashe's *Pierce Penilesse His Supplication to the Diuell* (1592) may be the most effective of the replies. Interestingly, his defense of drama recalls William Caxton's fifteenth-century defense of chivalric fiction. Plays, chronicle plays in particular, reprove the degeneracy of the present by bringing to life the great deeds of the past (Chambers, 1:260, 4:238–40).

The impact of Puritan complaints on public opinion has been debated. The objections Gosson and his allies cited continued to harry British drama and dramatists into the seventeenth century. They unquestionably exerted pressure on the theatrical profession and contributed to the antitheatrical sentiment of the Commonwealth authorities in the mid-seventeenth century.[4]

THE SUPPRESSION OF RELIGIOUS DRAMA. In his pioneering work *Mysteries End,* H. C. Gardiner emphasizes the role of the national government and the emerging Protestant leadership in the suppression of the Corpus Christi cycle plays. Church images related to the cult of the saints were early targets of the reformers, who easily associated them with biblical idol worship. Depictions of Catholic ceremonies and doctrine in the cycles were regarded as equally dangerous to the spiritual health of a precariously Protestant country. The surviving documents show the church authorities exerting their control over the town dramas. In 1543 appeared Henry VIII's statute forbidding the printing or performance of any plays contrary to the religious doctrine proclaimed in 1540. Plays "for the rebuking and reproching of vices, and the setting foorthe of vertue" remained lawful, a condition that would seem to exempt the moralities. This is only the first in a series of similar legislative pronouncements extending from Henry VIII through the reign of Elizabeth.[5]

As Professor Lancashire observes, different monarchs regulated different stages. Edward VI tolerated traveling companies that presented Protestant plays, while objecting to potentially Catholic town drama. In 1548 the feast of Corpus Christi was itself abolished. Mary I repressed the traveling players while allowing town-sponsored performances to resume (Lancashire, xxix–xxx). At the same time, local churchmen engaged in a series of determined struggles with town corporations. In 1575 Archbishop Edmund Grindal of York obtained three playbooks of the town Pater Noster play, ostensibly for revision; they have never been seen since. Grindal had recorded his objection to common players in a 1564 letter to Cecil: "that idle sorte off people, which have been infamouse in all goode common weales" (Chambers, *Elizabethan Stage*, 1:244). In 1580 the York city council postponed performance of the Corpus Christi play until the archbishop and the dean of York Minster approved the text; apparently they never did. At Wakefield in 1576 an ecclesiastical commission told the town authorities to excise the Trinity, the sacraments of baptism and communion, and any form of idolatry from the Whitsun performance of their Corpus Christi play. Following these stern instructions, it is not clear that the show went on. A few isolated instances of performances can be detected in the seventeenth century, but for the most part the Corpus Christi cycles had been discouraged by 1580.

Parallel efforts can be observed on the Continent, for instance in Paris, where the 1548 prohibition of biblical *mystères* shows particular distaste for comic developments within the scriptural plays. Elsewhere in France similar plays gradually faded out. The German *mysterienspiel* survived only in a few remote areas like Oberammergau, where it profited from the Catholic revival of the seventeenth century.

Economic factors have been stressed by later scholars as a corrective to Gardiner's focus on religious and political causes for the disappearance of the Corpus Christi plays. The decline of provincial centers relative to London certainly contributed to the demoralization of their citizens. As the *Treatise on Miraclis pleying* had observed nearly two centuries earlier, these plays were expensive to produce. Many towns could no longer afford them. Competition from London-based professional companies may also have depressed local performances. Among the effects of their disappearance is a distinct loss of diversity on the British stage. Civic pageantry was diverted into other directions: it remained lavish and inventive throughout the Tudor and Stuart eras. A variety of biblical plays were mounted on the professional London stages, though they tended to avoid the life of Jesus or other solemn matters of doctrine. Biblical puppet shows, "motions," also seem to have survived. Shakespeare refers to "a motion of the Prodigal Son" in *The Winter's Tale,* while Ben Jonson's puppeteer Lanthorn Leatherhead in *Bartholomew Fair* reminisces nostalgically about a series of biblical spectacles he had performed: "Jerusalem was a stately thing, and so was Nineveh . . . and Sodom and Gomorrah, with the rising of the prentices, and pulling down the bawdy-houses there upon Shrove-Tuesday."

HUMANIST DRAMA: THEATER AND LEARNING

The history of school plays in sixteenth-century England is intimately related to the Italian humanists' reorientation of education to center it on Greek and Roman classical literature. Manuscript copies of the plays of Plautus and Terence had been preserved in British monastic and university libraries since the early Middle Ages. There they were read with interest, and imitated on occasion by men or women of letters. What transpired at the end of the fifteenth century was a large-scale educational reform movement. British schools and universities began to insist on the study of Latin and then Greek drama as a key element in their curricula. Performance often accompanied study. The tradition of presenting a school play may have been inspired by the Feast of Fools. Enactments of classical plays had become widespread at English schools and universities by the mid-sixteenth century. The Westminster Play has continued the tradition into the twentieth century.[6]

New plays in the classical mode, composed in both English and Latin, were also written by scholars or schoolmasters for performance by their students. Many celebrated humanist educators were dubious about the moral effect of undiluted classical drama, particularly that of Plautus, on their young charges. Erasmus and Juan Luis Vives, the Spanish humanist who supervised the education of Princess Mary, both favored judicious expurgation. In 1523 Vives decided that the Latin comedies of Plautus and Terence were unsuitable for Mary's educational program. Roger Ascham, Princess Elizabeth's tutor, objected to the content of the Latin comedies at the same time that he praised their language. The ideal drama would combine Christian morals and subject matter with polished classical Latin and classical dramatic form.

Initially the dramatic works of authors associated with the humanist movement employed many of the same conventions of the stage that we find in the moral plays or courtly pageants. Humanist playwrights only gradually attempted to write comedies and tragedies in the classical mode. The earliest humanist plays are, for the most part, interludes, like their fourteenth-century precursor *The Interlude of the Clerk and the Girl:* short dramatic pieces, perhaps originally entertainments between the courses of a banquet. Later the same term would be applied to short pieces inserted between acts of a longer play.

Much of the interest in earlier sixteenth-century humanist drama centers on Sir Thomas More and his circle. Henry Medwall (ca. 1500), the author of the *Interlude of Nature* and *Fulgens and Lucres,* served as chaplain to Cardinal John Morton, Henry VII's chancellor and inventor of that useful fundraising device, "Morton's Fork." Thomas More was reared in Morton's household, where he is reported to have entertained the assembled company by stepping into a performance and improvising a role for himself. One of the most attractive features of Medwall's interlude *Fulgens and Lucres* is the similar intrusion of two young spectators, who begin by casually introducing the action and then become participants in it. *Fulgens and Lucres* has been associated by F. S. Boas and A. W. Reed with Morton's 1497 Christmas festivities for the Spanish and Flemish ambassadors (Creeth, xvi). It was printed between 1513 and 1519; a single copy survives. Its printer, John Rastell (1476–1547) was married to More's sister Elizabeth, and Rastell's son-in-law, John Heywood (1497?–1580), was a protégé of More. Still another author of humanist interludes, John Redford (1486–1547), may have been acquainted with Heywood as a fellow musician.

Heywood himself was employed at the court of Henry VIII between 1519 and 1528 as a singer and player on the virginals. Heywood has generally been regarded as a useful transitional figure linking medieval and Elizabethan theater. Six plays have been ascribed to him; *Johan Johan the Husbandman,* adapted from the French farce *Pernet qui va au vin,* may be his. Heywood definitely wrote interludes: *The Playe called the foure P.P.; a very mery enterlude of a palmer, a pardoner, a potycary, a pedler* (printed ca. 1544) was acted in 1520, perhaps at court. Other words include *The Play of the Wether, A Play of Love, The Pardoner and the Frere* (printed 1533–34 by John Rastell's son William), and the manuscript interlude-debate *Wytty and Witless,* first printed in 1846 by the Percy Reprint Society. Of the early Tudor dramatists, only Heywood and John Redford can be described as professional performers. No plays appear in his *Woorkes* (1562), suggesting that he did not consider his interludes an important aspect of his literary activity (Creeth, xvii–xxii).

Much of Heywood's work is characterized by its liveliness, economy, and charm. Like Skelton, Heywood was evidently a reader and admirer of Chaucer, as his modes of social satire and use of Chaucer's rhyme royal stanza both suggest. *Johan Johan* begins and ends with the cuckolded husband, whom we meet at the beginning in a dramatic monologue of great length, in which he assures himself and the audience that he is about to beat his faithless wife, Tib. The ribald comedy of the ensuing *fabliau* employs the crudest of sexual imagery. Tib displays her mastery over her husband by directing him to jump through a series of hoops: Johan Johan must set the table, fetch the unctuous priest Sir Johan who is his wife's lover, fetch water in a leaky bucket, and at last finds himself crouching by the fire, struggling to soften the wax of a candle to mend the bucket, while the priest gorges on his wife's pie. Pie, bucket, and candle are all exploited as blatant symbols of intercourse. The action ends appropriately in slapstick violence: "Here they fight by the e[a]rys a while, and then the preest and the wife go out of the place" (Bevington, *Medieval Drama,* 989). In the final speech of the play Johan Johan hurries off in search of his wife and the priest once again; and the audience can imagine the same farce repeating itself over and over. The comic characterization of the husband, wavering between truculence and shrinking cowardice, carries the play.

David Bevington divides Heywood's works into two categories, suggesting that *Johan Johan* and the anticlerical debate of *The Playe called the foure P.P.* were intended for popular audiences, whereas *The Play of the Wether* would appear chiefly to courtly spectators. As he notes himself, this distinction can be made only with care: the work of Per Nykrog on the French *fabliaux* and an acquaintance with the career of Chaucer suggest that aristocratic audiences frequently enjoyed *fabliaux* like *Johan Johan* as much as any bourgeois, perhaps more. Probably an interlude designed for a banquet, *The Play of the Weather* presents a courtly debate, the descendant of a long medieval tradition. Indeed, this work demonstrates how medieval debate poems like those mentioned in chapter 1 might have been performed as dramas. In Heywood's interlude a series of petitioners ask Jupiter to provide them with weather suitable for their activities: Jupiter's servant, "the vice" Merry-Report, escorts the gentleman, the merchant, the ranger, the water-miller, the wind-miller, the gentlewoman, the launder, and "a boy, the lest that can play" before the presiding god. Naturally their requests are mutually incompatible. The play stresses the natural diversity of needs and desires within the state, and the godlike role of royal authority in mediating among them. The theme would appeal naturally to Henry VIII (Bevington, *Medieval Drama,* 990).

The publisher John Rastell has himself been identified as the author of *Calisto and Meliboea* (adapted from de Rojas's *Celestina*) and *The Dialogue of Gentleness and Nobility.* Both interludes were performed in his garden at Finsbury and printed by him in 1527. Rastell evidently had set up some type of stage in Finsbury Fields, for which there are 1424–26 records of costumes for plays and disguisings.

During the reign of Henry VIII John Redford was master of the choristers at St. Paul's Cathedral; his interludes may have been intended for their performance. Regrettably for the study of early Tudor drama, most of his works have remained unedited up to the present. *Wit and Science* of around 1530–48 dramatizes the allegorical adventures of "Wit, as student," in his quest for the hand of Lady Science, daughter of Reason. Wit's adversaries and helpers are also allegorical figures: Experience, Instruction, Honest Recreation on the side of the virtues, and Tediousness, Idleness, Ignorance as vices. Dame Idleness's role as "the very roote of all viciousnes" has an extensive background in medieval literature, religious and secular; she was the gatekeeper of the garden of love in the thirteenth-century *Roman de le rose* and the mother of the vices in a number of penitential works. In *Wit and Science* Wit sleeps in her lap while she blackens his face and changes his gown of learning for the fool's coat of ignorance. As in *Mankind* and many other moralities, the change of costume marks a spiritual change. This comic interlude seems especially well adapted for Redford's boy actors, the forerunners of the boy companies of Shakespeare's day. Its numerous female roles, lively repartee, and specifications for sophisticated music and dance would admirably display the strengths of these child performers.

Most of these humanist interludes remain within the established dramatic conventions of the morality tradition. It is not until the 1530s at the earliest that the genres and conventions of classical drama begin to appear in experimental English works. Then, as Bevington demonstrates, the change is by no means wholesale. Moral plays and interludes remain in the majority. Indeed, it has been argued that the early attempts at comedy and tragedy in the style of the ancients have been often overemphasized in the history of British drama. They certainly point the way toward the large-scale adaptation of classical genres by later British dramatists, and they signal a movement especially among academics toward the practical application of classical literary theory in English compositions. They do not, however, represent the mainstream of mid-sixteenth-century drama by any means. To begin with, classical comedies and tragedies are sidelights to the popular morality plays.

Of the early Tudor comedies *Ralph Royster Doyster* should probably be read as a school play, perhaps written by Nicholas Udall (1505–56) while he was headmaster at Eton (1534–41), as a change from the Latin comedy normally performed there. It was not printed until 1566–67. Udall later became headmaster at Westminster and assisted in the Revels Office under Mary I. His other plays are lost, though a few snatches survive (Creeth, xxvii). *Ralph Royster Doyster* has been described as "the first play in English to deserve the name of comedy"

(*The Concise Oxford Companion to the Theatre,* 566). This distinction means, of course, that it is the first surviving play written in the English language to adopt the style and structure of Latin comedy, not by any means the first comic play in English or the first use of comic effects in an English play. The author's reading in the Latin comedies of Plautus and Terence is evident. The title character is "a Miles Gloriosus," modeled on Plautus' braggart soldier. Udall, like his fellow educators Erasmus and Vives, seems concerned to raise the moral tone of classical comedy. His prologue rejects "all scurilitie" in favor of mirth "mixed with vertue in decent comlynesse." The Roman courtesan of Plautus becomes a respectable and charming English widow, courted earnestly by the rather stuffy merchant Gawyn Goodlucke and ludicrously by Ralph Royster Doyster himself. The clever Roman slave who propels Plautus' intrigue becomes Udall's Matthew Merygreeke, who announces memorably in his opening line, "As long lyveth the mery man (they say) / As doth the sory man, and longer by a day." Royster Doyster is a direct ancestor of Jonson's Captain Bobadil and Shakespeare's Falstaff. Udall's play further reflects the progress of the domestication of Latin comedy through the five-act framework in which its text presents itself. The Renaissance principles of dramatic organization into acts and scenes, first apparent in editions of classical plays, here order an English comedy. Printing English plays in the same format as Plautus or Terence lends them the visual dignity of the Roman texts. These literary divisions do not necessarily correspond to anything in the actual dramatic structure or in its original performance; that depended on the playwright and the actors. In some cases the five-act design reflects the rhythm of the play. In other cases it seems to have been imposed by the printer. The shape of the individual sixteenth-century play often needs to be reassessed independent of these artificial divisions.

The second pioneering humanist comedy, *Gammer Gurton's Needle,* is ascribed to a "Mr. S., Mr. of Art." It was evidently performed at Christ's College, Cambridge, at some time between 1552 and 1563. A William Stevenson (d. 1575), who was fellow of Christ's College, may have been the author, though the play has also been ascribed to others. It was printed by Thomas Colwell in 1575, possibly as a reprint of an earlier edition. As Creeth notes, within the format of classical comedy,

Gammer Gurtons Needle presents a farce, somewhat reminiscent of *Johan Johan* in the physical comedy of its village humor. As in *Ralph Royster Doyster* the comedy ends in communal reconciliation (Creeth, xxvii).

The first English tragedy still seems to be *Gorboduc,* also known as *Ferrex and Porrex,* acted in the hall of the Inner Temple during the Christmas revels of 1560–61 and repeated on 18 January 1561–62 before Elizabeth I at Whitehall. The first three acts were written by Thomas Norton (1532–84), a member of the Inner Temple, and the last by his fellow law student Thomas Sackville (1536–1608), first earl of Dorset. Sackville also wrote the "Induction" and "The Complaint of Buckingham" in the second edition of the *Mirror for Magistrates* (1563) and went on to a political career under Elizabeth. *Gorboduc* stands as the earliest known attempt to compose an English Senecan tragedy in blank verse. Chaucer had been the first English poet to explore the usefulness of the iambic pentameter line. In 1540 Henry, earl of Surrey, wrote his translation of Virgil's *Aeneid* in unrhymed iambic pentameter, our "blank verse," perhaps in imitation of Molza's translation of the same Latin epic into unrhymed Italian hendecasyllabic lines. Surrey's work was printed by Tottel in 1557. *Gorboduc* adapts this recent attempt to approximate in English the unrhymed Latin line of Virgil, itself modeled on the Greek dactylic hexameters of Homer. This key metrical innovation leads to the blank verse of Marlowe and Shakespeare. *Gorboduc* also follows its classical models in the indirect reporting of action and by its use of a chorus. The basic plot derives from Geoffrey of Monmouth's useful compendium of early British historical mythology, the *Historia Regum Britanniae.* It parallels *King Lear,* another offshoot from the same source. King Gorboduc divides Britain between his sons, who proceed to fight one another. Ferrex kills Porrex and is killed offstage by Videna, his mother. The people rise and murder the king and queen, inaugurating an era of civil war and pointing the play's moral. The tragedy is medieval in the sense that it centers on the fall of a prince, yet adapted to the sixteenth century in its stress on the need for divinely ordained royal authority to impose order. Each act is prefaced by a "dumb show" accompanied by music, perhaps an attempted re-creation of Roman pantomime. *Gorboduc* seems to have been an ambitious, innovative production, a clear model for dramatists of the age of Elizabeth (Creeth, xxvii).

Close on the heels of *Gorboduc* came Thomas Preston (fl. ca. 1570). His *A Lamentable Tragedy Mixed Full of Pleasant Mirth of Cambises, King of Persia* of around 1569 seems to have been in the repertory of a professional troupe, the Earl of Leicesters' Men. This early tragic work was popular enough for Falstaff to refer to "King Cambyses vein" of declamation (*Henry IV*, part 1). Preston may also have been the author of *Sir Clyomon and Sir Clamydes* (ca. 1570). *Cambises*'s political concerns are not remarkably different from those of *Gorboduc*, but the styles of the play could not be more dissimilar. *Cambises* narrates the crimes and sudden death of King Cambises of Persia, mixing historical and allegorical characters in a manner reminiscent of Bale. Violent deeds are executed onstage. The popular "fourteeners" Preston employs were familiar in sixteenth-century Britain as a "ballad meter," and were still popular for narrative verse a century later in Puritan New England. They attracted the parodies of later Elizabethan playwrights, but they were easy to memorize and suitable for a fast-moving narrative. *Cambises* shows us classical tragedy as it might have been attempted by a professional company of actors (Creeth, xxxiv–v).

Many colleges and the London Inns of Court continued the medieval tradition of appointing an abbot or lord of misrule to supervise the Christmas and New Years' festivities, in the spirit of the old Feast of Fools. University scholars and law students were also involved in the production of classical and neo-Latin plays. At Cambridge, Kirchmayer's *Pammachius* was presented at Christ's College (1546), and Plautus' *Aulularia* (1564) in King's College Chapel. Oxford also produced plays in Latin; the first is recorded at Magdalen around 1490. Several colleges performed Latin plays in the 1540s. They also devised English plays. In 1566 Elizabeth I saw Edwardes's *Palaemon and Arcyte*, a dramatization of Chaucer's *Knight's Tale,* at Christ Church. A 1567 Merton College comedy, *Wylie Beguylie,* has regrettably disappeared. The university authorities viewed professional troupes of actors with suspicion, but Strange's Men are known to have played at an innyard at Oxford in 1590–91, and other visits have been documented.

These academic communities have been viewed as key precursors of the Elizabethan professional theater, the source of University Wits and classical influences. Their records, documenting both internal events and performances for important visitors, show a high degree of dramatic activity into the seventeenth century. Among the most astonishing productions of the Inns of Court was *The Misfortunes of Arthur* of 1587, a notable attempt at Arthurian Senecan tragedy in which Francis Bacon collaborated with Thomas Hughes and others. Here Arthur is presented in the style of *Gorboduc*. The dramatic experiments of the colleges and Inns of Court persisted into the seventeenth century. New editions of dramatic records of the Inns of Court and of Cambridge University will enable scholars to trace the dramatic activities there in much greater detail. These academic stages should not be seen merely as formative influences on Elizabethan public drama, but as training grounds and alternative theaters. The critical division that has been drawn in the past between academically trained playwrights like the University Wits—Marlowe, Greene, Nashe, Peele, and Lodge—and their contemporaries who had not been exposed to higher education—Jonson and Shakespeare, for instance—merits reexamination, but it should not be summarily discarded.

The dramatic influence of the Inns of Court may prove even more impressive in the long run than that of the universities. The law students of Gray's Inn and the Middle Temple were to become notable dramatists: by the end of the century John Marston and John Ford had both transferred their allegiance from the law to the stage. P. J. Finkelpearl's *John Marston of the Middle Temple* effectively describes the intellectual atmosphere of the Elizabethan Inns of Court, which had become centers for the education of sons of gentlemen, not only for specialized legal training. The gentlemen in residence there had begun to display an interest in contemporary Italian drama as well as in the classics. Lodovico Ariosto's (1474–1533) *I Suppositi* (*The Supposes*) was performed at Gray's Inn in 1566 in a translation by George Gascoigne; the same play was not revived at Oxford until 1582. The gentlemen of Gray's Inn also enacted an acclaimed series of revels, *Gesta Grayorum,* at the court of Elizabeth; the poet Thomas Campion participated as actor in 1588 and composer in 1594. The Inns of Court continued to appoint a lord of misrule at Christmas on and off until around 1660.

For the most part, academic pageants and plays were intended to be performed in halls, perhaps during feasts, or in chapels. In stagecraft they are logical extensions of medieval indoor drama, and show strong affinities with contemporary court pageantry.

COURT PAGEANTRY AND THE RISE OF THE MASQUE

The two previous chapters described basic varieties of court and civil pageantry from the thirteenth through the fifteenth century. In court theater, critics often contrast the sporadic and idiosyncratic experiments with royal patronage under earlier rulers with the systematic Tudor approach. As far as the evidence allows us to judge, the royal forays into political pageantry under Edward I, Edward III, and Richard II provide the closest medieval parallels to Henry VII's energetic initiatives. Sydney Anglo's *Spectacle, Pageantry, and Early Tudor Policy* is still the key study of court pageantry of this period. Anglo uses the extensive records of the Tudor Revels Office to advantage in his investigations. Henry VII appointed the first master of the Revels as an officer in the royal household under the lord chamberlain in 1494. From then on, the Revels Office becomes a voluminous source of material, revealing the backstage workings of early Tudor court pageantry. Later in the sixteenth century the Revels Office would be directed to censor the public stages; it was eventually superseded in this role by the lord chamberlain himself. In this way the Tudor court came to exert control over its own productions and over popular drama as well. As Henry VIII's statute of 1543 indicates, the authorities were more concerned to censor religious or political speech than obscenity. As in ancient Rome, political satire was a dangerous business.[7]

Court pageantry of the sixteenth century quickly developed its own variations on the medieval courtly entertainments discussed earlier in this volume. A lord of misrule still supervised the court's Christmas and New Year's entertainments, as at the Inns of Court. Court jesters had been visible earlier, but they became an institution in the sixteenth century, when they influenced Shakespeare's fools. Most significantly for the future, perhaps, the fifteenth-century term *disguising* for a masked entertainment, courtly or otherwise, begins to be replaced in the literature by "mask" around 1512. Ben Jonson would be the first English author to use the French spelling *masque* in the seventeenth century. In the course of the sixteenth century, this masked pageant developed into a complex courtly spectacle, to be further refined by the courts of James I and Charles I in the seventeenth century. A brisk overview of the Tudor monarchs and their court pageantry is all that can be attempted here. Even such a quick survey suggests some of the variety and virtuosity of court entertainments throughout this period.

Henry VII (1485–1509) has been credited with establishing the Tudor policy of using pageants for political propaganda. The tenuous nature of his claim to the throne may have contributed to a sense of insecurity and the need for an active publicity campaign. The records suggest that, in addition, he genuinely enjoyed drama. He attended the Corpus Christi plays twice at Coventry, in 1487 and 1493, and at York in 1487. Henry VII also supported clerical drama. In 1493 comes the first record of the *Lusores Regis* (the Players of the King's Interludes). They evidently performed during the wedding celebrations for Henry VII's daughter Margaret Tudor and King James IV in Scotland (1503) and are also recorded on tour in various private houses. At Greenwich, Richmond, and Westminster, educated authors were employed by the king to produce court performances: John Skelton, Henry Medwall, John Heywood, John Redford, and the two William Cornyshes were all actively engaged in writing for Henry VII. The Revels accounts of Richard Gibson tabulate performances, materials, and expenses more extensively than ever before. Detailed records document the pageants, disguisings, jousts, and interludes mounted by the court and by the city of London to celebrate the arrival of Catherine of Aragon and her wedding with Prince Arthur in November of 1501. One attractive item was the disguising in which a lady resembling Princess Catherine appeared on a ship accompanied by Hope, Desire, and a bevy of sailors (Lancashire, 187). The impression Henry VII's court leaves on the historian of drama is that of theatrical inventiveness and energy enlisted in the service of royal prestige.

Major dramatic activities at the court of Henry VIII (1509–47) also cover a wide range. The athletic young king engaged in grandiose tournaments embellished with processions and opulent disguises. The vivid images of *The Great Tournament Roll of Westminster* portray a joust of February 1511 in which four knights of the Queen Noble Renown, including Henry VIII as Coeur Loyal, appeared as principal challengers. In 1520 in the course of the multiple pageants of *The Field of the Cloth of Gold* at Ardres in France, Henry matched himself and his pageant makers against Francis I of France, as sophisticated and theatrical a monarch as he was himself. One pageant cast Henry VIII as Hercules, leading the Nine Worthies. George Cavendish's *Life of Wolsey* describes a disguising in which Henry VIII paid a surprise visit to Cardinal Wolsey. Mayings also gave opportunities for dramatic entertainment. Several court entertainments of Henry VIII's day incorporated Robin Hood and paralleled village Robin Hood plays associated with May Day. Pageant and drama provided Henry VIII with useful support in his controversial religious and political decisions (Lancashire, 199).

Many of the same types of pageant that had entertained his father were produced at the court of Edward VI (1547–53), often by the same entertainers. The records of costumes used in court Revels during Edward's reign are particularly detailed and suggestive. In one striking passage, Anglo describes the sinister mask of "Medioxes," half death and half man, that appeared before the young king shortly before his death in 1553. Other pageants on this occasion included players disguised as bagpipes, cats, and tumblers hopping on their heads. Evidently someone in Edward VI's entourage appreciated fantastic or grotesque effects.

With the accession of Mary I and her marriage to Philip II of Spain in 1554 came further pageants and further records. Familiar names appear in the dramatic documents of Mary's reign (1553–1558). Nicholas Udall, the headmaster and author of *Ralph Royster Doyster,* participated in the activities of the Revels Office. In one of the climactic pageants for Mary's coronation, John Heywood appeared sitting under a vine in the churchyard of St. Paul's, where he greeted the new queen in English and Latin. The London pageants for Philip II's royal entry culminated in a castle, where Mary and Philip appeared, crowned by Sapientia (Wisdom), and accompanied by Justicia, Equitas, Veritas, and Misericordia (Justice, Equity, Truth, and Mercy).

Both court and civil pageants used the characters and conventions of moral drama and chivalric mythology to enhance the public images of the reigning couple (Lancashire).

With Elizabeth I (1558–1603) we reach the ultimate example of Tudor political pageantry, the "cult of Elizabeth." Once again the reigning monarch is active as a performer. In all of her many personae, as "Gloriana" and "the Virgin Queen," Elizabeth and her court cultivated the aura of splendor and majesty that still surrounds her today. Several of their main tendencies were already apparent in the January 1559 civic pageants for Elizabeth's coronation. The new queen's own likeness appeared on "the seate of worthie gouernance," in a kind of moral tableau, allied with Pure Religion, Love of Subjects, Wisdom, and Justice against Superstition and Ignorance, Rebellion and Insolency, and their like. A later pageant contrasted two mounts, "a decayed common weale" and "a florishyng commonweale" together with Truth the daughter of Time, who offered a Bible to the queen. In the next scene the biblical judge Deborah appeared with the three estates of nobility, clergy, and commons (Lancashire, 217–18). All of these scenes complimented Elizabeth as a divinely appointed female ruler while they alluded delicately to the return of the Protestant faith.

We know the names of many of the court officers who created Elizabeth's court pageants. Sir Thomas Cawarden supervised the entertainment at Elizabeth's coronation and was appointed master of the Revels for life (1545–59). His successor was Sir Thomas Benger (1559–72). At this time the functions of the Revels Office were limited, as other departments of the royal household began to take over many economic and technical aspects of court entertainment. There was a new master in 1572; Thomas Blagrove in fact ran the office, while the title went to Sir Edmund Tilney (1579–1610). It is important to recall that the master of the Revels was also a censor of plays and drew fees for public performances (Chambers, *Elizabethan Stage,* vol. 1).

Among the more celebrated Elizabethan court events were the Accession Day tilts, commemorating Elizabeth's accession to the throne and encouraging Protestant chivalry. Sir Philip Sidney was perhaps the most famous English knight to participate. Like most earlier British courts, Elizabeth's was mobile. The queen's "progresses" across the country gave her noble and plebeian subjects a chance to contribute appropriate offerings for her entertainment. George Gascoigne helped to devise a particularly celebrated series of 1575 entertainments at Woodstock and Kenilworth, the seat of the earl of Leicester. These July 1575 Kenilworth Revels are notable for their mixture of courtly and popular elements. They include a Captain Cox in a revival of the Coventry Hocktide play, which had been traditionally held on Hock Tuesday, the third Tuesday after Easter Sunday. The version witnessed by Elizabeth showed English knights on hobby horses in combat against Danes, after which Danish prisoners were led off by English women. Probably this dramatizes a later historical explanation grafted onto an early folk custom involving men's capture, "hocking," by women. (A Worcester prohibition of this activity dates to 1450.)

Sixteenth-century court pageantry was not confined to the royal court of England. Scotland under James IV and James V had its own reputation to maintain in the area of royal magnificence. The fifteenth and sixteenth centuries were the great era of Middle Scots literature, and we expect to find some reflection of the sophisticated poetry of Henryson, Dunbar, and Gavin Douglas in the court pageantry of their day.

James IV of Scotland jousted notably at Edinburgh in 1507 and again in 1508, in two tournaments of *The Wild Knight and the Black Lady*. The second event culminated in a three-day festival at Holyrood House, with a grand banquet punctuated by farces, plays, or spectacular illusions. As the finale Andrew Forman, bishop of Moray, appeared as a sorcerer and spirited away the Black Lady in a cloud that descended from the ceiling of the hall (Lancashire, 316).

We have already seen how Sir David Lindsay's *Ane Satire of the Thrie Estaitis* may have functioned first as a palace interlude for the feast of the Epiphany and then reappeared at Edinburgh twelve years later as a grand communal event under the auspices of Queen Mary of Guise. Sir David Lindsay evidently devised other court spectacles in the course of his career as herald and poet. At Mary of Guise's royal entry to St. Andrews in 1538 he is reported to have devised the pageant at the New Abbey Gate in which a cloud descended from the heavens, opening to reveal an angel who offered Queen Mary the keys of the kingdom.

Connections between sixteenth-century court pageantry and professional theater have been explored by a number of scholars. Professor Wickham stresses the importance of professional performances at court throughout the century. Sophisticated scenic effects concocted by the craftsmen of the Revels Office were known to the professional companies. Wickham argues that this technical expertise served as a resource for the professional theater, as well as for the court pageants of the seventeenth century. Many characters and allusions in Elizabethan and Jacobean plays derive from the ongoing tradition of the court performance. The well-established connection between the court jester and the fool of Shakespeare's plays is only the most obvious of these links.

THE RISE OF ELIZABETHAN PLAYHOUSES AND COMPANIES

For small companies of traveling players of the fourteenth and fifteenth centuries, aristocratic patronage had become a necessity, without which wandering performers risked arrest as vagabonds. Local and national efforts to control wandering bands of performers continued through the sixteenth century. Players were often regarded as disorderly characters, in need of repression. The suspicions of town authorities were aroused rather than quieted by the building of the first public playhouse of Elizabethan London, the Theatre. This chapter briefly summarizes the development of the professional theaters and companies in London, leading up to the first reference to Shakespeare as a playwright in 1592.[8]

TRAVELING PLAYERS AND PERFORMANCES.   In many respects the professional companies who gravitated toward the London of Elizabeth resembled their counterparts of the fifteenth and earlier sixteenth centuries. They tended to be small, nomadic groups, often of no more than four or five actors. Officially they served some noble patron, as members of his or her household. They were expected to perform for their patron on certain important occasions; otherwise they were free to tour the country. The earlier discussions of the moral plays and humanist drama give some idea of their repertories.

Earlier scholarship, searching for models for the Elizabethan playhouses, stressed the role of inn courtyards as early theaters. Yet many of the provincial records investigated in the course of the REED project suggest that outside of London the innyards were rarely used for performances. Traveling plays preferred to perform in halls whenever they could find them. Parish houses with large assembly rooms upstairs, guildhalls, and churches occur more often than innyards as places of performance. Anyone acquainted with the variability of British weather should not be surprised at this preference for indoor performance. Nevertheless, there is clear evidence that innyards in London were used as theaters in the later sixteenth century: performances occurred on occasion at the Bel Savage on Ludgate Hill (1579–1588 and later), the Bell in Gracious (Gracechurch) Street (1576, 1583), the Boar's Head in Aldgate (1557, when *A Sack Full of News* was halted for lewdness and the players imprisoned), and several others (1557–1608).

Indoor hall theaters were as desirable in London as they were outside of the capital. The first Blackfriars theater was constructed on the site of the old Blackfriars monastery, possibly in a small hall. It was first used by several companies of boy actors between 1576 and 1584. A second hall at Blackfriars was fitted up by James Burbage in 1596 and leased by the Children of the Chapel from 1600 until 1608. From 1608 to 1642, it served as the indoor, winter home of Shakespeare's company, the King's Men.

Temporary outdoor stages in marketplaces and fairgrounds also seem to have been used by resourceful companies of actors. Fairgrounds theaters persisted after the appearance of the playhouses. London summer fairs always attracted performances, whether puppet-plays or live actors. (In addition to Bartholomew Fair were the Smithfield, Southwark, Greenwich, and May fairs, to name a few.) Fairgrounds theater is more prominent in French and German theatrical history, but it should not be ignored as an aspect of British dramatic experience.

THE LONDON PUBLIC PLAYHOUSES, 1576–1603. Playhouses like the Globe and the Fortune have attracted an immense amount of critical attention as scholars attempt to reconstruct the theatrical experience of the age of Shakespeare. It is important to remember that the public playhouses were not the only places where Shakespeare and his rivals performed. Essentially outdoor theaters, they accommodated mass audiences in the summer months. In the winter the players sensibly preferred hall theaters like those at Blackfriars. Performances at court, continuing the long medieval tradition of indoor staging, would also take place in a hall. The Globe was no place for Elizabeth I, let alone for the most respectable matrons of London.

A review of the geography of London contributes to an understanding of the development of the Elizabethan theaters. Generally the players established themselves on the outskirts of the city, at the outer limits of civic authority. To the north, they occupied Finsbury Fields, the site of Burbage's Theatre. When the local authorities made things too "hot" for the players there, they crossed the river to Bankside, a still less reputable neighborhood. To the south of the city productions were mounted at Newington Butts, a popular resort for archery practice and other recreational activities. It is difficult to tell whether there was any type of theatrical building there.

The building of the Theatre, the first English playhouse, in 1576 has been seen as inaugurating a new era in the history of British drama. Professor Lancashire observes that not since the days of the Romans had there been such theatrical buildings in Britain. This prototypical building was the work of James Burbage (ca. 1530–97), a carpenter who had joined the earl of Leicester's players around 1572. His son, Richard Burbage (ca. 1567–1619), would become one of the most celebrated actors of his age. The Theatre's location was determined by the lord mayor's opposition to actors performing in innyards within the city of London. It was built outside the city limits, between Finsbury Fields and the road from Bishopsgate to Shoreditch Church. As far as modern scholars have been able to determine, it was a wooden structure of unknown dimensions, with several galleries of tiered seats that surrounded a circular inner yard. Professor Wickham's research leads him to the conclusion that its principal models were bear- and bull-baiting houses, similar structures whose central yard was used for the animal baiting itself. These animal-baiting houses were in their turn influenced by arenas for tournaments, again a central space surrounded by scaffolds for spectators. A number of the Elizabethan playhouses also served as animal-baiting houses; their stages could be dismantled, leaving the arena clear. The Theatre itself was used for exhibitions of martial skills—fencing and quarterstaff contests—as well as for performances by several acting companies who leased it before the Chamberlain's Men took up occupancy in 1594. The Theatre cost Burbage roughly £650 to build. His admission fees are known: one penny was charged for standing room on the ground level, two pennies for the galleries, and threepence for a seat in the gallery area. The *Hamlet* that preceded Shakespeare's and jigs and drolls by Kempe and Tarleton were performed there. The local authorities continued to object to the presence of the Theatre. In 1597 Cuthbert Burbage dismantled it, had it ferried across the Thames to Bankside, and built the Globe from its timbers.

The rival theater, the Curtain, was put up in 1576, a year after the Theatre, and its erection was in itself testimony to the promise of the idea. The Curtain seems to have been much more successful in attracting a high quality of drama, in which it rivaled the Fortune. Initially the Curtain was the home of the Chamberlain's Men under Burbage. It is associated with Jonson's *Every Man in His Humour* (1598), a production in which Shakespeare took the part of Knowell. The first productions of *Romeo and Juliet* (ca. 1595) and *Henry V* (1599) were possibly also given here.

The Globe is unquestionably the most celebrated of the Elizabethan playhouses. Here Richard Burbage appeared in most of Shakespeare's plays. Burnt down in 1613, the Globe was rebuilt with a tiled roof instead of the flammable thatch and reopened in 1614. Its later history belongs to the Stuart era.

The Fortune, the Hope, the Rose, and the Swan are the other Elizabethan public playhouses that figure in the dramatic history of Elizabethan London. The Fortune, the Hope, and the Rose were all owned by Philip Henslowe (d. 1616), whose diary (now at Dulwich College) is a principal source of information on the running of his Elizabethan theaters. Henslowe was a major theatrical entrepreneur and is also described in contemporary sources as an exploiter of his actors and playwrights. Henslowe's forceful economic control of his companies led to accusations of embezzlement in 1615. His methods contrast with the joint ownership policy of the rival Chamberlain's Men.

Of Henslowe's theaters the Swan was not the most brilliant theatrically, but it is the theater for which we have the most information. It was built by Francis Langley in Bankside, at Paris Garden, near the Bear Gardens, much to the disapproval of the lord mayor. It opened in 1594. Johannes de Witt, on a 1596 visit from the Netherlands, sent a sketch of the interior of the Swan back to Utrecht; his friend Arend von Buchel preserved a copy of it in his commonplace book. This is the only surviving contemporary drawing of the inner area of an Elizabethan theater building. It shows an open stage, three galleries, and a stage building. Its pillars were wooden, painted in imitation of marble. Possibly the Swan did hold three thousand spectators, as de Witt estimated. The Fortune was even larger. The Swan was used for a variety of entertainment and sports events. It was closed in 1597 after Pembroke's Men produced the *Isle of Dogs* there; Ben Jonson, implicated as both actor and playwright, was imprisoned along with some of his fellow performers.

In spite of the scarcity of visual representations or clear descriptions, many scholars have attempted to reconstruct the basic structure of the Elizabethan public playhouses. Recent archaeological excavations of the Rose and Globe sites should test their conclusions. Each playhouse clearly had individual features, but they shared the same general shape and mode of construction. They were wooden buildings, circular or octagonal, with central unroofed spaces into which projected platform stages. A single door controlled access to the theater and ensured payment of the admission fee. Three galleries with thatched roofs surrounded the central area, offering shelter and seating to affluent spectators. The "groundlings," the lowest class of auditors, who had paid a penny for admission, surrounded the stage on three sides. Spectators might also pay for seats onstage. The first reference to this practice appears in 1596; it can be noted in the induction to Shakespeare's *Taming of the Shrew*. The custom continued in English theaters as late as 1840.

The stage itself seems to have been skirted by boards or draperies to screen the area beneath it from spectators standing in front. Below the stage, machinery for raising special effects through trapdoors could be housed. Railings sometimes protected the stage above. The area behind the stage remains the most difficult to envision. It seems to have had an elegant architectural facade, the stage wall, with pillars supporting a roof, "the Heavens," that extended over all or part of the

The Harvard Theatre Collection model of Shakespeare's First Globe
Playhouse (1599–1613), as reconstructed by C. Walter Hodges and built by
John Ronayne and his associate, John Mills (1980).
*Reproduced by permission of the Harvard College Library from a slide of the
Harvard model photographed by Ed Jacoby*

stage. This roof would have been brightly painted and supplied with colorful curtains. The possibility of an "inner stage" has generated the most controversy, a debate reflected in the alternative term "discovery space." Was it a separate room or merely the corridor behind the stage, hidden by a curtain? Or were temporary structures set up onstage to serve as caves or tombs, tents, or interiors? Stage directions for plays like *The Tempest* demand the drawing of curtains to reveal a scene. Behind the stage wall, there was a dressing room, the "tiring house," for the actors.

Above the stage was an upper room, like the musician's or minstrel gallery of a nobleman's banquet hall. This acting space was useful for balcony scenes, Romeo and Juliet's being the most celebrated. On the level above this there was a room for machinery and sometimes musicians, above this a tower for the trumpeter to announce performances, and a flagpole. The playhouse's flag flew while a play was in progress.

The Elizabethan public playhouse served as a resource for its dramatists and influenced the shape of sixteenth-century drama. The debate over its relative impact compared to that of the indoor theaters is probably incapable of solution. Certainly the large, varied audiences of the playhouses fired the imagination and challenged the ingenuity of most Elizabethan dramatists. The inspiration of the public playhouse and its audiences is reflected in numerous references; so are expressions of disgust and disillusionment. Ultimately the playhouses would prove more influential in the twentieth-century revival of interest in stage history and Shakespeare's theater than they may have been in the immediate future of British drama.

PROFESSIONAL ACTING COMPANIES AND THE LONDON STAGE. The rise of professional companies of actors in the London area can be traced in official and unofficial sources. Their reliance on noble protectors links many of these companies with the medieval household troupes. The complexities that perplex the student of the Elizabethan acting companies can be seen in the following illustration. A group of players called Oxford's Men first appear on record in 1492. The earl of Oxford's players, presumably a later troupe, shocked London in 1547 by performing in Southwark in competition with the dirge for Henry VIII at St. Saviour's. Still another company, also Oxford's players, are known to have performed at the Theatre in 1580. Their patron, Edward de Vere (1550–1604), the seventeenth earl of Oxford, was himself a poet and is still considered in some quarters the actual author of Shakespeare's plays. For brawling, this troupe was banned from London until 1584, when they made a court appearance with John Lyly. It disappears from the records altogether in 1602 (Chambers, *Elizabethan Stage,* 2:99–102). Given the present state of the documents, it is as difficult to construct a continuous history for many British acting troupes of the period as it is for Oxford's Men.[9]

Records do indicate the size and basic structure of some of the theatrical companies. Often their organization varies strikingly. Documents occasionally permit scholars to speculate about the influence of certain aristocratic patrons. We can sometimes recover the names of principal actors and detect the work of specialists. Musicians were employed both for songs within plays and for "act music," musical interludes between acts. No professional actresses appeared in the public London theaters until the continental influence of the Restoration took hold in 1660, though ladies, from the queen on down, participated in court pageants.

Every theater company needs a good supporting staff. Behind the scenes, the tireman supervised costumes in the tiring house, attended to lights in the indoor theaters, and produced stools for onstage spectators. The companies had their own singers and instrumentalists, but professional musicians may also have been hired by theaters from the city corporation for particularly impressive musical effects. Carpentry was also an essential skill in the Elizabethan theater. It may not be accidental that two of the most influential figures in the architectural history of the British stage, James Burbage and Inigo Jones, seem to have been trained as carpenters.

It seems appropriate to focus attention at this point on the two major companies that dominated the Elizabethan stage in the 1580s and 1590s, the Admiral's Men and the Chamberlain's Men. These two troupes became the most powerful forces in the Elizabethan professional theater, their influence continuing into the reign of James I. A compact overview of their respective characters can help the modern reader to envision the competitive environment of the London stage in the last two decades of the sixteenth century.

The Admiral's Men operated under the patronage of Lord Charles Howard (1536–1624), earl of Nottingham, who had been appointed admiral in 1585, when the troupe made its first court appearance. Edward Alleyn (1566–1626) was its most prominent actor, and Christopher Marlowe the most celebrated playwright associated with the company. Alleyn made his reputation in the title roles of Marlowe's tragedies *Tamburlaine the Great* (1587–88), *The Tragical History of Doctor Faustus* (1589?), and *The Jew of Malta* (1590?). It has been suggested that Alleyn's style tended to be declamatory. Offstage, Alleyn founded Dulwich College (1613) and married as his second wife a daughter of the poet John Donne. Through his first wife, Philip Henslowe's stepdaughter, he inherited the papers, now preserved at Dulwich, that are key sources for Elizabethan stage history. These records allow modern readers to observe the Admiral's Men in operation; they include contracts between Henslowe and his actors and playwrights, receipts, names of plays, and dates of performances. The troupe migrated from Burbage's Theatre to Henslowe's Rose, under Alleyn's leadership, then on to the Fortune, where the Admiral's Men acted under the joint direction of Henslowe and Alleyn. As the owner of the theater, Henslowe seems to have exercised financial and artistic control over many productions. After 1603 the troupe became Prince Henry's Men. They survived the 1621 fire that destroyed the Fortune, and attempted to continue in the rebuilt Fortune (1623). They finally dispersed after the death of James I (Chambers, *Elizabethan Stage*, 2:134–192).

The Chamberlain's Men were organized in 1594, when they apparently enticed Shakespeare away from Pembroke's Men. Their first patron was Henry Carey, Lord Hunsdon (1524–96), lord chamberlain 1585–96. They gave early performances in Burbage's Theatre, but in 1599 they transferred to the Globe, built and managed by Cuthbert Burbage. Cuthbert's brother Richard probably began his career with the rival Admiral's Men before joining the Chamberlain's Men in 1594. Probably the most celebrated English actor of his day, Richard Burbage was the first to portray Shakespeare's Hamlet, Lear, Othello, and Richard III. He also appeared in plays by Jonson, Kyd, and Webster. The company became the King's Men under James I. Upon Shakespeare's retirement Beaumont and Fletcher seem to have taken over as company playwrights; *Philaster* (1610) is their earliest surviving collaborative work. The first Globe burnt in 1613, set afire by the cannons in Shakespeare's *Henry VIII;* it was rebuilt by 1614, when John Webster's *Duchess of Malfi* premiered there. Court patronage of the troupe continued under Charles I and Henrietta Maria. Their indoor performances had been produced at the second Blackfriars theater since 1608, and often also at court, in the Cockpit at Whitehall. Massinger became the main dramatist of the company's Caroline period, followed by James Shirley. The King's Men continued to perform up to the closing of theaters in 1642.

Besides Richard Burbage, we know a fair number of the actors for whom Shakespeare wrote, and we can speculate about their capabilities. The clown was by this time an indispensible stock comic character in Elizabethan drama, by turns a court jester, a scoundrel, or an idiot. Will Kempe, Shakespeare's original Dogberry, had toured Holland in 1585–86 and went on to appear at Elsinore in Denmark. He left the Chamberlain's Men after six years in 1600, to conduct his morris dance from London to Norwich (1600). The comedian Robert Armin (1568?–1611?) succeeded Kempe as the company's chief clown, taking his turn as Dogberry. This change in the comic lead seems to coincide with changes in Shakespeare's treatment of the principal comic roles in several of his plays (Chambers, *Elizabethan Stage,* 2:192–220).

The boy companies offered Elizabethan audiences a sophisticated alternative to the adult players. The dramatic records of educational institutions document children's performances back to the earlier part of the sixteenth century. The first public performance of the Children of the Chapel at Blackfriars is recorded in 1576. Ostensibly choirboys, these young professionals apparently attracted a following through the cultivation of a parodic combination of styles. Certain playwrights preferred to write for the children's companies. They performed Jonson's *Cynthia's Revels* (1600) and *The Poetaster* (1601), to name two better known examples. The children's companies also trained future actors. One of the finest actors of Jacobean London, Nathan Field (1587–1620) went from St. Paul's School to the Children of the Chapel in 1600; he appeared in both Jonson plays. Nine years later he is recorded in the cast of Jonson's *Epicoene; or, The Silent Woman.*

The REED series is beginning to permit students of Elizabethan theater to appreciate the professional companies' full range of performances, including the ways these troupes continued to operate in their traditional role as nomadic entertainers, frequently on tour. Provincial drama after the disappearance of the Corpus Christi cycles is also receiving more attention. It is in these fields that the study of the Elizabethan and Jacobean stage seems to demand the greatest future development. Without further analysis of these matters we cannot really understand how the professional actor functioned in Elizabethan England, or how the British Isles beyond the metropolis of London experienced drama.

English touring companies also ventured abroad. A series of troupes known by the generic title English Comedians (in German, the *Englische Komödianten*) appeared in Europe from the later sixteenth century on. One company, under Will Kempe, appeared at Elsinore, Dresden, and other towns across Germany beginning around 1586. In the 1590s the actor Robert Browne (fl. 1583–1620/40?) and his protégé John Green were among the best-known English performers on the Continent. Browne was a member of the Earl of Worcester's Men in 1583. He visited the Netherlands and Germany in 1592 at the head of a troupe of actors whose repertoire consisted of jigs, biblical drama, Marlowe, and early comedies including *Gammer Gurton's Needle.* At Wolfenbüttel, Heinrich Julius, duke of Brunswick (1564–1613) wrote plays for a household troupe of actors; like their leader, Thomas Sackville, many of the performers were English. Eleven of the duke's plays survive. George Jolly (fl. 1640–73) turned up in Germany in 1648, leading the last company of English Comedians yet detected. Jolly was especially associated with Frankfurt. Two printed collections of the English Comedians' repertoire were published, significantly influencing German drama. At the same time these expeditions exposed the actors to new continental sources, which influenced British drama in their turn. Besides their role in European dramatic history, the careers of the English Comedians bear witness to the energy and enterprise of the English acting profession.

THE EXPERIENCE OF ELIZABETHAN THEATER: AUDI-ENCES AND PLAYGOING. The London audiences of the Elizabethan era have been strenuously discussed since Ann Jennalie Cook's 1981 challenge to Alfred Harbage's analysis of Elizabethan theatrical attendance. Cook argues against the idea that Elizabethan audiences were drawn to any great extent from the laboring classes. She sees both the public playhouses and the smaller, more expensive indoor theaters as the preserves of the privileged, members of the gentry, the peerage, merchants, lawyers, and other educated, relatively leisured Londoners. When Martin Butler reassessed the evidence in 1984, his conclusions differed. He documents the presence of underprivileged Londoners, of apprentices and servingwomen, cutpurses, craftsmen, soldiers, and sailors. Even in the indoor theaters, the rear of the audience seems to have harbored a quantity of disreputable characters. At the moment the critical consensus seems to lean toward maintaining the idea of the "two traditions" of Elizabethan theater, with some new modulations and qualifications.[10]

Conditions of playgoing in Elizabethan London certainly varied between the indoor and outdoor theaters. In both cases admission fees separated playgoers into distinct classes. An actor onstage at the Globe would expect to look across a more or less disreputable mob below the stage, to address the genteel auditors in the galleries. At the Blackfriars theaters, the privileged spectators would occupy the front of the house, while the vulgar crowded in behind. The spaces each group was assigned gave them very different vantage points. *Othello* changes when seen from onstage compared to the center of the crowd in front of stage or a stool in the second gallery. Refreshments were available. Audience members munched nuts and apples during performances, and on occasion threw the cores at actors who happened to annoy them. The 1989 excavators of the Rose playhouse site unearthed a substantial number of hazelnut shells scattered by Elizabethan spectators.

Public performances of plays would often end with a jig: the comic actors Tarleton and Kempe are particularly associated with this form of entertainment. A forerunner of the ballad opera, the Elizabethan jig was basically a farce, set to a popular tune of the day, sung and danced by three or four actors. After the closing of the theaters in 1642 jigs

lingered on in fairground performances. They may have been introduced by the English Comedians to Germany, where they achieved
great popularity beginning in the later sixteenth century. The dance of
Bottom and his friends at the end of "Pyramus and Thisbe" approxi-
mates the jig's effect as a method of closing the performance.

The London stage was subject to the seasons; summer was the
height of theatrical activity, as it had been for many older forms of
outdoor theater like the May games and the Corpus Christi play.
During major plague epidemics the theaters were closed, leaving the
actors to fend for themselves. Three acting companies—Queen Elizabeth's, Pembroke's, and Sussex's Men—all seem to have been casualties of the plague of 1592–93. The theaters were required to hold their
own against rival attractions: bear and bull baiting, cockfights, tournaments, civil and court pageants, fairs, executions, sermons. All of
these stresses helped to shape the dramatic companies and conditioned
the work of their playwrights.

DRAMA IN SHAKESPEARE'S LONDON

The temptation to view Shakespeare in isolation, as a solitary presiding genius of the British drama, is difficult to resist. The tendency of
dramatic criticism and stage history to revolve around him, so that all
roads, past, present, and future, lead back to Shakespeare, compounds
the problem. In the past these attitudes rather warped the study of
early British drama. The tendency has also affected many later dramatists, critics, and historians, who see anything after Shakespeare—
particularly his immediate successors—as a woeful declension from
the sublime to the mediocre. In this final section of the chapter I seek
to re-place Shakespeare in context, to do justice to his genius without
allowing him to overshadow everything around him.

Shakespeare and his contemporaries need to be viewed as heirs of
the native tradition as well as of the learned humanist theater. To adopt
this perspective it is important to develop a sense of the varieties of
Elizabethan drama, playwrights, and performances within and beyond
the Shakespearean canon. At the same time, it is clearly undesirable to
emulate encyclopedic works like E. K. Chambers's alphabetically orga-

nized collection of Elizabethan playwrights, major and minor, which occupies the final three hundred and eighteen pages of the third volume of *The Elizabethan Stage*. Here I seek to provide a concise introduction to the subject rather than comprehensive documentation, as there is simply too much going on.

Ordinarily plays were bought outright by the owner of the theater, a financier like Henslowe, or by the company itself. The startling proliferation of plays during the 1590s may be due to the under-payment of their authors, who had to keep scribbling in order to eat. Thomas Heywood received only six pounds from Henslowe for the script of *A Woman Killed with Kindness*. The pound was certainly worth more in 1603 than it is now, but the sum is still modest. More than one playwright might work together. Often, old plays would be brought up to date by current writers. None of this activity was lucrative. The fortunate author might be an actor and shareholder in the company as well as a writer. Shakespeare is one of the few Elizabethan playwrights to obtain such a position. He is also the only Elizabethan playwright who seems to have made a fortune in the theater.

The printing of plays tended to be frowned on by the companies that owned them. Publication gave other troupes access to scripts, otherwise the exclusive property of the original actors. As a result, many early published versions of Elizabethan plays, mostly in "quarto" format, seem to be pirated. In 1600 the Admiral's Men paid a printer forty shillings to halt the publication of Dekker's *Patient Grissel*. On the other hand, publishers might pay the author or the company a modest fee. Large-scale collections of contemporary dramatic works in English were not printed until Ben Jonson introduced the idea in 1616. Royalties, benefits, or an "author's night" are all later developments (Chambers, *Elizabethan Stage*, 3:157–200).

Once a play had been written, the acting companies needed to employ copyists to write out actors' copies. The names of a few have survived in the records. A Ralph Crane (ca. 1550–1624), officially employed as an underwriter in the Privy Seal office, is also known to have copied a number of plays; several of his copies executed between 1615 and 1624 survive in the Bodleian and British libraries. Posted backstage during the performance would be a "platt," a prompter's outline of a play indicating major divisions, entrances, and exits. Some have been preserved in Henslowe's papers. All of these varieties of documentation help in tracing the complex genesis of Elizabethan plays.

EARLIER ELIZABETHAN PLAYWRIGHTS. When Shakespeare's name first appears in the annals of the London stage in 1592, the public playhouses had been operating there for sixteen years. This first selection of Elizabethan dramatists is intended to suggest something about the character of professional drama in London before Shakespeare became active as a playwright. Most of these authors continued working into the 1590s and became Shakespeare's collaborators or competitors.

The quarrels and alliances of the London literary community of the 1580s and 1590s are still discernible in dramatic literature and nondramatic works. Controversial pamphlets, letters, and romans à clef indicate some of the interactions among these authors as they struggled for literary survival in the London of Elizabeth. Shifting alliances unite and divide cliques of writers. Some of the University Wits mock the less erudite, popular school of dramatists, represented by Kyd and Munday. They also quarrel virulently among themselves. At the same time authors actively collaborate in the writing of plays, civic pageants, and a great deal of nondramatic literature. It is hardly surprising that the literary community of late sixteenth- and early seventeenth-century England has attracted later authors as a subject in itself. The conflicts of flamboyant personalities, the political, religious, and philosophical stresses of the period, and the economic realities of life as an Elizabethan professional writer all come into sharp focus in any examination of the lives of Shakespeare and his contemporaries.

It is important not to be too draconian in dividing Elizabethan playwrights into social or literary categories according to their level of higher education, even though the playwrights themselves sometimes drew this distinction. In some cases university training did produce a writer whose view of dramatic theory and practice had been shaped by advanced classical studies. In other cases, this criterion can be totally deceptive. Ben Jonson, one of the most erudite dramatists of this era, was unable to go on to university. Conversely, some university-trained writers retained a strong attraction toward popular theatrical conventions. Each author presents his own problems.[11]

Anthony Munday (ca. 1553–1633), the son of a London draper, is reported to have begun his theatrical career as an actor, perhaps with the Oxford's Men. He was perhaps better known for strenuous efforts in the field of nondramatic popular literature than for his plays. Besides translations of romances and ballads, Munday has been suspected of having written an antitheatrical pamphlet, *The Third Blast of Retrait from Plaies* of 1580. Evidently he left the stage and later returned to it. Much of his dramatic writing was undertaken for Henslowe. Francis Meres called him "our best plotter" and one of "the best for comedy." *John a Kent and John a Cumber* (ca. 1594) may have suggested Bottom. One Robin Hood play of Munday's is lost, but *The Downfall of Robert Earl of Huntingdon* and *The Death of Robert Earl of Huntingdon* (1598), collaborations with Chettle for the Admiral's Men, give some idea of his approach to this popular subject of British drama. Munday enjoyed a long career in the service of the city of London as a deviser of lord mayor's pageants like *Chryso-Thriambos, The Triumphes of Golde*, paid for by the company of Goldsmiths, for the installation of Sir James Pemberton as lord mayor in October 1611. Ben Jonson and John Marston, both eminently literary playwrights, amused themselves in satirizing Munday's popular mode of theater. His surviving plays at least suggest that the traditional Robin Hood play remained an attractive genre for the Elizabethan public and its authors. With the renewal of attention to the powerful popular element on the sixteenth- and seventeenth-century English stage, Munday should receive renewed critical attention.

Robert Greene (ca. 1558–92) studied at both Oxford and Cambridge, and claimed the title *Academiae Utriusque Magister in Artibus*. He is most often recalled today for his bitter comment on Shakespeare in his pamphlet, *A Groatsworth of Wit Bought with a Million of Repentance*, the earliest reference to Shakespeare as a rising dramatist. Greene possibly resented the actor Shakspeare's revisions of earlier plays in which he may have had a hand, for instance *Henry VI;* he describes "an upstart crow beautified with our feathers, and in his opinion the only Shakescene in the country." At the same time Greene attacks Marlowe and other practitioners of "English blank-verse" even more violently. Greene may have collaborated with Kyd on *The Spanish Tragedy.* Undoubtedly his own were *Alphonsus* (ca. 1587); *The Honourable History of*

Friar Bacon and Friar Bungay (ca. 1589; published 1594), perhaps a response to Marlowe's *Doctor Faustus; Orlando Furioso* (ca. 1591; Alleyn's
actor's copy survives at Dulwich College); and *James IV of Scotland* (ca.
1591). *Friar Bacon and Friar Bungay* was the most successful of Greene's
dramatic works and was revived a number of times until 1630. Its happy
combination of comedy and a pair of rival magicians with British historical material in a romantic adventure of the future Edward I are still
effective onstage. Several of Greene's plays seem to reflect his admiration for Marlowe's success and his frustration with his own failure to
match it.

Christopher Marlowe (1564–93) has been identified as the most
important of Shakespeare's predecessors. The son of a prominent
member of the Canterbury Shoemaker's Guild, Marlowe was educated at Corpus Christi College, Cambridge. The first mention of
Marlowe's involvement in some type of espionage mission, perhaps
among the English Catholics at Rheims, occurs in a letter from the
Queen's Privy Council to the university in 1587, asking that Marlowe
be granted his master's degree. Following this mysterious episode,
Marlowe migrated to London, taking his place in the circle of Cambridge contemporaries already at work there—with Greene and Nashe
and the Oxonian Peele. The history of Marlowe's remaining six years
of life traces a series of violent clashes with the law. Marlowe and his
friend, the poet Thomas Watson, were charged in the murder of the
son of an innkeeper in 1589 and were acquitted on the ground of self-
defense. He seems to have annoyed the constables of Holywell Street
in 1592. At this time accusations of atheism began to be directed at
him, initially in 1588 by Robert Greene, and repeated in 1592. In May
1593 the dramatist Thomas Kyd was arrested on suspicion of atheism
and was examined under torture. Desperate to divert suspicion from
himself, Kyd accused Marlowe vehemently: critics have been fascinated by the question of Marlowe's heterodoxy ever since. Before he
could be called upon to answer these serious charges, Marlowe was
murdered at Deptford while dining in the dubious company of several
of Walsingham's spies.[12]

Marlowe is still most often praised as the first master of dramatic
blank verse in England. "Marlowe's mighty line" conclusively demonstrated the power of blank verse as a medium for tragic drama on the

public stage, not merely as a pedantic fancy. Beyond this accomplishment he is of particular interest for his reshaping of the plot devices of the morality tradition into new forms of tragic drama. Marlowe's philosophical audacity goes well beyond the norms of the Elizabethan stage; as a thinker he is much more controversial than Shakespeare. His enormously successful *Tamburlaine the Great,* part 1 (ca. 1587) may have been first produced by the Admiral's Men with Edward Alleyn; its sequel, *Tamburlaine the Great,* part 2 (ca. 1588) certainly was. *Tamburlaine* continued to be performed through 1642. The first play chronicles the inexorable rise of the Mongolian conqueror Tamburlaine (Timur Khan; 1336–1405), long considered by Western historians an instrument of God's providence sent to save Europe from the Turks. Here and in his later tragedies, Marlowe is preoccupied with the idea of a Renaissance superman, the individual who gains ultimate power through his innate force of character. Tamburlaine's death is not tragic in the same sense that Faust's would be. He dies at the height of his power, bequeathing a legacy of personal dominance to his sons. "So reign, my son; scourge and control those slaves, / Guiding thy chariot with thy father's hand" (Ribner, 174). Harry Levin's elegant discussion of Marlowe's heroes and Richard III as types of the "over-reacher" is still one of the most readable and illuminating studies of Marlowe and Shakespeare.

The *Tragical History of Doctor Faustus* has been dated variously between 1589 and 1592. It was printed in 1604. The play's classic morality structure has been commented on by generations of critics. Marlowe probably based his play on the English version of a Frankfurt chapbook of 1587, relating the fabulous adventures of Johann Faust (ca. 1488–1541), a traveling conjurer whose name had become attached to earlier legends of the man who sells his soul to the devil. Marlowe's Faust play survives in mangled condition, interlarded with crude comic episodes that Marlowe probably did not write, though in their present form they effectively undercut the hero's magical experiments. *Doctor Faustus* remains the most celebrated and most often anthologized of Marlowe's plays. Here the playwright reworks the morality tradition, playing against audience expectations and familiar structural conventions. Faustus's own intellectual ambitions lead him into temptation, but like the hero of *The Castle of Perseverance,* he is attended by good and evil angels.

The audience is led by clear signals to expect the redemption that should normally follow humanity's temptation and fall. Where the demon Mephistopheles is a truthful witness to the orthodox Christian universe, the human philosopher Faustus vacillates between skepticism and a longing for faith. His despair of the mercy of God ultimately damns him, but not until the last instant of the play. The final moments of suspense, as the hour approaches midnight and Faustus struggles to escape his inexorable doom, are memorably presented in his last feverish monologue.

The Jew of Malta (ca. 1590) is a more difficult work for modern readers. Again, Marlowe chooses a hero who dominates his world from beyond the bounds of Christianity. His prologue calls Barabas, the Jew of Malta, "in all his projects, a sound Machiavel." Critics have complained that the entirely conventional punishment of the Jew in the last act jars against the earlier sections of the play. Barabas has been seen as a forerunner of Shylock; in his revenge on his Christian enemies he should also recall the long tradition of perverse, cunning, and fabulously rich stage Jews of the British Middle Ages, especially those of the Croxton *Play of the Sacrament.* British audiences of the 1590s would recognize the convention from both dramatic and nondramatic sources. Barabas's position outside Christianity certainly gives Marlowe an opportunity to criticize Christian belief and behavior.

Edward II (ca. 1591–92) has been linked by some scholars with *Richard II.* It ranks with *Doctor Faustus* as Marlowe's best work. The play's allusions to Edward II's homosexuality have attracted modern critical interest. *Edward II* deserves to be read as well for its balancing of the rise of the younger Mortimer, who gradually becomes corrupt as he rises to power, with the corresponding fall of an increasingly more vulnerable, human, and appealing King Edward. These counterbalanced tragedies give the play much of its dramatic force.

Thomas Nashe (1567–1601) is best known for his nondramatic prose, particularly his controversial exchanges with the Harveys. As an exuberant virtuoso in the art of prose Nashe has few equals. Nashe was born the son of a minister at Lowestoft in Suffolk and educated at St. John's College, Cambridge. In London he seems to have associated with Peele, Greene, and Lyly, the University Wits. He engaged in a number of notable dramatic collaborations: with Marlowe on *Dido,*

Queen of Carthage in the 1580s for the Children of the Chapel, and with Jonson and others on *The Isle of Dogs* (1597).[13]

Nashe's only surviving independent dramatic work, *Summer's Last Will and Testament,* was written to be performed for Archbishop Whitgift at Croydon, probably in the late summer of 1592 while the London theaters were still closed on account of the Plague. An idiosyncratic, courtly play of great charm, it is unfortunately less often read as a drama than pillaged for its lyrics: "Spring, the sweet spring is the year's pleasant king," and Nashe's "litany in the time of plague"— "Dust hath closed Helen's eye: / I am sick; I must die. / Lord have mercy on us." In its basic form it recalls the humanist interludes of Redford and Heywood, particularly *The Play of the Wether*'s debate. Summer proposes to make his will, leaving his rule to Autumn. In the process a series of seasonal characters appear as Summer's officers and successors: Ver, the spring, Solstitium, Orion the hunter, Harvest, Bacchus, and as the play's mood darkens, a Puritanical Christmas followed by the sinister Backwinter. Nashe succeeds in combining elements of seasonal folk play, court pageantry, lyric, and social comment. The play's title puns on the name of Will Summers, Henry VIII's celebrated court jester, who appears as the play's narrator. Will Summers provides a running commentary, sometimes undercutting and sometimes entering the action. *Summer's Last Will and Testament* falls somewhere between play and masque. Its evidence for the continuing vitality of earlier sixteenth-century dramatic form is worth remembering. Most of all, the play's attempt to face the terrors of the approaching Plague, the common fear of author, actors, and audience, helps to make it memorable.

Thomas Kyd (1558–94) is best known for *The Spanish Tragedy* (ca. 1585–89), a work immensely popular at the time of its first production and generally acclaimed in British dramatic history as a progenitor of a series of "revenge tragedies." Other celebrated examples of the genre include *Hamlet,* Tourneur's *The Revenger's Tragedy,* Webster's *The White Devil* and *The Duchess of Malfi,* and Middleton's *The Changeling* of 1622. Revised by Ben Jonson and revived, *The Spanish Tragedy* was produced as late as 1668. Many of the play's compelling characters and plot conventions were to become commonplaces of the later British drama, notably its revenger Hieronimo, driven nearly insane with grief at the murder of his son, who devises revenge in the form of a court play, in the course of which the murderers, the heroine Bel-Imperia, and Hieronimo himself die. Other plays formerly ascribed to Kyd are now considered the work of other authors (for instance, *The First Part of Ieronimo*, a 1605 publication). Kyd was the son of Francis Kyd, a London scrivener. He was educated at the Merchant Taylor's School. Apparently a friend of Marlowe, he was also accused of atheism; his understandably frantic efforts to repudiate any connection with Marlowe's dangerous ideas have not commended his personality to later critics.

George Peele (ca. 1556–96), like Nashe, is remembered as a fine lyric poet as well as a playwright. His father James Peele was clerk of Christ's Hospital and an author of civic pageants. Like his friend Robert Greene, Peele valued his Oxford degree highly. His plays include *The Arraignment of Paris* (1581, at court); *David and Bethsabe* (ca. 1587); *Edward I* (1591, poor text extant); and *Soliman and Perseda* (ca. 1609), once ascribed to Kyd. *The Old Wives' Tale* (1590), his most famous play, is today considered particularly striking for its alluring interplay of comedy, romance, and multiple folk motifs like the legends of the Grateful Dead and the Three Heads at the Well. The recent critical attention and degree of admiration that *The Old Wives' Tale* has attracted contrasts startlingly with earlier views of the play as hopeless nonsense. A work of great charm and deceptive skill, Peele's lyrical, romantic drama entrances its latest readers into a world of dream and legend. As a dramatic fantasy it presents an unexpected facet of the Elizabethan drama for our consideration. His reputation as a wit was high among his London contemporaries; a jest book, *The Merry Conceited Jests of George Peele* (1607), suggests something about his fame in this arena.

John Lyly (ca. 1554–1606), the author of that trend-setting Elizabethan prose romance *Euphues: The Anatomy of Wit* (1578), was also acclaimed during his lifetime as a courtly playwright and noted for the elegance and refinement of his style. A gentleman and a scholar, trained at Magdalen College, Oxford, he eventually entered the service of the earl of Oxford. Lyly's dramatic work was evidently influenced by the Italian pastorals of Tasso and Guarini, a trend that would continue to develop in the seventeenth century. He is suspected of much collaborative writing for the stage. Lyly's extant plays were composed for the children's companies: *Alexander and Campaspe* and *Sapho and Phao* (both of 1584) were performed by the Children of Paul's and the Children of the Chapel, at court and at Blackfriars. His *Endimion, the Man in the Moon* (published 1591; acted at court ca. 1588) is considered his major dramatic work. Other notable plays of Lyly were *Midas, Mother Bombie* (an attempt at Terentian comedy) and the attractively titled *The Woman in the Moon,* which was apparently never acted. Lyly's prose style left its mark on most of his contemporaries. His plays are invariably classical. Lyly has been credited with the development of a new court comedy in English, characterized by the witty repartee of his child actors.

Henry Chettle (ca. 1560–1607), was a playwright and printer, following in the footsteps of John Rastell. Chettle seems to have produced mostly collaborative and mostly lost works; Henslowe's diary (1598–1603) lists forty-eight works, along with many small personal loans suggesting Chettle's extreme financial dependence, which is also suggested by his imprisonment for debt in 1599 and by the number of times he pawned his manuscripts. Meres classifies him among the best comic writers of his acquaintance. A "revenge tragedy," *Hoffman* or *Revenge for a Father* (ca. 1602), follows the model of Kyd. As a printer, Chettle is chiefly remembered for publishing the pamphlets of Thomas Nashe and Robert Greene's *Groatsworth of Wit* (1592) and for apologizing to Shakespeare afterward.

WILLIAM SHAKESPEARE IN THE REIGN OF ELIZABETH, 1564–1603. This volume's chronology assigns Shakespeare's early career to this chapter and his later years to the following one. As a result of this division Shakespeare and his younger rival Ben Jonson appear once again as both Elizabethan and Jacobean dramatists. This emphasis on chronological change tends unfortunately to obscure the continuity of both authors' development. As a counter measure it is important to stress the sustained quality of Shakespeare's work and the variety of his dramatic achievements over the course of more than twenty-one years in the theater. The purpose of this first discussion of Shakespeare is to present his drama under the reign of Elizabeth in some approximation of historical context.

The overpowering mass of four centuries of Shakespeare scholarship and criticism cannot be even adequately suggested here. The World Shakespeare Bibliography project conducted by Professor Harrison T. Meserole at Texas A & M University finds it strenuous enough to keep pace with twentieth-century scholarship with the aid of a supercomputer. Feminist, semiotic, structuralist, deconstructionist, Marxist, Bakhtinian, New Historicist, and every other approach available to twentieth-century theorists have been or are being applied to Shakespeare. This overview can only suggest some basic lines of approach.

William Shakespeare (1564–1616) was born at Stratford-on-Avon, the eldest son of the glover John Shakespeare. He seems to have attended the local grammar school. The parish records document his marriage in 1582 to Anne Hathaway and the births of his three children, a daughter Susannah and the twins Judith and Hamnet, in 1582–83. The next reference to him occurs in Robert Greene's pamphlet of 1592. Shakespeare is now a dramatist in London, successful enough to arouse the envy of his dying rival. Shakespeare may have been acting and writing in association with Pembroke's Men between 1592 and 1593; they were known to have performed Marlowe's *Edward II,* along with Shakespeare's *The Taming of the Shrew* and *Richard III,* possibly his revisions of earlier plays in the company's possession. Pembroke's Men were also associated with *Titus Andronicus* around 1592. Shakespeare's youngest brother Edmund (1580–1607) seems also to have become an actor in London. While the theaters were closed because of the Plague, Shakespeare published his Ovidian narrative poems, *Venus and Adonis* (1593) and *The Rape of Lucrece* (1594), both dedicated to Henry Wriothesley, third earl of Southampton. In 1594 Shakespeare joined the new acting company, the Chamberlain's Men, along with Richard Burbage and William Kemp. By 1595 he was a sharer. The remainder of Shakespeare's theatrical career with the Chamberlain's Men bears witness to his financial success and consequent rise in social status. In 1597 he bought New Place, one of the principal dwelling houses in Stratford; he retired there in 1610 and died in April 1616 after an evening, according to legend, of carousing with Jonson and Drayton. He is buried there in Holy Trinity Church.[14]

The apparently interminable debate in which the real author of Shakespeare's works is revealed to be a surprising variety of alternative authors, from Sir Francis Bacon and Christopher Marlowe to Edward de Vere, earl of Oxford, continues as the favorite conspiracy theory of British literature. The 1987–88 "Vere trials" were only the latest manifestation of a pursuit that has filled bookshelves in academic libraries since the Baconian Theory first appeared in the mid-nineteenth century. At the moment none of these theories seems capable of proof. Professor Levin has suggested that all this may stem from disappointment at the contrast between the commonplace facts of Shakespeare's biography and the thrilling, psychologically revelatory biographies of later authors, the romantics in particular. As a phenomenon in the history of Shakespeare studies this debate says more about the expectations of the investigators than about Shakespeare or his work.

The 1623 First Folio edition does not date Shakespeare's plays or present them in chronological order. While a total consensus among students can never be expected, a number of studies of the texts have suggested the dates of composition given in the discussion that follows. The First Folio does classify Shakespeare's plays as comedies, histories, and tragedies, to which the later category of the romances has often been appended. This scheme of classification can be correlated to some degree with trends in the development of Shakespeare's art and in the taste of his audience. Regrettably, it can also lead to the generic isolation of Shakespeare's plays from one another. It is often useful for critics to compare, like apples and oranges, tragedies and histories. None of the barriers between the genres should be considered impermeable.

Like most of his contemporaries Shakespeare pillaged a variety of sources for his plots. The devising of new and original plots was not yet considered an essential of literary merit, any more than it had been during the Middle Ages. Shakespeare was frequently called upon to revise earlier plays. When contriving new ones he had recourse to English chroniclers, especially Holinshed (1577) and Edward Hall; to Latin historians like Plutarch; to the existing classics of English literature, including the poems of Chaucer and Gower; and to a wide variety of modern romances. His Italian sources include Giovanni Battista Giraldi, "il Cinthio" (1504–73), the critical defender of Ariosto's romances and author of Senecan tragedies. Giraldi's play *Epizia* became George Whetstone's *Promos and Cassandra* (1578) and Shakespeare's *Measure for*

Measure (1604); his novella, *Disdemona and the Moor,* became *Othello* (1604). The English translation of Giraldi Cinthio's collection of stories, *Hecatommithi* (1565) also provided plots to Greene, Shirley, and Beaumont and Fletcher, by way of William Painter's *The Palace of Pleasure* (1566).

Professor Levin refers to Shakespeare's histories as a "cycle of plays," and the hint of a parallel with the late lamented Corpus Christi cycles deserves consideration. The first group of histories rank among Shakespeare's earliest plays: *Henry VI,* parts 2 and 3 (1591) and part 1 (1592), and *Richard III* (1594) hold together as a historical tetralogy. Richard Burbage seems to have achieved his early success in the role of the Machiavellian schemer Richard III, a heroic villain who owes much to Marlowe's heroes. With *King John* (1594) Shakespeare provided his cycle with a prologue. He began a second series of four plays around 1595: *Richard II* (later to become controversial because of its production in 1601 in support of Essex's rebellion), *Henry IV,* parts 1 and 2 (ca. 1597–98), and *Henry V* (1598). Shakespeare's last history play, *Henry VIII* (1613), was written in collaboration with John Fletcher. In addition, it seems probable that Shakespeare was called in around 1594 to revise two sections of the politically delicate play of *Sir Thomas More,* originally written by Munday and Chettle. British Library Harley MS 7368 preserves this 1594 version, of which 147 lines seem to be in Shakespeare's autograph. It is less likely that Shakespeare had a hand in *Edward III* (printed anonymously in 1596).

The main sources Shakespeare used for his British history plays were Holinshed's 1577 chronicle and Edward Hall's rather partisan account of the Tudor role in providential history, *The Union of the Two Nble and Illustre Families of Lancaster and York* (1548). For Hall, British history followed the divinely ordained pattern of biblical history. *King John* and *Henry VIII* stand a little outside the main historical sequence, which follows British history from the reign of Richard II to the accession of Henry VII, the first Tudor king. Still, God directs England's destiny. In the first tetralogy, the Tudor viewpoint is the strongest. In blank verse inspired by Marlowe, Shakespeare presents the Wars of the Roses as a descent into chaos, from which Henry Tudor is to deliver England. The plays about Henry IV and his son Prince Hal, later Henry V, are possibly most celebrated for the relationship Shakespeare develops between Hal and Sir John Falstaff. The education of the prince at the hands of this brilliant, witty, outrageous mentor, the plays' lord of misrule, has eternally fascinated audiences and critics. By contrast, the king he helps to create, Henry V, seems hampered by his established position in English chivalric mythology. (Sir Laurence Olivier's definitive if severely pruned 1944 film demonstrates how effective the play remains as a patriotic epic, suitable for wartime and other moments of national insecurity. Kenneth Branagh's 1989 film, equally impressive, conveys a realistic sense of the medieval setting, with less emphasis upon Elizabethan patriotism.) Most reminiscent of Marlowe is the Duke of Gloucester, who mounts the throne as Richard III over the bodies of his young nephews. The seductive powers of this dynamic, virtuoso role manifest themselves in the stage history of the play. *Henry IV* prepared the way for *Richard II,* where Shakespeare studies the mind and actions of the narcissistic poet-king. Like Marlowe in *Edward II,* Shakespeare balances the fall of the one prince with the rise of another, Richard against an active, pragmatic Bolingbroke. This was a dangerous play in the eyes of Elizabeth and her Stuart successors.

At the same time that he was writing the history plays, Shakespeare was making his first attempts at comedy. The earliest seem to be *Love's Labour's Lost* (1592); *The Comedy of Errors* (1593; based on Plautus' *Menæchmi*); *The Taming of the Shrew* (1593–94); and *The Two Gentlemen of Verona* (ca. 1594). In the late 1590s these experiments in the genre were succeeded by a series of great "lyrical comedies": *A Midsummer Night's Dream, Much Ado about Nothing, As You Like It, Twelfth Night* (all 1595–99; the last produced in 1602). *The Merry Wives of Windsor* (1597) is linked to the *Henry IV* plays through the personage of Sir John Falstaff. A tradition explains its creation by reporting that Queen Elizabeth wanted to see "the fat knight in love." Three "dark comedies" that blend tragic and comic effects also belong to the final years of Elizabeth's reign: *The Merchant of Venice* (1596–97), *All's Well That Ends Well* (1602) and *Measure for Measure* (1604 production). The rise in popularity of this last tragicomedy since the 1960s parallels a shift in literary taste. That dubious figure of authority, the Duke, has been compared to James I—sex and power politics. *Troilus and Cressida* (1602), perhaps a related work, presents an utterly cynical view of the world of the Trojan War. Acts of treachery and self-deception are coupled with effusions of meaningless language. The heroes of Homer (and Chaucer) comport themselves despicably. The tragedy of *Hamlet,* written around the same time, is in some ways the more optimistic of the two plays.

Comedy for Shakespeare was a more tightly organized, more classically inspired enterprise than tragedy. For the most part cast lists are shorter, plots more cohesive. Beginning with the examples of Plautus and Lyly, Shakespeare developed his own comic vision in several different directions, varying his effects to some extent to suit the talents of the company. Will Kemp's bumbling servants are replaced around 1600 by Armin's court jesters. Slapstick comedy, acute social satire, sophisticated verbal exchanges, comedies of intrigue or reversal all appear in Shakespeare's arsenal. Many of the comedies reflect the carnival tradition, moving through disorder and confusion to a new social harmony at the end of the play. Invariably Shakespeare offers his creations sympathetic understanding as well as laughter. The most ludicrous—Constable Dogberry, Sir Oliver Martext the country vicar, Sir Andrew Aguecheek and Malvolio, to name a few—each have their own dignity and integrity. The plays themselves display the same individuation. The Arcadian forest of *As You Like It* where Rosalind and Touchstone court Orlando and Audrey is a completely different place than the "wood near Athens" where Bottom meets Titania. The debased urban environment where the "duke of dark corners" counsels the nun Isabella in her struggle against Angelo carries comedy into a strange, inverted, claustrophobic setting. Shakespeare's comic worlds are complete in themselves, enclosed spaces in which the forces of chaos operate on human delusions and aspirations, teasing or mocking according to the play's mood and design.

At virtually the same time that he was composing both comedies and histories, Shakespeare was at work on his darkest tragedies. The early play of *Titus Andronicus* (ca. 1592) is contemporary with the "lyrical comedies." Presumably next comes *Romeo and Juliet* (ca. 1595), followed by a cluster of tragedies and Roman plays; *Julius Caesar* was performed about 1599 and witnessed by a Swiss traveler, and *Hamlet* came immediately afterward.

Again, the variability of Shakespeare's Elizabethan tragedies expanded the limits of the genre. *Titus Andronicus,* the earliest, is the least successful of the group, but itself marked an advance on its predecessors. It is as "Senecan" as anything the century produced in its horrifying toll of murder, rape, mutilation, cannibalism, and suicide. Many critics have seen its most memorable figure as the Moor Aaron, "chief architect and plotter of these woes," Shakespeare's answer to Marlowe's Barabas. In its combination of a setting in Roman history and an echo of Ovid's account of the rape of Philomela, *Titus* is almost self-consciously classical. *Romeo and Juliet,* by contrast, experiments with a contemporary tragic subject. Giraldi Cinthio had suggested the idea; Shakespeare is as far as we can tell the first Elizabethan dramatist to make the attempt. In many respects his young Italian lovers step out of comedy or romance, and into an unaccustomed atmosphere of fatality. Frank Kermode has commented on the contrast between the complex rhetorical language that surrounds them and the straightforward speech in which the lovers speak to one another (*Riverside Shakespeare,* 1056–57). Linguistically and emotionally they become dislocated from their society. With *Julius Caesar* Shakespeare returned to Rome and continued the exploration of power politics that would occupy him in different ways in *Antony and Cleopatra* and *Coriolanus. Hamlet* is considered the first—and is perhaps the most celebrated—of Shakespeare's four "great tragedies." It has been seen as marking an important departure from Shakespeare's earlier work. Family resemblances to *The Spanish Tragedy* would have struck an Elizabethan audience immediately. The ghost, the play, the heroine's insanity, were all familiar devices of revenge tragedy, ingeniously reinterpreted by Shakespeare. A psychological, analytical tragedy focusing in on the meaning of action, it brings together a group of difficult characters. Its hero, a witty theorist whose philosophical inquiries complicate his every attempt at direct action, must face his tyrant uncle, capable, sensual, coldly calculating and secretly anguished with guilt. *Hamlet*'s villain, by himself, tells us how far Shakespeare had developed as a tragedian; its hero is a completely unexpected species of revenger.

The later tragedies and romances belong to the history of drama under James I. Already in these Elizabethan plays, Shakespeare had manifested his genius for depicting a galaxy of distinctive individuals with conflicting loyalties, motivations, and quirks of personality. The subtlety and depth of his best characterizations make Shakespearean acting a particular challenge. In both poetic technique and prose style Shakespeare was already at least equal to the best of his contemporaries. He apparently did not share Marlowe's attraction to extreme philosophical positions, but in the astonishing range of his interests, his ability to understand and depict multiple viewpoints, Shakespeare remains alone in his class. The seventeenth century would witness further advances in the drama of Shakespeare. Still, the first eleven years of his career would have been enough, by themselves, to establish his dramatic reputation.

SHAKESPEARE'S YOUNGER CONTEMPORARIES. Details of the life of Thomas Dekker (ca. 1572–1632) remain obscure, though we know he was a Londoner and that as a collaborator he had a hand in more than forty plays, fifteen of which survive. He was certainly working for Henslowe from 1598 to 1602. His early "city comedy" *The Shoemaker's Holiday* (1599) is by all accounts his best work. Its affinities with the tradition of the October Lord Mayor's Show and with the earlier tradition of drama connected with the trade guilds are patent. Simon Eyre the shoemaker stands at the center of the play, a lavish, heroic characterization of the London tradesman. *Patient Grissel* (1600) attempts an appealing dramatization of the difficult Griselda story; *Satiromastix* (1601), a collaboration with John Marston, belongs to the literature of the "war of the theaters." Ben Jonson appears, much to his annoyance, as Horace. Three years later Dekker collaborated with Jonson on the pageants for James I's coronation entry. He turned to a successful series of pamphlets in the tradition of Nashe, the most famous of which is *The Gull's Handbook* (1609). Dekker continued to write plays, *The Honest Whore* (1604) and *The Roaring Girl* (1610) with Middleton. His *If It Be Not Good, the Devil Is in It* (1610) boasts one of the best seventeenth-century titles. *The Virgin Martyr* belongs somewhere between 1610 and 1620. Dekker also possibly assisted in writing *The Witch of Edmonton* (1621). He spent six years in debtor's prison (1613–19) after flirting with extreme debt several times.[15]

Ben Jonson (1572–1637) was the posthumous son of a minister, born at Westminster and educated there. Jonson's academic ability attracted him to the university, but family circumstances seem to have decided otherwise. His stepfather was a bricklayer; after a short and no doubt vexatious period of bricklaying, Jonson seems to have become successively a soldier in the Netherlands, an actor of questionable ability, and finally a playwright. Jonson's truculent character emerged in a series of famous quarrels. He was imprisoned for *The Isle of Dogs* (1597), which he wrote with Nashe. *Every Man in His Humour* (1598) established his reputation as the prime exponent of the "comedy of humors." Shakespeare appeared in the cast as Kno'well. The title suggests a connection with *Everyman* and the morality tradition of abstractions as characters. In this case, the "humors" are the reigning passions or propensities of the characters, who thus represent a different kind of abstraction. The play's most celebrated character, Bobadill, is Jonson's version of Plautus' Miles Gloriosus. On 22 September of the same year Jonson achieved further notoriety by killing the actor Gabriel Spencer of the Admiral's Men in a duel. (Spencer had killed a previous opponent in 1596). He seems to have only just escaped hanging. *Every Man Out of His Humour* (1599) and *The Case Is Altered* (1599) continued his series of early comedies and also inaugurated a sharp exchange of caricatures between Jonson and that ingenious amateur dramatist John Marston of the Middle Temple. *Cynthia's Revels* (1600) and *The Poetaster* (1601) were both performed using Marston's own preferred medium, the children's company, in this case the Children of the Chapel at Blackfriars, as part of this "war of the theaters." Dekker and Marston returned fire in *Satiromastix*. By the end of Elizabeth's reign all three dramatists were reconciled and in fact collaborators. Jonson's all-too-correct Roman tragedy *Sejanus* (1603), in which Burbage and Shakespeare both acted, was unfortunately considered seditious: the relationship between the scheming imperial favorite Sejanus and the emperor Tiberius seemed to have possible English parallels in high places.

In *Cynthia's Revels,* where his first attempt at a mask appears, Jonson seems to have been eyeing the domain of court poetry, a field he was to dominate and reshape from 1605 to 1631. Jonson's most significant achievements as a creator of satirical comedies and the court masque belong to the Stuart era. His early "humors" comedies display many of the gifts he was later to develop. Jonson is one of the most obvious continuers of the morality tradition. In his greatest comedies he was to arrive at a striking fusion of the native, medieval moral play with the classical comedies he so genuinely admired. Jonson's satire bites much deeper than Shakespeare's. He is by far the more didactic author and the more abstract thinker. All of these stylistic preoccupations led him inexorably toward the stylized world of the court masque and the comedy of social correction—both, in different ways, the heirs of the morality tradition.

CONCLUSION

The turbulent sixteenth century unquestionably witnessed startling developments in British drama and gave Britain its greatest playwright. By the end of the century its public playhouses were celebrated across Europe, and its professional players were carrying British influences to stages on the Continent.

This account, following in the footsteps of Stevens and Bevington, has attempted to reintegrate medieval and earlier Renaissance dramatic traditions into the history of the Elizabethan theater. This reassessment of the roots of sixteenth-century drama demands more than seeing the personified vices of the moral play as possible ancestors of Elizabethan clowns, or Marlowe's *Doctor Faustus* as a morality. The expansive sense of time and space, the purposeful narration of linear history, all the obstinately unclassical mental attitudes of the British stage are essential to its greatness during this period. The last English Corpus Christi cycles were suppressed just as Burbage was building the Theatre, but the British dramatic conventions developed over four centuries refused to die with them.

CHAPTER V

THE SEVENTEENTH CENTURY

This chapter begins and ends with problems of endings. To begin with, we must consider whether significant changes really differentiate the Elizabethan and Jacobean eras. Many careers, notably those of Shakespeare and Jonson, do span the two periods. Yet scholars have detected shifts in mood from an expansive, optimistic Elizabethan period to a pessimistic, effete spirit on the Jacobean and Caroline stages. The reinterpretation of sixteenth- and seventeenth-century history in recent years has led stage historians to readdress the question.

At the opposite extreme of this chapter, the problem of finding a conclusion recurs. How and when did the long, native tradition of British drama come to an end? What did the closing of the theaters in 1642 really mean for British drama? What, if anything, of the theatrical heritage of the past survived to influence the new theaters of the Restoration in 1660? The questions are essentially unaswerable, but it is important to ask them and to consider the possibilities with care.

G. P. V. Akrigg described James I as "one of the most complicated neurotics ever to come to the English throne."[1] James wrote on the subjects of theology, the education of princes, the divine right of kings, witchcraft, and the evils of tobacco. His collected works, excepting his poetry, were published in 1617. James's preoccupation with a series of young and handsome favorites—George Villiers, duke of Buckingham, was the most celebrated of the group—has led modern psychological historians to view him as at least a latent homosexual. The padding he wore to ward off possible assassins' daggers made him appear a good deal stouter than he really was. His ungainly physical appearance and eccentricities tend to obscure his shrewdness and tolerance.

Charles I, like Henry VIII, was a second son, not expected to come to the throne. His magnificent elder brother, Prince Henry, overshadowed him as he grew up. Henry's death from typhoid fever in 1612 brought the twelve-year-old Charles to the center of the stage, where he came under the influence of Buckingham. His 1625 marriage to the French princess Henrietta Maria brought England a queen well versed in the latest continental stagecraft and court pageantry. Charles appeared with her in masques and the royal family attended plays assiduously. Charles is remembered as the most sophisticated art collector ever to reign in England. A notable horseman, he appears at his most elegant in the portraits he commissioned from Sir Anthony van Dyck (1599–1641). Charles's conception of himself as a divinely appointed ruler and his obstinate refusal to compromise his belief led him into the conflict with Parliament that became the English civil war.

The direct patronage of the Stuarts affected both public acting companies and court theater. The Lord Chamberlain's Men became the King's Men, and lesser dramatic companies came under the patronage of other members of the new royal family. English dramatists set out to exploit a new popular and aristocratic interest in Scotland. *Macbeth* is emphatically Jacobean in its subject matter and even in the role of its witches. Over a longer term James's queen, Anne of Denmark, became important as both patroness and performer of the Jonsonian masque. Charles I and Henrietta Maria inherited her interests.

Continuing the Elizabethan tradition of dramatic censorship, the Stuart government tried to regulate the activities of the public theaters. *Eastward Ho!, The Isle of Gulls,* and Middleton's *A Game at Chess* offered the most flamboyant challenges to the authorities. At the center of these controversies sat the clerks of the Revels Office, who continued to supervise drama up to 1642.

The earlier seventeenth century has often been described in the history of British drama as a decadent period, shading into actual enervation with the accession of Charles I. Court masques, romances, pastorals, and even gorier "revenger's tragedies" dominate dramatic history. Part of the business of this chapter must be to reassess these dramatic genres in the context of the period as a whole.

THE JACOBEAN PUBLIC THEATERS

LATER SHAKESPEARE, JONSON, AND THEIR CONTEMPORARIES. Many of the same playwrights who had reached prominence in the 1590s worked along the same lines after 1603. Shakespeare's later tragedies and romances belong to the reign of James I but represent a logical development of Shakespeare's ideas about tragedy. Three "great tragedies" were yet to come. *Othello* was performed at court in 1604, *King Lear* (1605), and Macbeth (1606) shortly thereafter.[2]

In *Othello* Shakespeare revisited the territory of *The Jew of Malta,* and in doing so demonstrated that Marlowe was not merely an early influence but a preoccupation throughout Shakespeare's career as a playwright. In *Titus Andronicus* Shakespeare had adopted Marlowe's pattern, making the Moor the Machiavellian predator on Roman society. In *Othello* the Moorish general is led to murder through a maze of jealousy and misapprehension by his Machiavellian lieutenant. Iago plays the role of a personified vice in corrupting Othello's vision of the world; in his final speech Othello recognizes that he has been deluded into the role of the alien enemy of civilization.

King Lear tends to dominate any discussion of Shakespeare's tragedies. The pessimism of its vision made the play too painful for generations of playgoers; the long stage history of Nahum Tate's revised version of *Lear* is also a history of the tragedy's reception that illuminates its viewers' ambivalence. *Lear* demanded to be performed; it could not simply be neglected by later theaters. At the same time Shakespeare's unflinching insistence on the cruelty of nature, human and animal, and the suffering of the innocent in a chaotic universe, disturbed readers as sophisticated as Samuel Johnson and Tolstoy, in much the same way that the Book of Job disturbs its readers. *Lear* is in many ways the most biblical of Shakespeare's tragedies, though paradoxically it is set in pre-Christian Britain. Frank Kermode has observed that Lear's suffering parallels Job's, except that God never speaks to him (*Riverside Shakespeare,* 1253).

Macbeth appealed directly to James I, not only through its prophecies of the rise of the House of Stuart but also through the machinations of its trio of witches. It is possible to interpret Macbeth himself as another noble figure, tempted by power and corrupted by the means he employs to attain it. Other readings present Macbeth as evil from the start. Shakespeare's study of the psychological toll of crime on both Macbeth and Lady Macbeth elaborates his portrait of Claudius in *Hamlet*. The genuine menace of the witches for Shakespeare's audience should not be discounted by modern readers. They are analogues at once of the Furies and the native tradition of devils onstage, grotesque emblems of evil and actual forces of destruction.

In his last tragedies Shakespeare returned to the classical world. *Antony and Cleopatra* (1606–7) further explores the alliance of love and power. In Cleopatra Shakespeare created one of his most demanding female roles, requiring a versatile and mature boy actor. *Coriolanus* (1607–8) takes on yet another subject from Plutarch. Its sullen war hero, the aristocratic Caius Martius "Coriolanus," is tested and found grotesquely wanting as a peacetime leader of Rome. Faced with the need to conciliate the mob he despises, Coriolanus cannot transcend his antipathy. Rome desperately needs his guidance, but his nature and training both incapacitate him. He is a ruler who cannot function in society, who inevitably becomes both traitor and victim. In the course of this century *Coriolanus* has come to be regarded as one of Shakespeare's most important statements about human political behavior. It is a play that particularly interested both T. S. Eliot and Bertolt Brecht. That strange play *Timon of Athens* was written around the same time. Possibly the text as we have it represents Shakespeare's first draft, unrevised. Like *Coriolanus*, it studies a hero at odds with society at large. The disillusioned Timon rebounds from a credulous magnanimity to misanthropic rage. The formality of the play's design and its use of banquets as symbols show affinities with the masque. Its curious, repeated comparisons of Timon to Christ also complicate the play.

The romances had classical nondramatic models as well as extensive precedents in popular and learned medieval and Renaissance literature. Many of Chaucer's and Gower's narrative poems, Malory's *Morte Darthur*, Ariosto's *Orlando Furioso*, Sidney's *Arcadia*, and Spenser's *Faerie Queene* were available to Elizabethan and Jacobean readers as models of the genre. The romance's thematic principles of organization have led to critical misunderstanding of Shakespeare's romances and those of his contemporaries. At the same time the genre's wide popularity from the Hellenistic period to the present bears witness to perennial literary attractions. Northrop Frye's *The Secular Scripture* is perhaps the most prominent critical attempt to analyze the principles of romance construction to date. More needs to be done.

Shakespeare's romances retain the sweeping geographic scope notable in romance-influenced plays like *Mary Magdalen* from earlier British drama. The four later plays that fall under this heading all combine tragic potential with serene conclusions. *Pericles* (performed 1606) was based on John Gower's narrative of Apollonius of Tyre from the *Confessio Amantis,* and introduced that fourteenth-century poet as commentator. As in *Lear* and in the romance tradition from which it stems, the innocent suffer spectacularly, but in this case are miraculously preserved, restored, and even, in the case of Pericles's lost wife Thaisa, resurrected. *Cymbeline* (1609–10) returns to ancient Britain for another drama of familial separation and reunion, accompanied by the slander of the innocent heroine; *The Winter's Tale* (produced 1610–11) carries these plot devices further, again using the destructive power of jealousy to propel the action. Its attractive pastoral scenes reflect a new interest in this popular Renaissance genre on the British stage. *The Winter's Tale* is a romance of apparent death and rebirth, winter and spring, deliberately evoking the folk plays of the changing seasons. *The Tempest* was produced at court in November 1611 and revived as part of the wedding festivities for Princess Elizabeth and the Elector Palatine in 1612–13. It has attracted much critical attention as Shakespeare's last major play, a valedictory to the stage in which Prospero represents the poet. Shakespeare used a recent account of Sir George Somers's shipwreck in the Bermudas in his account of Prospero's enchanted island. He also observed the unities of time and place for the first time since *The Comedy of Errors.* Within these confines, *The Tempest* employs music and spectacle as it plays reality against illusion, freedom against enslavement, natural against supernatural. The two contrasting spirits, Ariel and Caliban, suggest the abstract figures of a masque at the same time that they are convincingly developed characters. *The Tempest* teases its viewers with suggestions of allegory, but ultimately refuses to be bound by any restrictive scheme of correspondences.

Shakespeare retired to New Place, where he died in 1616. The publication of the First Folio of Shakespeare's plays in 1623 marks a notable advance in the status of contemporary drama as literature. It may well have been inspired by Ben Jonson's publication of a collected edition of his own works in 1616. The First Folio was the largest collection of contemporary plays yet to be published in England; in itself it bears witness to Shakespeare's standing among the dramatists of his own day. The prime movers in its publication seem to have been Heminge and Condell, who were Shakespeare's fellow actors, managers of the Chamberlain's Men, and major shareholders in the Blackfriars and Globe theaters. The collection of thirty-six plays was reprinted in 1636.

Ben Jonson had continued his rise to a position of literary prominence, if not dictatorship, in the early years of James's reign. He had a hand in the pageants for James's coronation. Jonson's explicit display of classical learning in his plays and nondramatic works may have helped to commend him to the somewhat pedantic Scots monarch. In his own estimation this militant classicism differentiated Jonson from his friendly rival Shakespeare and most of his other competitors. At the same time Jonson's satirical proclivities continued to embroil him in difficult situations. He collaborated with Marston and Chapman on *Eastward Ho!* (1605); Scottish references were not appreciated by the court, and the playwrights were jailed. Jonson's major comedies were yet to come: *Volpone; or, The Fox* in 1606, *Epicoene; or, The Silent Woman* in 1609, *The Alchemist* in 1610. In *Catiline His Conspiracy* (1611) Jonson attempted another Roman tragedy in the high style and was again frustrated. *Bartholomew Fair* (1614) and *The Devil Is an Ass* (1616) followed. *Volpone, The Alchemist,* and *Bartholomew Fair* are most admired and revived today, although Dryden singled out *Epicoene* for analysis in *An Essay of Dramatic Poesy* as the most perfectly constructed English comedy he could find. *Volpone* and *The Alchemist* both employ trickery to unmask the greed and self-deception of a variety of urban characters. In *Bartholomew Fair* Jonson depicts the London summer fair as a playground for his rogues' gallery of gamesters, cheats, bawds, thieves, hypocrites, and their dupes. Jonson's satirical portraits are sharply observed and exaggerated for comic effect. His Puritans, Tribulation Wholesome, "A Pastor of Amsterdam" in *The Alchemist,* and Zeal-of-the-Land Busy in *Bartholomew Fair* have attracted particular interest: in *Bartholomew Fair* Busy's debate with Lanthorn Leatherhead the puppet master encapsulates and ridicules generations of contention between preachers and playwrights. Jonson is equally devastating in his depiction of Sir Epicure Mammon in *The Alchemist.* That hedonist knight's astonishing exposition of his fantasies and their comic frustration remain highlights of the play. The tightness of Jonson's best plots and the driving force of his satirical vision make him one of the best and most distinctive English authors of comedy.

The 1616 edition of Jonson's works differs notably from the later collections of English plays it inspired, including the First Folio of Shakespeare. Where Shakespeare's and Lyly's English dramatic works were published posthumously, and Marston's appeared in his lifetime without his approval, Jonson set out to edit his own plays, masques, and poetry with the same care that would be lavished on an edition of Terence. This fact in itself tells us how seriously Jonson regarded his art. The grant of a royal pension in 1616 gave Jonson some of the status of a poet laureate, though the title and office were later developments. By this time he was a literary institution, surrounded by an attendant train of disciples, among them his secretary Richard Brome and the poet Robert Herrick. Jonson's later plays of 1625–33 were less successful onstage than his earlier work; they include *The Staple of News, The New Inn,* and *The Magnetic Lady.* In 1631 he quarreled with Inigo Jones and began to publish a second volume of his works, which he did not live to complete. Jonson's dominating personality stamped his neoclassical vision on English comedy, lyric poetry, and literary criticism during and after his lifetime. In the case of the court masque, to be considered later in this chapter, he re-created the genre.[3]

George Chapman (ca. 1560–1634) is best known in English literary history as the translator of Homer whose work inspired Keats's sonnet. His monumental translation, begun around 1598, was not completed until 1624. Chapman held a position in the household of Prince Henry until the prince's death in 1612. Many of Chapman's early plays are lost, including a number written for Henslowe between 1596 and 1599. Of his surviving plays the Terentian comedies *May Day* (1602) and *All Fools* (1604) were both presented at Blackfriars. Chapman's *Bussy d'Ambois* (1604) is one of his best plays, a tragedy of French court intrigue centered on the betrayal and murder of a daring young hero. It and *Eastward Ho!,* the collaborative venture with Jonson and Marston, were both performed by the Children of Paul's. *The Conspiracy and Tragedy of Charles, Duke of Byron* (1608) disturbed the ambassador of France as much as *Eastward Ho!* had annoyed King James. In his later years Chapman may have assisted James Shirley at the same time that he was engaged in revising his own plays for publication.[4]

Frontispiece, Ben Jonson, *Workes* (London: Will Stansby, 1616). From
a copy in the Rare Book Collection of the O. Meredith Wilson
Library, University of Minnesota.
Reproduced by permission of the University of Minnesota Library.

Cyril Tourneur (or perhaps Turner) (1575–1626) remains one of the most mysterious of Jacobean authors. His origins are unknown. He seems to have been engaged in some type of secret service employment in connection with the Cecils. A Cyril Turner was secretary to Sir Francis Vere sometime before 1614, and in 1625 sailed as secretary to Sir Edward Cecil when he raided the Spanish treasure fleet at Cadiz. Turner was one of the sick put ashore at Kinsale in Ireland, where he died in 1626. His major play may be *The Atheist's Tragedy; or, The Honest Man's Revenge* (ca. 1611), a work clearly influenced by *King Lear*. Tourneur was named in 1656 as the author of *The Revenger's Tragedy* (ca. 1606; published anonymously), but many scholars now ascribe it to Middleton. Some attractive connections link the two plays but do not prove they were written by the same author. Neither play has a definite source. In some ways they are composite works, recombining motifs from earlier revenge plays. The amazing reversal in the conclusion of *The Atheist's Tragedy* in which the "atheist" D'amville brains himself accidentally with the axe he is about to use on the hero, Charlmont, looks to a modern reader like either romance or farce. In *The Revenger's Tragedy* Vindice pursues his vengeance through a tortuous series of schemes, culminating in a dance of revengers recalling the dance of Death and, again, the contemporary masque. Its high poetic skill and invention have found many modern admirers.

Thomas Middleton (ca. 1570–1627) contributed important plays in the Jonsonian veins of satirical comedy and revenge tragedy. His editors suggest that Middleton's perspective may have been warped by his personal difficulties. His mother's disastrous second marriage to the adventurer Thomas Harvey jeopardized Middleton's inheritance and cut short his education at Oxford. Middleton turned to writing in 1597 and found employment with Henslowe. He was Dekker's collaborator on *The Honest Whore* (1604) and *The Roaring Girl* (1610). His own comedy, *A Trick to Catch the Old One* (1604–5) influenced Massinger's *A New Way to Pay Old Debts* (1623). In *A Chaste Maid in Cheapside* (1611–13) Middleton's black comedy of sexual perversion reaches a cynical climax. His revenge tragedies *Women Beware Women* (1621) and *The Changeling* (1622) remain among the most celebrated of their day. They reveal their author's concern to anatomize human motivations as well as the brutal economics that undermine all human transactions. *A Game at Chess* (1624), satirizing negotiations for an English-Spanish royal marriage, precipitated a political crisis. Its run at the Globe in August 1624 was longer than that of any other Jacobean play, as far as we know. The Spanish ambassador strongly objected, and Middleton went into hiding. It was his last play. Middelton's masques and the lord mayor's pageants he composed between 1620 and 1626 are no longer extant.

William Rowley (ca. 1585–1637) is best known as Middelton's collaborator on *The Changeling* (1622). Rowley was an actor, specializing in fat comic parts like the stout clown in his own *All's Lost by Lust* (1622), Plumporridge in *The Inner Temple Masque,* or the fat bishop in Middleton's *A Game at Chess* of 1624. A strange but attractive Arthurian play, *The Birth of Merlin; or, The Child Has Found His Father* (1620) was ascribed to Rowley and Shakespeare, and recent scholars have attempted to detect Shakespeare's hand in it. The play is most interesting to Arthurian specialists for its use of the legend of the birth of Merlin as a subplot, culminating in a spectacular scene in which Merlin rescues his mother from the devil who fathered him.

John Marston (1576–1634) was the son of a prominent lawyer and his Italian wife. He completed his education at Brasenose College, Oxford, and proceeded to disappoint his father by wasting his time in the Middle Temple in "plays and vain studies and fooleries" (Marston, *Selected Plays,* x). Marston's first theatrical composition may have been *Histriomastix,* written for Christmas revels at the Middle Temple around 1598. Marston was one of Jonson's principal antagonists in the "war of the theaters," though he seems to have admired Jonson's work. The studied artificiality of his tragedies *Antonio and Mellida* and *Antonio's Revenge* (1599) seems to have been particularly suited to the talents and style of the boy actors who performed them. His comedies *The Malcontent* (1603) and *The Dutch Courtesan* (1604) are now considered Marston's best work. Like Jonson, Marston was involved in *Eastward Ho!* but was not imprisoned. He married the daughter of one of James I's chaplains and left the theater for the church in 1609. In 1633 he insisted that his name be removed from an edition of his plays. As his editors remark, the fact that his works had been collected for publication reveals his high reputation among his contemporaries: Lyly, Jonson, and Shakespeare were the only other English playwrights of his day whose works were printed in collected editions. *The Dutch Courtesan* was adapted as a droll, *The Cheater Cheated,* in the days of the Commonwealth, and later inspired Aphra Behn's *The Revenge; or, A Match in Newgate* (1680).

Thomas Heywood (ca. 1570–1641) of Lincolnshire, the son of a barrister, had studied at Cambridge before embarking on his theatrical career. Any connection between Thomas Heywood and the early Tudor court musician John Heywood still remains unproven. Heywood worked energetically for Henslowe as a member of the Admiral's Men and Queen Anne's Men. He claimed in 1633 to have had "either a hand or at least a maine finger" in two hundred and twenty plays. He collaborated with Chettle on *Edward IV* (1599); his *If You Know Not Me, You Know Nobody* (1605) set out boldly to dramatize the early years of the late Elizabeth I. His romance *The Four Prentices of London* (ca. 1600) seems to have been one of the primary targets of Beaumont's *The Knight of the Burning Pestle.* The rare domestic tragedy *A Woman Killed with Kindness* (1604) is today considered his best play. Its double plot depicts feuding, adultery, and betrayal between country neighbors, in a sophisticated study of guilt and generosity. His other works include *The Wise Woman of Hogsdon* (1604), *The Rape of Lucrece* (1607), and *The Fair Maid of the West* (1610). Heywood retired in 1619 when Anne of Denmark died but returned to write *The English Traveller* (1625) and revive some of his earlier works. His masque of 1634, *Love's Mistress,* with scenery by Inigo Jones, made an attractive contribution to court drama. Heywood was employed for a long time as writer of pageants for the Lord Mayor's Show. His 1612 *Apology for Actors* is Heywood's considered response to the unabating antitheatrical pressures of the Jacobean years.

SHAKESPEARE'S IMMEDIATE SUCCESSORS. The names of Beaumont and Fletcher still come to mind as Shakespeare's most important successors. This received idea reflects several misconceptions. First, a chronological outline of their careers makes it clear that Beaumont and Fletcher achieved their greatest success as a team in the final years of Shakespeare's theatrical activity rather than after his retirement; their collaboration may have ended as early as 1613. Second, it should be pointed out that Beaumont and Fletcher also did much distinguished work independently. Sir Francis Beaumont (1584–1616) apparently wrote *The Knight of the Burning Pestle* (1607) singlehandedly. It directly parodies not only Thomas Heywood's *The Four Prentices of London* but also the wilder clichés of romantic drama at large. One of the funniest plays of the period, it presents the grocer's apprentice, Ralph, as a London Don Quixote. John Fletcher (1579–1625) was the son of a cleric who later became bishop of London. Fletcher wrote a pastoral, *The Faithful Shepherdess* (1608), before joining forces with Beaumont. This lovely play has been described as the earliest English pastoral drama, a worthy descendant of Tasso's *L'Aminta* (1573) and Guarini's *Il Pastor Fido* (1590; acted 1596–98). Pastoral plays were otherwise not successful in England, where they never succeeded in dislodging the romances. They enjoyed a much greater vogue in France, as did massive pastoral romances like Honoré d'Urfé's *Astrée*.

Beaumont and Fletcher's earliest surviving collaborative work seems to be *Philaster; or, Love Lies A-Bleeding* (1610). This attractive romantic drama reworks a number of stage conventions already familiar from Shakespeare. The heroine disguised as a page, in love with Philaster but sent to take service with the lady of his heart, Arethusa, recalls the situation of Viola in *Twelfth Night*. *Philaster* was followed by *The Maid's Tragedy* and *A King and No King*, both of 1611, and *The Scornful Lady* (1613). Fifty-three plays were attributed to these celebrated collaborators in collections of 1647 and 1679, but later scholarly opinion has stripped them of many of these dramas, sometimes whittling the Beaumont and Fletcher canon down to only six or seven works. Beaumont seems to have retired from writing for the public stage in 1613, when he married, though he still contributed to some court performances. Fletcher continued his career as a playwright, probably assisting with Shakespeare's *Henry VIII* (1613). In the Stationer's Register he is listed with Shakespeare as a co-author of the lost *History of Cardenio*, also in 1613. *The Chances* of 1623, based on a story by Cervantes, was revived in 1666, in a version rewritten by George Villiers, second duke of Buckingham. Samuel Pepys reported on the production in one of his many remarks on the Restoration stage. So it is neither chronologically accurate nor a fair picture of Beaumont's or Fletcher's careers to regard them as an inseparable team.

John Webster (ca. 1580–1634) was the son of a wealthy Smithfield coachmaker with premises close by the horse market in the neighborhood of Bartholomew Fair. His lucrative business involved John Webster senior in hiring out wagons to the Alleyns, perhaps for theatrical purposes. His son, the playwright, entered the Middle Temple in 1598. In 1615 he became a freeman of the Merchant Taylor's Company. Webster's career as a respectable tradesman contrasts starkly with his reputation as the wild man of the Jacobean theater. Webster's plays test and reject many accepted social and religious tenets. His reputation rests on two celebrated tragedies. *The White Devil* (1612) is loosely based on a 1585 Italian murder case. *The Duchess of Malfi* (1614) also takes up a sixteenth-century Italian story of crime and punishment. The demanding central role of the brutally victimized duchess often attracts modern actresses. Both of these major tragedies combine blood-curdling narratives of seduction, madness, and mass murder with striking linguistic fireworks. Both are "night pieces" that can easily topple into self-parody and melodrama if not carefully handled in performance. Of Webster's other plays, *Appius and Virginia* (ca. 1608) and *The Devil's Law Case* (1623) are considered the best.

THE PRINCIPAL CAROLINE DRAMATISTS. Caroline drama has suffered from critical neglect. Efforts to trace the causes of the English civil war in the artificiality and isolation of Charles I's court find parallels in critical determination to stress a courtly dislocation from social realities in the plays of the 1630s and early 1640s. Features of the Restoration stage have been detected in the theater of Charles I, among them the loss of a popular audience and the imposition of continental dramatic conventions to please a coterie of courtiers. Court dramatists like Davenant, Lodowick Carlell, and Walter Montagu receive perhaps more than their fair share of attention, at the expense of the public theaters. Martin Butler's study of the London stage between 1632 and 1642 presents a counterinterpretation. For Butler the Caroline theater was an arena of lively political debate where first-rate dramatists investigated the tensions between court and parliament, country and city, royal power and personal interest. Butler stresses the continuing importance of large public audiences at the playhouses and of the popular strain in Caroline theater. Butler's new perspective on the age of Charles I invites the investigator to reevaluate the playwrights of the Caroline decades.

Only a few of the principal dramatists active under Charles I can be sketched here to illustrate the range of drama in the years up to the closing of the theaters.

Like Marston, John Ford (1586–1639) became a member of the Middle Temple. His earliest plays have been lost. Ford may have collaborated with Thomas Dekker and Samuel Rowley on *The Witch of Edmonton* (1621) and *The Sun's Darling* (1624). His four romantic plays still rank among the best of their kind: *The Lover's Melancholy* (ca. 1625), *Love's Sacrifice* (ca. 1627), *The Broken Heart* (1629), and the most famous, *'Tis Pity She's a Whore* (ca. 1628; revived 1661). This dark tragedy centers on the brother-sister incest of Giovanni and Annabella, examined with psychological acuity. *Perkin Warbeck* (published 1634) continued Shakespeare's chronicle histories with the later history of Henry VII.

Philip Massinger (1589–1640) wrote fifty or more plays in the course of his twenty-seven years in the theater; twenty are still extant. He was working for Henslowe in 1613. He collaborated with Field on *The Fatal Dowry* (1619) and with Dekker on *The Virgin Martyr* (1620). John Fletcher seems to have been his main collaborator. They worked together on Shakespeare's *Henry VIII* and *The Two Noble Kinsmen*. In the 1620s Massinger achieved his independence as a dramatist, writing mostly for the King's Men. After Fletcher's death he became the company's main playwright, continuing in this role until his death in 1640, when he was buried in Fletcher's grave (Gibson, *Selected Plays*, ix). Among Massinger's best received plays were *The Duke of Milan* (1620), a romance; *The Bondman* (1623) and *The Renegado* (1624), tragicomedies; and the long-lived satirical play *A New Way to Pay Old Debts* (1625). Sir Giles Overreach's greed and corruption were modeled to some extent on qualities of Sir Giles Mompesson (1584–1651), whose extortions had been exposed in 1621. The portrayal of Overreach as a malicious social climber seems to be Massinger's own invention, however. Massinger's *The Roman Actor* (1626), *The Great Duke of Florence* (1627), *The City Madam* (1632), and *The Guardian* (1633) are all romances. Butler sees him as the most politically astute playwright of the era, after Brome.[6]

James Shirley (1596–1666) replaced Jonson as writer of scenarios for court masques. He worked with Queen Henrietta's Men, Christopher Beeson's company, between 1625 and 1636. His forty-odd plays include the tragedies *The Maid's Revenge* (1626); *The Traitor* (1631; it incorporates a masque of Furies and Lusts); *Love's Cruelty* (1631); *The Cardinal* (1641); and the comedies *The Witty Fair One* (1628), *Hyde Park* (1632), *The Gamester* (1633; adapted by Garrick in the eighteenth century), *The Lady of Pleasure* (1635), and *The Sisters* (1642). When the London theaters were closed in 1636–37 on account of the Plague, Shirley traveled to Dublin, where he wrote *St. Patrick for Ireland, The Royal Master, The Constant Maid, The Doubtful Heir,* and *The Politician* for the new Werburgh Street theater. After Massinger died, Shirley succeeded him as playwright for the King's Men. Shirley's comedies of manners, particularly *Hyde Park* and *The Gamester,* connect Jonsonian with Restoration comedy. By 1642 he was the most prominent London playwright. His *The Sisters* and *The Court Secret* were ready for production when the theaters were closed. Under the Commonwealth Shirley worked as a schoolmaster in the London area. He was also preoccupied in editing and publishing his own works and those of Beaumont and Fletcher. Shirley's reputation survived the Puritan interregnum; at least eight of his works were performed soon after the Restoration. Shirley was a casualty of the Fire of London in 1666; he died of exposure.

Richard Brome (d. ca. 1562), Ben Jonson's protégé and perhaps his secretary, became one of the outstanding playwrights of the Caroline theater. Fifteen of his plays survive, *The Northern Lass* (printed 1632) being the earliest, followed by *The Sparagus Garden* (1635), *The City Witt* (printed 1653), *The Queen's Exchange,* and *The Queen and Concubine.* Butler admires Brome's acute political sensitivity and underlines the importance of his work for a proper understanding of drama under Charles I. His attractive plays repay the investigator. Of all Caroline playwrights, Brome may have the most to offer critics engaged in the rehabilitation of mid-seventeenth-century English drama.

The Joviall Crew of 1641 remains Brome's masterpiece. In refreshing contrast to his urban comedies of manners, it presents a country scene. The sympathetic Squire Oldrents is harboring a band of beggars in his barn. Oldrents's daughters and their lovers decide to play at begging themselves, only to discover the real dangers of life among actual rogues and vagabonds. They are saved from disaster by Springlove, Oldrents's steward, king of the "beggars' Commonwealth." Butler's extensive analysis of the play focuses on Brome's interest in the viewpoint of the countryman. He sees the play not as a "Cavalier escapist fantasy" but as a perceptive review of British social divisions. In fact, Cavalier escapism itself is scrutinized in the lovers' dalliance among the beggars. The good squire finds foils in his irresponsible neighbors, Justice Clak and his repellent son Oliver. Butler suggests that Brome is presenting his own ideal of social responsibility under the guise of a deceptively deft and charming play (*Theatre and Crisis*, 269–79).

THEATERS AND ACTORS, 1603–42. The passage of time altered the personnel of the acting companies. The King's Men lost many of their best in the second decade of the seventeenth century. In 1611 Armin died and John Shank took his place as chief comic actor. Audiences enjoyed Shank's singing, and he continued the Elizabethan practice of dancing jigs as afterpieces.[7] Another fine actor, Nathan Field (1587–1620) joined the King's Men in 1615, perhaps replacing Shakespeare. Known for his success as Chapman's dashing hero Bussy d'Ambois, Field had already written two plays, *A Woman Is a Weathercock* (1609) and *Amends for Ladies* (1611) and collaborated with Massinger and Fletcher on several others. The deaths of Shakespeare in 1616 and Richard Burbage shortly thereafter came as blows to their colleagues. Robert Benfield (d. 1649) replaced Ostler in 1615 as a member of the company and took over his role of Antonio in *The Duchess of Malfi* in 1619. When Heminge and Condell died, the business of the company devolved upon three actors, Eliard Swanston (d. 1651), John Lowin, and Joseph Taylor (ca. 1585–1652). Taylor succeeded to a number of Burbage's roles, notably Hamlet and Ferdinand in *The Duchess of Malfi*, after he joined the company in 1619. Taylor also played Iago, Truewit in *Epicoene*, and Face in *The Alchemist* and excelled in the plays of Beaumont and Fletcher. The high reputation of the King's Men and perhaps the patronage of the king himself enabled the troupe to attract talented younger performers to replace the great names of the past.

The old Admiral's Men were also disrupted in 1616, by the death of Henslowe. Alleyn formed a new company, Prince Charles's Men, which migrated from the Phoenix in Drury Lane (the Cockpit) to the Curtain. It dispersed when Charles I became king. The principal players joined the King's Men. A second company of the same name formed under the patronage of the future Charles II in 1631.

Theaters were also subject to time and chance. The Fortune burnt in 1621, but was rebuilt in brick and reopened in 1623. A new London theater, the Cockpit in Drury Lane, was originally built for cockfights in 1609 and converted into a private, roofed theater in 1616 by the actor Christopher Beeston (ca. 1570–1638). This stage should not be confused with the Cockpit in Court at Westminster, an entirely different building. As a structure, the Cockpit in Drury Lane resembled the Blackfriars theater. In 1617 it was vandalized during the London apprentices' Shrove Tuesday festivities. It was rebuilt and appropriately renamed the Phoenix, though it was also still referred to by its original name. After leasing the Phoenix out to a variety of companies, Beeston formed Queen Henrietta's Men (1625–36) and from 1636 forward a boy company, Beeston's Boys. William Beeston (ca. 1601–82) took over the company upon his father's death. The Cockpit was reopened in 1660, managed by John Rhodes of the Blackfriars, with a children's company including the young Thomas Betterton (ca. 1635–1710), who was to become perhaps the most celebrated Restoration actor. The old Cockpit was gradually abandoned after 1663. Similarly, the Hope, built for bull and bear baiting, was converted by Henslowe into a theater in 1613, possibly to capitalize on the recent Globe fire; the stage remained removable, and the stables for bulls and horses were left in place. Queen Elizabeth's Men appeared at the Hope in 1614–15; Jonson's *Bartholomew Fair* was presented there for the first time in the same year. After Henslowe's death in 1616 dissension arose between the actors and their management; as a result, the Hope reverted to an animal-baiting arena. Partly torn down in 1656, its remains were still visible in 1682–83.

Salisbury Court, a roofed, brick "private" playhouse at Salisbury Square (Fleet Street), was the last theater opened before the civil war. It operated energetically between 1629–42; the list of troupes who performed there included the King's Men, between 1629 and 1631. Underground performances were held there during the Commonwealth; to prevent future illegalities, a party of soldiers ripped up the interior in 1649. The building was reopened by William Beeston in 1660 and survived until the Fire of London in 1666.

Between 1632 and 1642 six London theaters were in operation: Martin Butler characterizes the Red Bull and the Fortune as the most conservative, popular stages. They could be relied upon to revive the Elizabethan warhorses that London audiences continued to demand. The second Blackfriars theater remained the most elegant and fashionable house. The versatile Phoenix and Salisbury Court resist classification, in terms either of their audience or the plays performed there. In the summer the King's Men resorted to the Globe, where they still attracted mass audiences for whom they developed a special repertory (Butler, 304–5).

There is a hypothesis that moveable scenery like that introduced at court by Inigo Jones was used for the first time on the public stage at the second Blackfriars theater. It is at least first referred to in 1637 in connection with Suckling's *Aglaura*. If such a system was attempted, it was clearly an exceptional event and suggests again that the second Blackfriars was the most courtly of the London theaters.

Drama elsewhere in the British Isles during the Jacobean and Caroline periods deserves more attention than it has yet received. This volume unfortunately cannot pursue the subject. The REED series is making primary materials up to at least 1642 available to facilitate the future study of British dramatic activity outside of London. A few basic observations can at least be offered here. Scots Protestantism resisted the establishment of any public theater throughout the seventeenth century; the history of drama in Scotland anticipates the repressive measures that English stages encountered under the Commonwealth. Dublin's first public theater building was put up in 1635 and employed James Shirley between 1636 and 1640. It closed in 1642, together with its London counterparts. Public theater returned to Ireland with the Restoration. One astonishing record from Kilkenny documents the performance of a Corpus Christi play there as late as 1639. Such an event suggests that the chronology of British drama is far from straightforward.

MASQUES AND UNIVERSITY DRAMA,
1603–42

The English masque reached its fullest development at the courts of James I and Charles I. The Jacobean and Caroline masques elaborated on the early Tudor disguisings and Elizabethan masks. Through the introduction of "Italian scenery" and fresh visual expectations they exerted influences on Restoration theater design, as well as on ballet and opera. For Glynne Wickham, they present a fundamental shift in the philosophy of theater, away from a symbolic, emblematic stage to pictorial verisimilitude, away from the medieval pageants and toward the cinema.

BEN JONSON, INIGO JONES, AND THE STUART MASQUE. Ben Jonson first achieved celebrity in the public theaters for his comedy of humor, beginning with *Every Man in His Humour* of 1598. He began to play with the idea of court pageantry as early as *Cynthia's Revels,* which included an experimental attempt at a masque. Jonson contributed to James I's coronation pageants in 1604, and by 1605 he had presented the first of his memorable masques at court.

As Stephen Orgel's classic study *The Jonsonian Masque* demonstrates, Jonson regarded the masque as an important form of theater. It is doubtful that his courtly audiences ever appreciated this notion. From the fourteenth through the sixteenth centuries the courtly practice of mummings or disguisings had gradually developed into an effective and widely appreciated aristocratic amusement. The earlier court pageants had involved diguise and dance; now they began to acquire poetic texts. They still retained the distinctive features of the form: they were held in banqueting halls, the sovereign or some important member of the court often took a principal role, and in the end the group of performers would merge with the audience in a general dance, bringing the spectators into the pageant. Most of the three hours occupied by a masque would be devoted to dancing. The masque was seen as an ephemeral, occasional genre, appropriate to festal occasions like weddings or Christmas revels, invariably spectacular and exciting for its participants. Besides all this, it performed an important social function, expressing an ideal of national harmony and of the union of ruler and ruled (Orgel, 108).

With Ben Jonson, the masque attained its highest point as a form of drama. In his first royal commissions, *The Mask of Blacknesse* (6 January 1605), held in the Elizabethan banqueting house at Whitehall, and *The Mask of Beautie* (10 January 1608), Jonson built his entertainments around specific royal requests. Anne of Denmark had expressed a wish that she and her ladies should appear as "Black-mores": Jonson presented them as African river nymphs seated in a giant scallop shell. The audience did not approve: "you cannot imagine a more ugly Sight"; "a very lothsome sight, and I am sory that strangers should see owr court so strangely disguised." While they disapproved the queen's whim, the courtly audience recognized this as a more theatrical masque than any they had seen before (Orgel, 65, 68, 119).

Of Jonson's dramatic innovations the most memorable was the antimasque (or antic masque) introduced in the *Mask of Queens* (2 February 1609). As "a spectacle of strangeness . . . producing multiplicity of gesture and not unaptly sorting with the current and whole fall of the device," Jonson began his production with a smoky Hell scene, devised by "mr jones," and populated by eleven ghastly witches. These hags sang charms to blast the evening's entertainment, and danced "a magicall Daunce, full of praeposterous change, and gesticulation." A sudden scene change converted the stage from hell to the House of Fame, the scene of the masque's pageant of famous queens leading up to Anne of Denmark. In 1609 Jonson had only begun to explore the possibilities of the striking contrast between antimasque and the main subject. His later masques developed the clash of opposites more dramatically, as in *Mercury Vindicated from the Alchemists* (6 January 1615) or *The Gypsies Metamorphos'd* (1621), apparently James I's favorite, since he ordered it to be repeated twice. Unlike the other members of his family, the king never participated. Instead, he became the chief member of Jonson's audience, the center point toward whom all effects converged.

Jonson's collaborator, Inigo Jones (1573–1652), had studied art and architecture in Italy. He was briefly employed in Denmark in 1604–5. Before that his background is obscure, though Jonson accuses him of starting out as a theatrical technician, perhaps a carpenter. Jones's first recorded English court appointment was in the household of Prince Henry. Inigo Jones is celebrated for introducing Italian innovations to England, both in architecture and in the related fields of stage design and machinery. He greatly admired the Italian architect Palladio, the designer of the Teatro Olimpico in Vicenza. Indeed, Jones translated Palladio's *Quattro libri dell'architettura* (Venice 1570) into English. Jones adopted Buontalenti's use of painted backcloths and sliding panels for scene changes. He profited from the designs and theories of Sebastiano

Serlio (1475–1554), publicized in his *De architettura,* part 2 (1545; English translation 1611). Jones's theaters and sets employed strong perspective effects, framed within a proscenium arch. They dazzled audiences with revolving screens, shutters, turntables, and grooves for changes of scenery. Aside from a few experiments, public theaters in England did not adopt this technology until after 1660. Jones's "set scene" has become our "set" or "setting." The collection of Jones's designs in the library of the duke of Devonshire at Chatsworth preserves some of his stage effects and costume sketches for many Stuart pageants. A comprehensive study of the surviving designs was published in two folio volumes by Roy Strong and Stephen Orgel.

The collaboration between Jones and Jonson began to break down in a quarrel over the "credits" for *The Mask of Augurs* (1618). Neither of these imperious artists would compromise on the central question: Which of the component arts should dominate the masque? By the 1630s Jonson was satirizing Jones as In-and-In Medlay of *A Tale of a Tub,* and artistic cooperation had become impossible. Charles I only commissioned two masques from Jonson, preferring the spectacular art of Inigo Jones and the less assertive poetry of Carew, Davenant, and Townsend (Orgel, 77–80). According to Allardyce Nicoll, the antagonism between Jonson and Jones was "symbolic of an ageless conflict between the scene-designer and the playwright" (*Stuart Masque,* 23). According to Wickham, it also represented the confrontation of two dramatic traditions. The court decided for Jones. Even for Martin Butler, this exemplifies a disjunction of Charles's court from the daring minds of the Caroline public stages: "This was a court that had preferred to be without Ben Jonson" (284).[8]

Other authors wrote masques and court pageants in competition with Jonson, though none challenged his preeminence. Among the most distinguished was the poet Thomas Campion (or Campian) (1567–1620), who wrote his own music. While studying law at Gray's Inn, he had taken part in revels presented at court 17 January 1588 in the roles of Melancholy and Hidaspes. He contributed songs for *Gesta Grayorum* in 1594. Campion began his literary career as a follower of Sir Philip Sidney. He is chiefly remembered for his lyric poetry and his arguments in favor of the adoption of classical quantitative meter by English poets. His friendship with the lutanist Philip Rosseter, master of the Queen's Revels, brought him into contact both with the court and possibly with the public stage. In *The Lord Hay's Masque* of 6 January 1607 Campion celebrated the wedding of James Hay (or Hayes; d. 1636), first earl of Carlisle and Baron Hay, one of James I's favorites, with Honora Denny, daughter of Sir Edward Denny, high sheriff of Hertfordshire (Davis, 1969, 204). Campion is responsible for *The Lords' Masque* (performed 14 February 1613) and *The Caversham Entertainment* (27–28 April 1613), published together in reverse order. *The Lords' Masque* commemorates the marriage of James I's daughter, Princess Elizabeth, and Frederick, the Elector Palatine, on 14 February 1613. *The Caversham Entertainment* took place on Queen Anne's progress to Bath to be treated for the gout. Helpful notes on costumes and scenery assist students in envisioning these performances.[9]

John Milton's *A Mask presented at Ludlow Castle* (*Comus*) is described in its anonymous 1637 edition as a masque, though Greg in *Pastoral Poetry and Pastoral Drama* regarded Milton's work as a pastoral drama. It survives as a lovely example of private occasional entertainment, suggesting the exceptional poetic and musical talents that might be marshalled for such events. The original performance took place on Michaelmas night, 29 September 1634, before John Egerton (1579–1649), earl of Bridgewater and lord president of Wales. Henry Lawes composed the music for the songs and played the Attendant Spirit. The Lady and her two brothers were played by the earl's children, John, lord Brackley (1622–86); Thomas; and Alice Egerton. The elder son, John, was twelve years old. These special circumstances give the masque the charm of a family event and some of the stylistic effects inherent in the use of child actors. The lyric beauty of the language has long been recognized. In his plot Milton plays on British legend and the debate and morality traditions. The center of the drama is the confrontation of the Lady, the embodiment of chastity, and the enchanter Comus, the son of Bacchus and Circe, who tempts her to join him in bestial intemperance. Besides Milton's classical reading, *The Old Wives' Tale* and Spenser's *Faerie Queene* may all have contributed to the masque's individual magic.

UNIVERSITY PLAYS. Theater also persisted at English colleges and the Inns of Court. A Latin translation of Guarini's pastoral *Il Pastor Fido* of 1598 was performed at Cambridge in King's College

Chapel in 1605. Evidently Latin (or Greek) theater was still considered educational, but professional performances were discouraged in or near this Puritan stronghold. One record suggests that the Chamberlain's Men brought *Hamlet* there in 1603. An important visitor might provoke a theatrical effusion, analogous to the town drama of the royal entries or progresses. In 1613 the future Charles I saw *Scyros*, a Latin version of Bonarelli's *Filli de Sciro* on his visit to Cambridge. George Ruggles (1575–1622) wrote two comedies for student production at Clare Hall around 1600: the more successful was *Ignoramus*, a Latin comedy with English passages. Della Porta's *La Trappolaria* of 1596 is the main literary source for the play, which satirizes Francis Brackyn, Cambridge recorder, and lawyers generally. In 1615 James I was so delighted with *Ignoramus* that he came back and demanded it again the following week. The play was later translated into English for a 1662 court production; Ravenscroft adapted it as *The English Lawyer* in 1677. The last recorded college play at Cambridge before the Restoration was the Trinity College performance of Abraham Cowley's comedy of manners *The Guardian*, played for the entertainment of the future Charles II in 1642. Here the poet Cowley (1618–67) impartially mocks both Puritan and Royalist. The same play, retitled *Cutter of Coleman Street*, was performed in 1661 at the Duke's House; Samuel Pepys refers to it in his diary. Drama at Cambridge does not seem to have revived until 1855, when the Amateur Dramatic Club (ADC) was founded.[10]

At Oxford the annals of drama for this period are scantier. The proctor William Cartwright (1611–43) wrote four academic plays for performance at Christ Church between 1635 and 1638. Additional records of drama may still remain to be uncovered.

THE PURITAN REACTION:
DRAMA WITHOUT THEATERS, 1642–59

Puritan resistance to theater began long before 1642. Stephen Gosson's objections to the stage were echoed in their turn by numerous preachers and their congregations. William Prynne's massive *Histriomastix*, the most celebrated antitheatrical diatribe in the history of English literaure, appeared in 1632. The Star Chamber reacted by sentencing its author to imprisonment for life in the Tower and to the loss of his ears, imposing in addition the shocking fine of five thousand pounds. These penalties seem to have been imposed not on account of Prynne's view of plays, but because of outspoken references to the clergy, to the queen as an actress and possibly like them a "notorious whore," and to the need for wide-ranging social reform. In the past students of the period believed that the associations of the stage with Charles I and the Royalist party were as important as antitheatrical feeling in precipitating the parliamentary order of 1642 closing all public theaters. Martin Butler, however, points out that Puritan opposition to the stage had subsided a good deal since Gosson, particularly after James I forbade public performances on Sundays. The 1642 closing resembled earlier temporary orders shutting down the theaters during epidemics like those of 1592–93 and 1636–37. The onset of civil war represented a similar national state of emergency. That the closure was to last for eighteen years no one could then anticipate (Butler, 84ff.).

A complete cessation of all theatrical activity for eighteen years could hardly be achieved. English Puritans were by no means a monolithic group, unified in opposition to drama. School plays continued with Oliver Cromwell's approval. Actors still attempted performances, altered in response to the legal realities of the day.

The Puritan Interregnum produced a curious dramatic form of its own—"droll humors," "drolleries," or "drolls," which first appeared in London under the Puritans and continued to reappear through 1660. Drolls were short, comic pieces, often excerpts from a larger play, ending in dance, much like the earlier jigs. Their subjects might range from the Bible to Shakespeare, as in "Bottom the Weaver" from *A Midsummer Night's Dream* or "The Gravediggers" from *Hamlet*. Robert Cox (d. 1655) was the best-known player of drolls, both in London and at country fairs. His performances also featured conjuring and rope dancing. Francis Kirkman's *The Wits; or, Sport upon Sport* (1662) presents Cox's chief drolls; a 1672 edition includes the earliest surviving picture of footlights on the English stage.

Underground theatrical performances after 1642 were attempted at the more popular London theaters. The Globe had been demolished in 1644, and the second Blackfriars theater in 1655. The Red Bull had been built around 1600, then repaired and possibly roofed in 1625. Robert Cox himself was arrested there in 1653 and imprisoned. Edward Shatterell participated in the production of illegal performances at the Red Bull in 1654; he had also acted abroad. Anthony Turner, once a minor actor with Queen Henrietta's Men, was arrested for acting at the Red Bull in 1659; he and Shatterell seem to have been ringleaders. There are also records of puppet plays at the Red Bull from this period. William Cartwright the younger (ca. 1606–86) appeared at the Cockpit after its official closing in 1642, and it was raided in 1649; John Lowin of the King's Men, a celebrated Falstaff of Shakespeare's day, and his colleague Joseph Taylor were apprehended playing there. The old Fortune was also the scene of illegal performances, and was also raided and smashed by Commonwealth soldiers in 1649; it had to be demolished in 1661. The Vere Street theater, built in 1634 as a tennis court, also held secret performances; the "ill Beest" who betrayed them to the Puritan authorities in 1652 was rumored to be William Beeston, himself associated with illegal theater at Salisbury Court. These performances and arrests reveal the persistence of interest in the stage, in the face of official repression.

Sir William Davenant's experiments with opera also belong to this period. Davenant (1606–68) seems to have enjoyed the rumor that he was Shakespeare's illegitimate son, his mother being the hostess of the Crown Inn, Cornmarket, at Oxford. Conceivably Shakespeare may have been his godfather. He became poet laureate in 1638, succeeding Ben Jonson, and composed plays and masques after the Jonsonian manner. Butler discusses him as a court dramatist under Charles I. Davenant was knighted by Charles I in 1643 for service in the Royalist army. In the final years of the Commonwealth, he obtained permission to stage events he described as "music and instruction," perhaps the earliest English operas. These equivocal entertainments were *The Siege of Rhodes* (1656), *The Spaniards in Peru* (1658), and *Sir Francis Drake* (1659), with scenery designed by John Webb (1611–72), who had studied under Inigo Jones. At the Restoration Davenant opened Lincoln's Inn Field's theater (The Duke's House) with Betterton as his leading actor. Davenant links Jonson and the Stuart masque to the age of Charles II, making absolute boundaries again difficult to set up.[12]

English actors, like English princes, found refuge abroad. George

Jolly may have appeared at the Fortune in 1640. Jolly's English Comedians appeared in Germany in 1648 and performed extensively in Frankfurt. In 1654 he was already employing women in his troupe. He reappeared in England at the Cockpit after the Restoration.

CONCLUSION

The earlier seventeenth century has been scrutinized for symptoms of the death of native British dramatic tradition. The European influences on the theory and practice of Inigo Jones, the influx of Italian and Spanish translations, the pressure of new aesthetic ideals were all propelling the British stage into a new era. Signs of experimentation, adaptation, stress, and debate recur in the diverse productions of the Jacobean and Caroline theaters. The closing of the theaters in 1642 and their suppression under the Commonwealth have been seen as a major break in British dramatic tradition.

Again, certain careers and lifetimes span the gap. William Beeston's post-Restoration company at Salisbury Court perhaps preserved some of the Elizabethan theatrical techniques of his father Christopher. The Restoration actor Michael Mohun (ca. 1620–84), was one of Beeston's boys, moving on to adult parts before 1642. A Royalist officer during the civil war, he returned to the stage in heroic drama. John Lowin (1576–1653) also links Elizabethan theater and later English drama. Lowin was a stalwart member of the King's Men until 1642 and played Falstaff and Volpone, Melantius in Beaumont and Fletcher's *The Maid's Tragedy* (1611), and the original Bosola of 1614. Downes (in *Roscius Angelicanus*) reports that Lowin passed on Shakespeare's instructions on the playing of Henry VIII to Davenant, who in turn instructed Betterton. Eighteen years had separated the Restoration stage from its Caroline precursors, but some echoes still made themselves heard.

CHAPTER VI

CONCLUSION

CURRENT CRITICAL REPUTATION

Not much has changed in the area of Romano-British drama. As with most late antique drama, little evidence of it survives. No major find has yet changed the critical reputation of the period; it is still of no literary repute whatsoever. This phase of British stage history remains largely the domain of the archaeologists. For drama in the centuries following the end of the Roman empire, we fall back on active speculations based on minimal documentary evidence.

The role of the folk play in the development of medieval drama has been stressed by scholars like Richard Axton. In the realm of liturgical drama the work of O. B. Hardison, Jr., has led to useful critical reevaluations. The chronological priority of surviving dramas, the liturgical drama's lines of development, and the role of the Mass itself as drama are still debated. Most recently critics of liturgical drama have focused on larger dramatic units rather than on snatches of dialogue or scenes like the *Quem quaeritis*. The *Quem quaeritis* is now considered within the larger setting of the drama of Holy Week, a sequence of purposefully choreographed rituals that should be evaluated as a dramatic totality. This approach expands our definition of liturgical drama, adding depth and resonance to the form.

Although liturgical drama is still seen as a mainspring of medieval drama in the West, the breakdown of the evolutionary approach has fragmented the field. Scholars now seem wary of connecting genres, preferring to treat each one separately. Early vernacular plays like the *Ordo representacionis Adae,* in particular, and *La seinte Resureccion* retain the high regard of specialists. Whether they are protocycles or not remains uncertain; their place in the development of vernacular drama is still under discussion.

The cycle plays have benefited from new critical insights, among them the appreciation of cycle form. Their individuality and coherence is now better recognized than ever before. The moralities, with their structure of temptation, fall, and redemption, have received new attention. Scholarship is also rediscovering other forms of drama. Robin Hood plays and court revels are newly admired. The canon of moral interludes of the early Tudor period is expanding as new authors are discovered and edited. Work like that of David Bevington ties together British dramatic history by exploring links between medieval and Renaissance dramatic forms.

Elizabethan dramatic criticism is beginning to assimilate these ideas. The mixed nature of Shakespeare's audiences and the varied appeal of the drama of this period have been reaffirmed by recent investigators. Shakespeare studies proceed apace on all fronts. New interest has been directed to a number of his contemporaries and successors, with Martin Butler's demand for a reevaluation of Jacobean and especially Carolinean drama. These phases of British drama are still often described as decadent and emasculated, but these are becoming perilous adjectives. Butler also proposes a reinterpretation of the closing of the theaters in September 1642.

The well-defined patterns of separate medieval and Renaissance stages, the successive rise and fall of genres, no longer provide an adequate explanation of this initial period of British dramatic history. Criticism loves to complicate as well as oversimplify. What it is doing here is generating a more complex, overlapping, and interconnected model of the earlier British drama.

FUTURE DIRECTIONS FOR RESEARCH

A great deal remains for the critics of the twenty-first century to attempt in the field of British drama to 1660. Much basic research on original texts and documents is ongoing or yet to be undertaken. At the same time, twenty years of activity in fourteenth- through seventeenth-century stage history is making much documentary evidence available to students. Its synthesis and application to the understanding of British drama remain high priorities. The dramatic scholarship of the future should benefit from a new appreciation of visual and musical elements of performance, and from archaeological and architectural analyses of buildings where these performances took place. Students will have to be able to form coherent pictures from technical financial and legal documents. This specialized research must be assimilated and evaluated by the critical community if it is to prove of more than antiquarian interest.

Large subjects like the town drama under the Tudors and the role of popular theaters in the seventeenth century deserve serious attention. Dramatic records of the Inns of Court will need to be integrated into the history of the drama. Assessment of archaeological finds like the Roman amphitheater of Londinium and the Rose playhouse site will deepen our understanding of British drama. The history of British drama should become less centered on London professional companies and balanced by evidence of provincial dramatic history. As later medieval and Caroline drama are reinvestigated, their relationship to Elizabethan theater necessarily changes, and important reevaluations of that central period become necessary. A more acute awareness of the strength of the drama of this period in actual performance and its relevance for the most advanced theatrical experiments should inform both scholarship and drama in the future. Precise reenactments and radical adaptations both test the power of the dramatic artifact. By encouraging the staging of early plays and pageant cycles, the critical community can contribute to contemporary audiences and dramatists.

THE DEVELOPMENT OF DRAMA IN BRITAIN, 100–1660

There were undoubtedly forms of drama in Britain before the Roman theaters—prehistoric dramas of procession along causeways like the magnificent example at Avebury, rituals enacted at altars and in cavern sanctuaries, hunting games using animal masks, and fertility or initiation rites. All this is now a "ghost drama," territory for speculation and theory based on fragmentary archaeological evidence and anthropological analogies. With the drama of Roman Britannia we are on surer ground. The theaters and amphitheaters that survive suggest some of the resources of Roman stagecraft, the potential size of audiences, and the physical relationship of the theater to Romano-British communities. Masks and inscriptions hint at a variety of dramatic activities. There is still no contemporaneous literature of drama, a problem shared by late Roman theater throughout the empire. Possibly imperial Rome had no dramatic literature to speak of. This era, then, in the dramatic history of Britain remains only slightly less hazy than the succeeding centuries of Anglo-Saxon migration, Celtic retreat, and the resettlement of the British Isles.

No doubt some nomadic entertainers did outlive the Roman era in Britain. Their oral transmission of classical dramatic conventions may be one link in the continuing history of British drama. So is the preservation of Roman plays in manuscript by Irish and Anglo-Saxon monastic scribes, major custodians of Latin culture throughout this period and primary influences on the revival of learning across Europe. It is important to remember, too, that Anglo-Saxon vernacular literature, pagan and Christian, was performed before audiences by professional poet-composers or their amateur admirers. If not drama in our sense of the term, such performance contained strong elements of impersonation and dialogue, easily enhanced in oral delivery. The folk plays of the Germanic tribes, ritualized combats in particular, celebrated communal agricultural rites of fertility and seasonal change. The Christian calendar adapted these ingrained agricultural patterns, lending the year a new narrative structure and new forms of drama. The events of the liturgy, the Mass as the reenactment of the sacrifice of Christ, and the special commemorations of key moments in the lives of Jesus and the saints demanded and gradually received dramatic expression. The *Quem quaeritis* scene retains its importance as an early English example of this development. Recent research has given us a new understanding of large dramatic patterns and a wide range of dramatic effects within the liturgy, making liturgical drama a larger scale phenomenon altogether.

The twelfth century was a period of dramatic innovation in Britain. Though the extant plays are difficult to place it seems clear that types of drama that only crystallized later found their beginnings here. Saints' plays, possible protocycles, classically inspired comedies, royal entries, and aristocratic revels all appear for the first time in twelfth- or early thirteenth-century British records. By the end of the thirteenth century, there are signs of secular farce, "king and queen games," and a corps of versatile professional entertainers and aristocratic amateur performers at tournaments and banquets. London audiences trampled the priory gardens at Clerkenwell to see scriptural plays. Edward I pioneered Arthurian entertainments and political pageantry.

With the feast of Corpus Christi in 1311 a new religious celebration attracted a major dramatic form, the Corpus Christi cycle. The fourteenth-century development of trade guilds and provincial town government reworked the Corpus Christi processions into a biblical drama that ranks among the most significant achievements of the British stage. Symbolic morality dramas could be undertaken on a similarly epic scale, as in *The Castle of Perseverance,* or packed into small-scale, fast-moving productions like *Mankind.* Professional troupes, protected by their noble patrons, and clear evidence of a commercial theater public in London both belong to this era. At the same time pageantry became a powerful form of dialogue between rulers and their subjects. Richard II's 1392 reconciliation with the Londoners reveals the dramatic potential of this highly charged medium of exchange. The pageantry of the fourteenth and fifteenth centuries contrasts interestingly with the Tudor political drama studied by Sydney Anglo. Around this time traces of popular Robin Hood plays and May games became more distinct, ancient festival play in new dramatic garb.

All of these activities persisted under the aegis of the Tudors, with royal, political, and social theater acquiring bureaucratic structure and documentation. The vigorous morality tradition extended its range into overt secular political comment. The humanist educators' renewed interest in classical drama as a subject of instruction led to the performance of classical plays in schools and universities and to scholarly Latin and English imitations of Plautus and Seneca. British literary theorists became acutely conscious of Italian and classical models. The religious controversies of the Reformation broadened the range of Christian theater at the same time that government censorship sharply limited it by shutting down the Creed and Pater Noster plays and, by 1580, most of the mystery cycles themselves.

The dramatic conventions of the British stage could not be suppressed along with the content of religious drama. They went on to influence the professional companies and playwrights of Elizabethan London. The "new" genres of classically inspired comedy and tragedy may seem self-consciously Roman, but in fact owe much to medieval farce, cycle play, and morality play. The distinctively British developments of chronicle history plays, sometimes occurring in cycles, and romances and tragicomedies betray their parentage even more conclusively. Much of the power and versatility of the Elizabethan drama stems from its combination of Latin and Italian models with a sense of time and space, symbol and structure developed in Britain over the past four centuries.

We still acknowledge Shakespeare as the greatest Elizabethan author, as the major dramatist of his day or of British dramatic history, as a potent force among his contemporaries. Alongside the public playhouses with their varied audiences we need to place the indoor hall theaters and the active court drama. Across the country, local pageants kept up a long sociopolitical tradition of "drama as offering" to a sovereign, with the elaboration of Elizabeth I's role as Great Harry's Daughter, Gloriana, the Virgin Queen.

In the latest studies the complications of Jacobean theater and the effects of a change of royal patronage are still recognized. Inigo Jones's design innovations and the influence of the court masques and later courtier plays all point the way toward the drama of the Restoration. The devaluation of the Jacobean and Caroline stage needs to be resisted. Instead, just as Johan Huizinga's seductive vision of the decadent *Waning of the Middle Ages* is now viewed by most specialists as a potent caricature, so the "decadence" of the stage under James I and Charles I may well have been overstated for effect. Martin Butler describes a politically alert drama of the period 1632–42, one that found room for popular Elizabethan stage conventions as well as European innovations.

Between 1642 and 1660 it is important to see not the imminent death of native British dramatic traditions but their struggle to survive, their vitality in the face of hostile political and social forces. The often denigrated "drolls," the illicit performances, and the ingeniously redefined "musical entertainments" of Davenant prevent us from viewing the theater after 1660 as a completely alien creation. The Restoration stage differed in many ways from any earlier British theater. Drama became an elegant amusement for a small elite group, a near-monopoly: the six or so London theaters of the early seventeenth century shrank to two or three. As the Restoration playwright and critic John Dryden observed, manners became a major preoccupation of authors and their audiences, as did the production of spectacular representational effects and attention to neoclassical correctness of design. The classical unities concerned British playwrights as never before. This notable change must preoccupy the historian of drama for the immediate future. Early British drama looks ahead to our own day in its respect for the symbolic, its wide-ranging vision of the universe, and its sophisticated resources of technique and language, passion and dignity.

BRITISH DRAMA AND THE SPIRIT
OF THE AGE

As a reflection of its own times drama can be immensely expressive. It can also display combative tendencies, reacting violently against the current of contemporary thought. We cannot tell much about these issues before the tenth century, when we begin to have dramatic texts to analyze. The most we can say is that even in the distant province of Britannia Roman communities found drama a useful adjunct to political control, an essential element of civilized life, from the beginning of the Roman occupation to its fourth-century retreat. After that time the societies of early medieval Britain saw little need for large-scale theater buildings, except as rubbish dumps or arenas for animal baiting. Instead, in the intervals between combats different varieties of dramatic entertainment continued to appeal to isolated scholars and to close-knit communal groups.

It is no longer at all fashionable to describe the Middle Ages as a monolithic age of faith or to view the religious drama thereof as an unvarying, singleminded, and rather touching expression of that faith. Medieval and Renaissance religious drama responds sensitively to local and international social and spiritual developments. The cycle plays share their cyclic structure, that most ambitious and perhaps most gothic of medieval artistic structures, with the *Canterbury Tales* and Malory's *Morte Darthur* and are characterized by diversity within an overarching unity of design. Their symbolic force and universal scope attract many twentieth-century admirers to the mystery cycles, though the sophistication of their construction is only now beginning to be appreciated. Medieval British dramatists are attentive to immediate social stimuli: a drama of social protest begins to be articulated in more than one cycle and in the social reversals of the Robin Hood plays.

Clashes of opinion charge the early sixteenth-century stage. Few plays of any age are as daring in their social and political criticism as John Skelton's *Magnyfycence* or Sir David Lindsay's *Ane Satire of the Thrie Estaitis,* both taking aim at their targets from the shelter of familiar morality plot structures. Reformation debates find reflection in the polemical plays of John Bale. Ecclesiastical and secular authorities exerted themselves from 1543 on to muzzle the drama as a medium of debate; these suspicious auditors found drama's flexibility, public character, and persuasive power more of a threat than an opportunity. Tudor monarchs enhanced their images on national or international stages by means of court theater. Elizabeth I might in some ways be regarded as the most successful dramatic creation of the period, a "performance artist" before her time.

It is only a commonplace of theatrical history to marvel at the comprehensive way the late sixteenth- and earlier seventeenth-century stage reflected the contradictory intellectual energies of its day— humanism and classical learning, religious speculation and political theory, the exploration of the New World and the new science, British nationalism and self-doubt.

Not all readers are convinced by Martin Butler's suggestion that the Caroline theater was politically engaged rather than escapist as the confrontation of king and Parliament developed. Still, his view demands our attention. Even when we are clearly dealing with a theater of fantasy and wish-fulfillment, the vehicle and its escape route say a great deal about the authors' and audiences' shared mental landscape.

Ben Jonson addressed Shakespeare both as "Soul of the age!" and as "not for an age, but for all time." A few dramatists encountered in the preceding pages remain inextricably bound to their own eras. Their work offers historical insights but little dramatic excitement. In most cases, though, the earliest drama retains the force to reexpress the spirit of its time and speak to the spirit of ours.

CHRONOLOGY

This brief chronology lists selected landmarks of British drama to 1660; it focuses on major plays, dramatists, and locations. My principal sources are Ian Lancashire, *Dramatic Texts and Records of Britain: A Chronological Topography to 1558* (Toronto: University of Toronto Press, 1984); G. Blakemore Evans, "Annals, 1552–1616" in *The Riverside Shakespeare* (Boston: Houghton Mifflin, 1974), 1853–93; Alfred Harbage and Samuel Schoenbaum, *Annals of English Drama, 975–1700* (London: Methuen, 1962).

55–54 B.C.E.	Julius Caesar's first and second invasions of Britain.
C.E. 1–99	Roman amphitheaters constructed: ten sites known today.
ca. 60–400	Roman theaters in operation: five sites known today.
ca. 605–640	Anglo-Saxon assembly place or theater at Yeavering, Northumberland, modeled on Roman theaters.
965–975	*Regularis Concordia* text of *Visitatio sepulchri.*
978–980	Winchester *Quem quaeritis* performance: liturgical drama.
1066	Battle of Hastings: William the Conqueror defeats Harold.
ca. 1100–1119	"Miracle" play of St. Catherine at Dunstable, Bedfordshire.
ca. 1146–1174	*Ordo representacionis Adae* (*Le Mystère d'Adam*), French play perhaps written and acted in England.
ca. 1160–1185	*Babio,* Latin "comedia" ascribed to Walter Map.
ca. 1170–1182	Miracle and martyr plays performed in London.
ca. 1180	*La seinte Resureccion,* French play written in England.
1207	Possible London pageantry for royal entry of Emperor Otto.
1210	King John pays for a play (or revel) at Stogursey in Somerset, possibly the first recorded English secular revel.
1236–1390	Lincoln Cathedral feast of Fools, celebrated with clerks' *ludos,* prohibited by Robert Grosseteste, bishop of Lincoln.

CHRONOLOGY

ca. 1265	Robin Hood plays are popular in Scotland.
before ca. 1272–1283	*Dame Sirith,* East Midland dialogue with narrative connections, possibly dramatized by minstrels.
ca. 1275–1325	Castilly (Cornwall) henge made into a "Plain an Gwarry," a playing place with a capacity of about two thousand.
1286	Hereford: possible performance of a play at a Jewish wedding. The bishop excommunicated the Christian guests. Earliest English reference to such a performance in a private household.
1299	Play or game of King Arthur at Edward I's wedding.
ca. 1300–1325	*Interludium de clerico et puella* (*Interlude of the Clerk and the Girl*), Middle English dialogue.
1311	Introduction of the feast of Corpus Christi by Clement V.
1348	The Black Death: first English epidemic of bubonic plague.
ca. 1350	*The Pride of Life,* possibly connected with Ireland.
ca. 1375	Cornish scriptural plays associated with Penryn.
1376–1580	Various versions of the York Corpus Christi play performed.
1392–1580	Coventry Shearmen and Taylors' Pageant and Weavers' Pageant.
1397–1440	*The Castle of Perseverance,* possibly associated with Lincoln.
1421–1575	Records of the Chester Corpus Christi play.
1424–1430	John Lydgate's series of "mummings."
1427–1589	Newcastle upon Tyne play of Noah.
1437–1438	Tito Livio Frulovisi, *Peregrinatio* and *Eugenius,* humanist Latin comedies.
1445	Henry VI marries Marguerite d'Anjou. London pageants for Marguerite's royal entry 28 May.
ca. 1450–1475	The N-town (or Hegge) cycle plays, formerly known as *Ludus Coventriae.*
ca. 1450–1576	The Wakefield cycle (Towneley plays).
1461–1520	The Croxton Play of the Sacrament.
1464	*Mankind,* performed near Cambridge.

1475	Norwich *Robin Hood and the Sheriff of Nottingham* play.
1476	William Caxton sets up press at Westminster.
1480–1520	*The Conversion of St. Paul,* from East Anglia or Cambridge.
1480–1520	*Mary Magdalene,* from East Anglia, possibly King's Lynn.
1490–1500	Henry Medwall, *Nature,* interlude.
1495	John Bale born at Cove, Suffolk, 21 November.
1495–1497	Richard Pynson prints six of Terence's comedies.
ca. 1496–1497	Henry Medwall, *Fulgens and Lucrece.*
1509	Henry VIII marries Catherine of Aragon. Beginning of Richard Gibson's detailed Revels accounts for court events.
1510–19?	*Everyman,* probably translated from the Dutch *Elckerlijk.*
1519–1520	John Skelton writes *Magnyfycence.*
1524–1526	John Rastell of Coventry, printer, sets up London public theater in Finsbury Fields.
1531–1547	John Redford active as author of interludes.
1533	Henry VIII marries Anne Boleyn. Henry VIII declares himself supreme head of Church of England. Elizabeth I born. William Rastell publishes John Heywood's plays.
1532	Religious relics and images destroyed in south of England.
1539	Bale's *King Johan* performed before Archbishop Cranmer.
1540	Statute forbids performance or printing of plays contrary to religious doctrine. Sir David Lindsay's *Ane Satire of the Thrie Estaitis* performed at Linlithgow Palace.
1547	Henry VIII dies. John Bale returns from Germany. Corpus Christi processions suppressed.
1547–1552	Nicholas Udall, *Ralph Royster Doyster.*
1551–1554	*Gammer Gurton's Needle* by "Mr. S." produced at Cambridge.
1555	Roman Catholicism officially restored in England.
1561	Preston, *Cambises.*

1562	Norton and Sackville, *Gorboduc,* first English Senecan tragedy in blank verse.
1564	Christopher Marlowe and William Shakespeare born.
1566	George Gascoigne, *The Supposes* (translated from Ariosto's *I Suppositi*).
1568	York corporation is advised not to produce the Creed play.
1572	Ben Jonson and Thomas Dekker born.
1573	Inigo Jones born.
1575	Archbishop Grindal confiscates the York Pater Noster play text. Final performances of the Chester Whitsun play cycle.
1576	The Theatre built in Shoreditch by James Burbage. The Children of the Chapel perform at the first Blackfriars theater.
1577	The Curtain playhouse opens at Moorfields in Shoreditch.
1580	Final performance of the Coventry Corpus Christi cycle.
1587	Marlowe's *Tamburlaine the Great, Part I* and Thomas Kyd's *The Spanish Tragedy* first produced.
1589	The master of the Revels is authorized to license and censor all plays presented in London. Shakespeare's *Henry VI, Part I* produced. Marlowe's *The Jew of Malta* produced.
1590	Shakespeare's *Henry VI*, parts 1 and 2, produced. Peele's *The Old Wive's Tale* produced.
1591	*Arden of Feversham* (anonymous), first "domestic" tragedy.
1592	Robert Greene, *A Groatsworth of Wit,* earliest reference to Shakespeare as an active playwright. Shakespeare's *Richard III* and *The Comedy of Errors* produced. Formation of the Earl of Pembroke's Men. Marlowe's *Doctor Faustus* produced. Philip Henslowe begins keeping his diary.
1593	Christopher Marlowe murdered.
1593–1594	Shakespeare's *Titus Andronicus* and *The Taming of the Shrew.*

1594	The first appearance of the Lord Chamberlain's Men; Shakespeare's *The Two Gentlemen of Verona, Love's Labor's Lost,* and *King John* all probably produced.
1595	Shakespeare's *Richard II, Romeo and Juliet,* and *A Midsummer Night's Dream* produced. The Swan playhouse built.
1596	Johannes de Witt drawing of the Swan playhouse. Shakespeare's *The Merchant of Venice* and *Henry IV,* part 1.
1597	Second Blackfriars theater built by James Burbage.
1598	The Theater at Shoreditch demolished, reused in the first Globe at Bankside. Shakespeare's *Henry IV,* part 2 and *Much Ado about Nothing;* Jonson's *Every Man in His Humour.* Shakespeare acts in Jonson's play.
1599	The Chamberlain's Men open the first Globe at Bankside. Oliver Cromwell born. Shakespeare's *Henry V, Julius Caesar,* and *As You Like It* produced.
1600	Shakespeare's *Hamlet* produced. The Fortune Theatre built.
1601	Shakespeare's *Twelfth Night* and *Troilus and Cressida* produced. The "war of the theaters": Dekker and Marston against Jonson.
1602	Shakespeare's *All's Well That Ends Well* produced.
1603	Elizabeth I dies 24 March; funeral 28 April.
1604	Shakespeare's *Measure for Measure* and *Othello* produced.
1605	Shakespeare's *King Lear* produced; Jonson's *The Mask of Blackness,* first collaboration with Inigo Jones.
1606	Shakespeare's *Macbeth* and *Antony and Cleopatra* produced; Jonson's *Volpone; or, The Fox* and *The Revenger's Tragedy* (ascribed first to Tourneur but later to Middleton). William Davenant born.
1607	Shakespeare's *Coriolanus, Timon of Athens,* and *Pericles;* Beaumont's *The Knight of the Burning Pestle.*
1609	Shakespeare's *Cymbeline* produced. The King's Men begin performances in the second Blackfriars theater. Beaumont and Fletcher's *Philaster; or, Love Lies a-Bleeding. Jonson's Epicoene* and *The Masque of Queens* (first antimasque).

1610	Shakespeare's *The Winter's Tale* and Jonson's *The Alchemist*.
1611	Shakespeare's *The Tempest* and Jonson's *Catiline* produced.
1612	Shakespeare collaborates on *Henry VIII*, perhaps with Fletcher. John Webster's *The White Devil* produced. Last Corpus Christi play at Kendal, Westmoreland.
1613	Shakespeare collaborates with Fletcher on *The Two Noble Kinsmen*. The Globe burns during performance of *Henry VIII*.
1614	Jonson's *Bartholomew Fair*; Webster's *The Duchess of Malfi*.
1616	William Shakespeare dies at Stratford (23 April). Beaumont and Henslowe die. Jonson's *Works* published.
1623	Publication of the First Folio edition of Shakespeare.
1628	Shirley's *The Witty Fair One*; Ford's *'Tis Pity She's a Whore*.
1630	Jonson's *Chloridia* (masque); Jonson's quarrel with Inigo Jones and loss of court patronage.
1632	William Prynne's *Histriomastix* published.
1637	Ben Jonson dies.
1639	Corpus Christi plays last performed at Kilkenny, Ireland.
1641	Brome's *The Joviall Crew*; Shirley's *The Cardinal*.
1642	Shirley's *The Sisters*. Parliamentary order closing theaters.
1642–1651	Civil wars between Royalists and Parliament.
1649	Raids on theaters by Commonwealth soldiers, 1 January. Trial and execution of Charles I.
1653	Oliver Cromwell installed as "lord protector." Robert Cox arrested for performing in drolls at the Red Bull.
1656	Sir William Davenant's *The Siege of Rhodes*.
1660	Restoration of Charles II: reopening of theaters.

NOTES AND REFERENCES

CHAPTER I: INTRODUCTION

1. John Dryden, "Essay of Dramatic Poesy" (1668, rev. ed. 1684), in Walter Jackson Bate, *Criticism: The Major Texts* (1952; New York: Harcourt Brace Jovanovich, 1970), 129–60.

2. See David Mills in A. C. Cawley et al., *The Revels History of Drama in English*, vol. 1, *Medieval Drama* (London and New York: Methuen, 1983), 80ff.; 304–7; R. W. Ingram ed., *Coventry*, Records of Early English Drama (Toronto: University of Toronto Press, 1981), xxv–xxx; G. Blakemore Evans in *The Riverside Shakespeare*, ed. G. Blakemore Evans (Boston: Houghton Mifflin, 1974), 32–36; Stanley Wells, "Shakespeare Criticism since Bradley," in Kenneth Muir and S. Schoenbaum, eds., *A New Companion to Shakespeare Studies* (Cambridge, Cambridge University Press, 1971), 249; Martin Butler, *Theatre and Crisis: 1632–1642* (Cambridge: Cambridge University Press, 1984). For the medieval revival of the nineteenth century see Alice Chandler, *A Dream of Order: The Medieval Ideal in Nineteenth-Century English Literature* (Lincoln: University of Nebraska Press, 1970).

3. Sir Walter Scott, "Essay on Drama," in *Miscellaneous Prose Works*, vol. 6 (Edinburgh: Cadell, 1827); Sir E[dmund] K[erchever] Chambers, *The Mediaeval Stage*, 2 vols. (Oxford: Oxford University Press, 1903); Butler, *Theatre and Crisis*, ix–24. I am indebted to an exceedingly useful discussion of critical principles and their application in Ronald W. Vince, *Ancient and Medieval Theatre: A Historiographical Handbook* (Westport, Conn. and London: Greenwood Press, 1984).

4. See Vince, *Ancient and Medieval Theatre;* H. C. Gardiner, *Mysteries' End,* Yale Studies in English, vol. 103 (New Haven: Yale University Press, 1946); F. M. Salter, *Mediaeval Drama in Chester* (Toronto: University of Toronto Press, 1955); Glynne Wickham, *Early English Stages, 1300–1660,* 3 vols. (London and Henley: Routledge and Kegan Paul; New York: Columbia University Press, 1980); O. B. Hardison, Jr., *Christian Rite and Christian Drama in the Middle Ages* (Baltimore: Johns Hopkins, 1965); V. A. Kolve, *The Play Called Corpus Christi* (Stanford: Stanford University Press, 1966); Rosemary Woolf, *The English Mystery Plays* (Berkeley: University of California Press, 1972); Martin Stevens, *Four Middle English Mystery Cycles: Textual, Contextual, and Critical Interpretations* (Princeton, N.J.: Princeton University Press, 1987).

5. See Butler, *Theatre and Crisis;* Leslie Hotson, *The Commonwealth and*

Restoration Stage (Cambridge, Mass.: Harvard University Press, 1928). For some examples of antitheatrical material, see Tertullian, *Apology and De Spectaculis*, ed. T. E. Page, trans. T. R. Glover, Loeb Classical Library (London: Heinemann, 1931); Clifford Davidson, ed., *A Middle English Treatise on the Playing of Miracles* (Washington, D.C.: University Press of America, 1981); W. Prynne, *Histriomaṣtix* (London, 1633). Excerpts from a variety of Elizabethan sources are reproduced in Sir E[dmund] K[erchever] Chambers, *The Elizabethan Stage*, vol. 4 (Oxford: Oxford University Press, 1923), 184–259.

6. On the social role of Roman drama see in general W. Beare, *The Roman Stage: A Short History of Latin Drama in the Time of the Republic* (London: Methuen, 1950); Margarete Bieber, *The History of the Greek and Roman Theater* (Princeton, N.J.: Princeton University Press, 1961); John Wacher, *The Towns of Roman Britain* (Berkeley and Los Angeles; University of California Press, 1974); Vince, *Ancient and Medieval Theatre;* and Ian Lancashire, *Dramatic Texts and Records of Britain: A Chronological Topography to 1558* (Toronto and Buffalo: University of Toronto Press, 1984), an immensely useful work to which I am indebted throughout this volume.

7. A variety of attempts to reconstruct early medieval drama can be found in Richard Axton, *European Drama of the Early Middle Ages* (London: Hutchinson, 1974); William Tydeman, *The Theatre in the Middle Ages* (Cambridge: Cambridge University Press, 1978); Glynne Wickham, *The Medieval Theatre*, 3d ed. (1974; rpt., Cambridge: Cambridge University Press, 1987); Allardyce Nicoll, *Masks, Mimes and Miracles* (London: Harrap, 1931); J. D. A. Ogilvy, "*Mimi, Scurrae, Histriones:* Entertainers of the Early Middle Ages," *Speculum* 38 (1963), 603–19. On the liturgical drama, see Hardison, *Christian Right;* C. Clifford Flanigan, "The Liturgical Drama and Its Tradition: A Review of Scholarship 1965–1975," *Research Opportunities in Renaissance Drama,* 18 (1975): 81–102; 19 (1976): 109–36. On the dramatic qualities of a particular Old English poem, see William Alfred, "The Drama of *The Wanderer,*" *The Wisdom of Poetry: Essays in Early English Literature in Honor of Morton W. Bloomfield,* ed. Larry D. Benson and Siegfried Wenzel (Kalamazoo, Mich.: Medieval Institute Publications, 1982), 31–44.

8. See Ian Lancashire's useful introduction to *Dramatic Texts and Records;* Chambers, *Medieval Stage;* R. M. Wilson, *The Lost Literature of Medieval England* (1952; rpt., London: Methuen, 1970), 209–33.

9. See Lancashire (*Dramatic Texts and Records*) for specific events and bibliography; Constance Bullock-Davies, *Menestrellorum Multitudo: Minstrels at a Royal Feast* (Cardiff: University of Wales Press, 1978); Nancy Cotton, "Katherine of Sutton: The First English Woman Playwright," *Educational Theatre Journal* 30 (1978): 475–81.

10. See Lancashire, *Dramatic Texts as Records;* and Wickham, *Early English Stages,* vols. 1–2, part 1. See also the volumes published in the Records of Early English Drama (REED) series on specific towns or regions, for example

Lawrence M. Clopper, ed., *Chester* (Toronto: University of Toronto Press, 1979); David Galloway, ed., *Norwich, 1540–1642* (Toronto: University of Toronto Press, 1984); Ingram, ed., *Coventry;* Alexandra F. Johnston and Margaret Rogerson, eds., *York,* 2 vols. (Toronto: University of Toronto Press, 1979).

11. See especially Butler, *Theatre and Crisis;* Peter Happé, ed., *Four Morality Plays* (Harmondsworth, England: Penguin, 1979); John Bale, *The Complete Plays,* ed. Peter Happé, 2 vols. (Cambridge: D. S. Brewer, 1986); Edmund Creeth, ed., *Tudor Plays* (New York: W. W. Norton, 1966). For pageantry of the early Tudor courts, see S. Anglo, *Spectacle, Pageantry, and Early Tudor Policy* (Oxford: Oxford University Press, 1969); G. E. Bentley, *The Jacobean and Caroline Stage,* 7 vols. (Oxford: Oxford University Press, 1941–66); Stephen Greenblatt, *Renaissance Self-Fashioning: From More to Shakespeare* (Chicago: University of Chicago Press, 1980).

12. Lancashire, introduction to *Dramatic Texts and Records;* Wickham, *Early English Stages.*

13. Wickham stresses the hall in *Early English Stages.* See also Chambers, *Elizabethan Stage,* and Bentley, *Jacobean and Caroline Stage,* on specific theaters.

14. Discussion of an extensive and ongoing debate over the extent of processional staging for the civic cycle plays can be traced in Alan H. Nelson, *The Medieval English Stage: Corpus Christi Pageants and Plays* (Chicago and London: University of Chicago Press, 1974); Stanley J. Kahrl, *Traditions of Medieval English Drama* (London: Hutchinson University Library, 1974); A. M. Nagler, *The Medieval Religious Stage: Shapes and Phantoms* (New Haven, Conn., and London: Yale University Press, 1976); and in discussions of staging in Wickham (*Early English Stages*), Lancashire (*Dramatic Texts and Records*), and Stevens (*Four Middle English Mystery Cycles*).

15. On the development of the Elizabethan stage, see Wickham, *Early English Stages,* vol. 2; Chambers, *Elizabethan Stage;* and Harry Levin's concise description in his introduction to *The Riverside Shakespeare,* ed. Evans.

16. See Lancashire (*Dramatic Texts and Records*) on specific archaeological finds and more generally Beare (*The Roman Stage*), Bieber (*Greek and Roman Theater*), Wacher (*The Towns of Roman Britain*), and Nicoll (*Masks, Mimes, and Miracles*).

17. See Nicoll, *Masks,* and Axton and Tydeman, *Theatre in the Middle Ages.*

18. See Karl Young, *The Drama of the Medieval Church,* 2 vols. (Oxford: Clarendon Press, 1933); Pamela Sheingorn, *The Easter Sepulchre in England,* Early Drama, Art and Music Reference Series, 5 (Kalamazoo: Medieval Institute Publications, 1987); David Bevington, ed., *Medieval Drama* (Boston: Houghton Mifflin, 1975), 3–29.

19. See Bevington, *Medieval Drama,* 75–121.

20. See Wickham, *Early English Stages;* Chambers, *Elizabethan Stage;* Levin, introduction to the *Riverside Shakespeare;* Philip Henslowe, *Henslowe's*

Diary, vol. 1, ed. R. A. Foakes and R. T. Rickert (Cambridge: Cambridge University Press, 1961), fos. 119v–120v.

21. See Allardyce Nicoll, *Stuart Masques and the Renaissance Stage* (New York: Benjamin Blom, 1968); Bentley, *Jacobean and Caroline Stage;* Butler, *Theatre and Crisis.* Inigo Jones's surviving designs have been reproduced and discussed in two most impressive volumes by Stephen Orgel and Roy Strong.

23. Much specific new information on the audiences of medieval drama will be forthcoming from the REED project volumes. Some of this is made available in compact form in Lancashire, *Dramatic Texts and Records;* see also Wickham, *Medieval Stage,* and Tydeman, *Theatre in the Middle Ages.*

24. On the Elizabethan audience see Alfred Harbage, *Shakespeare's Audience* (New York: Columbia University Press, 1941); Ann Jennalie Cook, *The Privileged Playgoers of Shakespeare's London* (Princeton, N.J.: Princeton University Press, 1981); and Butler, *Theatre and Crisis,* 293–306. See also Bentley, *Jacobean and Caroline Stage,* and Hotson, *Commonwealth and Restoration Stage.*

25. See Nicoll, *Masks;* Chambers, *Medieval Stage;* Ogilvy, "Entertainers of the Middle Ages"; Bullock-Davies, *Minstrels at a Royal Feast;* M. C. Bradbrook, *The Rise of the Common Player: A Study of Actor and Society in Shakespeare's England* (Cambridge, Mass.: Harvard University Press, 1962).

26. See the general comments of David Selzer on "The Actors and Staging" in Muir and Schoenbaum, eds., *A New Companion to Shakespeare Studies,* 35–54; for analysis of actors' opportunities in specific plays in Bevington, *Medieval Drama,* and more specific studies like Bevington's "Discontinuity in Medieval Acting Traditions," in *The Elizabethan Theatre,* Papers Given at the Fifth International Conference on Elizabethan Theatre, ed. G. R. Hibbard (Waterloo: University of Waterloo, 1975), 1–16; Joseph Bertram, *Elizabethan Acting* 2d ed. (Oxford: Oxford University Press, 1964); or Bertram's *The Tragic Actor* (London: Routledge, 1959).

CHAPTER II: EARLY DRAMA IN BRITAIN

1. See Vince, *Ancient and Medieval Theatre,* for a lucid discussion of the perils of anthropological inference; the major difficulties lie in the basic underlying principle that all early societies of the past or present day develop along the same lines. See also Hardison, *Christian Rite,* 1. On the early development of drama see Axton, *European Drama;* Wickham, *Medieval Theatre;* E. C. Cawte, *Ritual Animal Disguise* (Cambridge: D. S. Brewer, 1977).

2. On the social and economic development of population centers in Roman Britain in general, see Wacher, *Towns.*

3. See Collingwood, *Archaeology of Roman Britain;* see Bieber, *Greek and Roman Theater,* for a well-illustrated discussion of Roman theatrical architecture elsewhere in the empire. The recent London amphitheater excavations are

described in two articles for the general reader: Brian Hobley and Harvey Sheldon, "Big Bang Unearths London's Rich Past," *Illustrated London News* (May 1988): 40–45; John Maloney, "Fun and Games in Roman London," *Illustrated London News* (May 1988): 45–47. See Maloney, 48 in particular. For specific Roman theaters and amphitheaters see entries and useful analysis and bibliography in Lancashire, *Dramatic Texts and Records.* See also Kathleen M. Kenyon, "The Roman Theatre at Verulamium, St. Albans," *Archaeologia* 84 (1935): 213–61; Rosalind Dunnett, "The Excavation of the Roman Theatre at Gosbecks," *Britannia* 2 (1971): 27–47.

4. For the Roman religious calendar and its relation to drama see Beare, *The Roman Stage,* and Tydeman, *Theatre in the Middle Ages.*

5. Tertullian, *Apology and De Spectaculis,* ed. Page, trans. Glover.

6. See Beare, *The Roman Stage;* Bieber, *Greek and Roman Theater;* and Lancashire, *Dramatic Texts and Records,* for bibliography and concise discussion of specific archaeological finds in Britain.

7. Allardyce Nicoll attempts a reconstruction of the art of the Roman mimes in *Masks, Mimes, and Miracles.* For an overview of Roman legislation relating to the theater see the first section of Chambers, *Mediaeval Stage,* vol. 1.; for the final days of Roman drama see Peter Llewellyn, *Rome in the Dark Ages* (New York: Praeger, 1970), and Bevington, *Medieval Drama.*

8. See Wickham, *Medieval Theatre;* Ogilvy, "Entertainers of the Middle Ages."

9. See Lancashire, introduction to *Dramatic Texts and Records,* and specific entries listed by location.

10. See Jeff Opland, *Anglo-Saxon Oral Poetry: A Study of the Traditions* (New Haven, Conn.: Yale University Press, 1980); Ogilvy, "Entertainers of the Middle Ages"; Chambers, *Mediaeval Stage,* vol. 1; see also Edmond Faral, *Les Jongleurs en France au moyen age* (Paris: Champion, 1910).

11. See J. A. W. Bennett and G. V. Smithers, eds., *Early Middle English Verse and Prose* (Oxford: Oxford University Press, 1966), 77–95 and 196–200; Martin W. Walsh, "Performing *Dame Sirith:* Farce and *Fabliaux* at the End of the Thirteenth Century," in *England in the Thirteenth Century,* Proceedings of the 1984 Harlaxton Symposium, ed. W. M. Ormerod (Woodbridge, Suffolk, and Dover, N.H.: Boydell Press, 1986), 149–65.

12. See Opland, *Anglo-Saxon Oral Poetry,* and Alfred, "The Drama of *The Wanderer.*"

13. On medieval calendars and their importance to drama see Chambers, *Mediaeval Stage,* vol. 1; Wickham, *Medieval Theatre.*

14. On the folk play and its possible role in medieval drama, see Axton, *European Drama;* Wickham, *Medieval Theatre;* Tydeman, *Theatre in the Middle Ages;* Chambers, *Medieval Stage,* vol. 1. For some more specialized studies of the mummers' plays themselves, see Alan Brody, *The English Mummers and Their Plays: Traces of Ancient Mystery* (Philadelphia: University of Pennsylvania

Press, 1969, 1970); Alex Helm, *The English Mummer's Play,* Folklore Society (Cambridge: D. S. Brewer, 1981).

15. For more extensive discussion of the development of the liturgy and liturgical drama, see Young, *Drama of the Medieval Church;* Hardison, *Christian Right;* Flanigan, "The Liturgical Drama and Its Tradition"; Sheingorn, *Easter Sepulchre in England.* Major texts of the liturgical dramas under discussion in this section of the chapter appear in Young, *Drama of the Medieval Church;* Sheingorn; and Bevington, *Medieval Drama,* usually with helpful and accurate translations.

16. See Sheingorn, *Easter Sepulchre in England;* Thomas Symons, ed. and trans., *The Monastic Agreement of the Monks and Nuns of the English Nation: Regularis Concordia* (New York: Oxford University Press, 1953). "Break-through at Kalamazoo," *Medieval Music-Drama News* 7, no. 2 (Summer 1988):5–6, assesses Clifford and Audrey Davidson's 7 May 1988 production for the Society for Old Music reuniting the *Depositio* and *Elevatio* with the *Visitatio sepulchri.*

17. For additional twelfth-century background material, see Charles Homer Haskins, *The Renaissance of the Twelfth Century* (Cambridge, Mass.: Harvard University Press, 1927); Christopher Brooke, *The Twelfth-Century Renaissance* (1969; New York: Harcourt, Brace, 1970); Wickham, *Medieval Theatre;* Lancashire, *Dramatic Texts and Records,* xii. Major texts are helpfully edited and translated in Bevington, *Medieval Drama.*

18. See Walsh, "Performing *Dame Sirith*," *Thirteenth Century,* 149–65. Walsh connects *Dame Sirith* particularly with the twelfth-century Latin "elegiac comedies," in most cases written in the vicinity of the Loire valley, of which the most prominent are *Babio* and *Pamphilus.* The events mentioned can be found in geographical entries in Lancashire.

19. For Hilarius, see Young, *Drama of the Medieval Church,* 2:212–18; Bevington, *Medieval Drama,* 155–63; Lancashire, *Dramatic Texts and Records,* 335–36.

20. For two classic readings of the *Ordo representacionis Adae* see Henry Adams, *Mont-Saint-Michel and Chartres* (1904; New York: New American Library, 1961), 198–99; and Erich Auerbach, *Mimesis: The Representation of Reality in Western Literature,* trans. Willard R. Trask (Princeton, N.J.: Princeton University Press, 1953), 143–73.

21. See Young, *Drama of the Medieval Church,* vol. 2; Bevington, *Medieval Drama,* 79. For further background material, see Israel Abrahams, *Jewish Life in the Middle Ages* (New York: Athenaeum, 1969), 417–18; and Max L. Margolis and Alexander Marx, *A History of the Jewish People* (New York: Atheneum, 1973), 384–391. For further discussion of the background of medieval anti-Semitism and its appearance in later English literature see Robert Worth Frank, Jr., "Miracles of the Virgin, Medieval Anti-Semitism, and the 'Prioress's Tale,' " in *The Wisdom of Poetry,* ed. Benson and Wenzel, 177–88.

22. For texts and translations, see Bevington, *Medieval Drama,* 122–36.

23. For the "Shrewsbury Fragments," see Lancashire, *Dramatic Texts and Records,* 167; Norman Davis, ed., *Non-Cycle Plays and Fragments,* Early English Text Society (EETS) ss 1 (1970) (London, New York, Toronto: Oxford University Press, 1970), xiv–xxii, 1–7; Young, *Drama of the Medieval Church,* 2:514–23.

24. See Peter Dronke, *The Medieval Lyric* (1968: New York: Harper & Row, 1969), 186–206; Axton, *European Drama;* Chambers, *Mediaeval Stage.*

25. For the history of the tournament, see Larry D. Benson, *Malory's "Morte Darthur"* (Cambridge: Cambridge University Press, 1976), 163–85; Maurice Keen, *Chivalry* (New Haven, Conn.: Yale University Press, 1984), 83–101. For citations of other events I am again indebted to Lancashire, *Dramatic Texts and Records.* On the performers of this period, see Bullock-Davies, *Menestrellorum Multitudo.*

26. See B. J. Whiting, "The Vows of the Heron," *Speculum* 20 (1945): 261–78; Benson, *Malory's "Morte Darthur,"* 190; Keen, *Chivalry,* 213, 215. Other chivalric activities of Edward I are also discussed in Keen, 86, 93 97, 136–39.

27. Brian Stock, *The Implications of Literacy: Written Language and Models of Interpretation in the Eleventh and Twelfth Centuries* (Princeton, N.J.: Princeton University Press, 1983); on the Old English situation, see Katherine O'Brien O'Keeffe, "Orality and the Developing Text of Caedmon's *Hymn,*" *Speculum* 62 (1987): 1–20.

CHAPTER III: BRITISH DRAMA IN THE FOURTEENTH AND FIFTEENTH CENTURIES

1. For an overview of English history during this period see May McKisack, *The Fourteenth Century: 1307–1399,* vol. 4 in *The Oxford History of England* (London: Oxford University Press, 1959); and E. F. Jacob, *The Fifteenth Century: 1399–1485,* vol. 5 in *The Oxford History of England* (Oxford: Oxford University Press, 1961). On Shakespeare's reading of Chaucer, see E. T. Donaldson, *The Swan at the Well* (New Haven, Conn.: Yale University Press, 1985). See also Johan Huizinga, *The Waning of the Middle Ages,* trans. F. Hopman (1924; New York: Anchor Books, 1954); Barbara Tuchman, *A Distant Mirror: The Calamitous Fourteenth Century* (New York: Alfred A. Knopf, 1978); Charles T. Wood, review of Tuchman, in *Speculum* 54, no. 2 (April 1979): 430–35.

2. On the development and authorship of the Corpus Christi plays in general, see the useful discussions in Kolve, *The Play Called Corpus Christi;* Wickham, *Medieval Theatre;* Kahrl, *Traditions of Medieval English Drama;* Lancashire, introduction to *Dramatic Texts and Records;* Woolf, *English Mystery Plays;* and especially Stevens, *Middle English Mystery Cycles.* For specific locations,

see Lancashire and the appropriate REED volumes. References to tournaments in chronicles and letters of the period frequently supplement official documents.

3. For an overview of the critical history of medieval cycle plays, see Stevens, introduction to *Middle English Mystery Cycles*. For the debate for and against processional staging, especially of the York cycle, see Nelson, *The Medieval English Stage;* Kahrl, *Traditions of Medieval English Drama;* Nagler, *Medieval Renaissance Stage;* Wickham, *Early English Stages,* vol. 1; A. C. Cawley, "The Pageant Wagon and Processional Staging," in *The Revels History of Drama in English,* 1:23–30. The October 1983 Poculi Ludique Societas production of the York cycle at the University of Toronto tested the method of processional staging effectively and bore witness to the dramatic power of the cycle as a whole.

4. On the Cornish *Ordinalia* see Jane A. Bakere, *The Cornish Ordinalia: A Critical Study* (Cardiff: University of Wales Press, 1980); E. Norris, ed. and trans., *The Ancient Cornish Drama,* 2 vols. (Oxford: Oxford University Press, 1859); Markham Harris, trans., *The Cornish Ordinalia* (Washington, D.C.: Catholic University of America Press, 1969); Lancashire, *Dramatic Texts and Records,* 249; Cawley in *The Revels History of Drama in English,* 1:14–19, 309–10; R. Southern, *The Medieval Theatre in the Round* (London: Faber & Faber, 1957).

5. On the York cycle in general see Stevens, *Middle English Mystery Cycles;* Richard Beadle, ed., *The York Plays* (London: Edward Arnold, 1982); Johnston and Rogerson, eds., *York;* Lucy Toulmin Smith, ed., *York Plays* (Oxford: Clarendon Press, 1885). For the manuscript, see Richard Beadle and Peter Meredith, *The York Play: A Facsimile of British Library MS Additional 35290* (Leeds: University of Leeds, 1983). See also Clifford Davidson, *From Creation to Doom: The York Cycle of Mystery Plays* (New York: AMS Press, 1984); Clifford Davidson, *York Art: A Subject Index of Extant and Lost Art Including Items Relevant to Early Drama,* Early Drama, Art, and Music Monograph Series, 1 (Kalamazoo, Mich: Medieval Institute Publications, 1978). For York and other locations, see *Homo, Memento Finis: The Iconography of Just Judgment in Medieval Art and Drama* (papers by David Bevington, Huston Diehl, Richard Kenneth Emmerson, Ronald Herzman, and Pamela Sheingorn), Early Drama, Art, and Music Monograph Series, 6, (Kalamazoo, Mich.: Medieval Institute Publications, 1985); JoAnna Dutka, *Music in the English Mystery Plays,* Early Drama, Art, and Music Monograph Series, 2 (Kalamazoo, Mich.: Medieval Institute Publications, 1980); Martin W. Walsh, "Divine Cuckold/Holy Fool: The Comic Image of Joseph in the English 'Troubles' Play," *England in the Fourteenth Century: Proceedings of the 1985 Harlaxton Symposium,* ed. W. M. Ormerod (Woodbridge, Suffolk: Boydell Press, 1986), 278–97.

6. For Chester see Stevens, *Middle English Mystery Cycles;* Salter, *Mediaeval Drama in Chester;* Clopper, ed., *Chester;* Lawrence Clopper, "The History

and Development of the Chester Cycle," *Modern Philology* 75 (1978): 219–46; Peter W. Travis, *Dramatic Design in the Chester Cycle* (Chicago: University of Chicago Press, 1982).

7. For N-town, see Stevens, *Middle English Mystery Cycles;* Patrick J. Collins, *The N-town Plays and Medieval Picture Cycles,* Early Drama, Art, and Music Monograph Series, 2 (Kalamazoo, Mich.: Medieval Institute Publications, 1979); Kolve, *The Play Called Corpus Christi;* For the text see K. S. Block, ed., *Ludus Coventriae; or, The Plaie Called Corpus Christi,* EETS es 120 (1922 for 1917; rpt. 1960) (London, New York, Toronto: Oxford University Press, 1960). All quotations are taken from this edition. For the manuscript see Peter Meredith and Stanley Kahrl, eds., *The N-Town Plays: A Facsimile of British Library MS Cotton Vespasian D VIII* (Leeds: University of Leeds, 1977).

8. For the Towneley cycle see Stevens, *Middle English Mystery Cycles,* chapter 2. The text has been edited in A. C. Cawley, ed., *The Wakefield Pageants in the Towneley Cycle* (Manchester: Manchester University Press, 1958); George England, ed., *The Towneley Plays,* EETS es 71 (1897) (London, New York, Toronto: Oxford University Press, 1897); Martial Rose, ed., *The Wakefield Mystery Plays* (London: Evans Brothers, 1961); and selections appear in Bevington, *Medieval Drama.* For the manusript, see A. C. Cawley and Martin Stevens, eds., *The Towneley Cycle: A Facsimile of Huntington MS HM 1* (Leeds: University of Leeds, 1976). Critical studies include analysis in Woolf, *English Mystery Plays;* Jeffrey Helterman, *Symbolic Action in the Plays of the Wakefield Master* (Athens: University of Georgia Press, 1981); Arnold Williams, *The Characterization of Pilate in the Towneley Plays* (East Lansing: Michigan State University Press, 1950).

9. For Coventry material, see Ingram, ed., *Coventry;* Hardin Craig, ed., *Two Coventry Corpus Christi Plays,* 2d ed., EETS es 87 (1957) (London, New York, Toronto: Oxford University Press, 1957).

10. London records are forthcoming in the REED series. See Lancashire, *Dramatic Texts and Records,* xx, and specific entries for London and vicinity.

11. For records of drama at numerous locations outside London, see Lancashire and the REED series volumes. See also Davis, ed., *Non-Cycle Plays and Fragments.*

12. Davidson, ed., *A Middle English Treatise.* All quotations are taken from this edition.

13. For civic pageantry see Lancashire, *Dramatic Texts and Records;* Cawley in *The Revels History of Drama in English,* 1:31; Robert Withington, *English Pageantry, an Historical Outline,* 2 vols. (Cambridge, Mass.: Harvard University Press, 1918–20); Wickham, *Early English Stages,* vol. 1.

14. For the morality plays in general see Mark Eccles, ed., *The Macro Plays,* EETS os 262 (1969) (London, New York, Toronto: Oxford University Press, 1969); David Bevington, *Medieval Drama;* A. C. Cawley, ed., *Everyman and Medieval Miracle Plays* (London: J. M. Dent, 1956); Happé, ed., *Four*

Morality Plays, especially for the text and useful discussion of the *Castle of Perseverance*; M. R. Kelley, "Fifteenth-century Flamboyant Style and *The Castle of Perseverance*," *Comparative Drama* 6 (1972): 14–27; Sumiko Miyajima, *The Theatre of Man: Dramatic Technique and Stagecraft in the English Medieval Moral Plays* (New York: Avon, 1977); Robert Potter, *The English Morality Play* (London: Routledge & Kegan Paul, 1975).

15. On the saint's plays and miracle or conversion plays, see Donald C. Baker, John L. Murphy, and Louis B. Hall, Jr., eds., *The Late Medieval Religious Plays of Bodleian MSS Digby 133 and E Museo 160*, EETS os 283 (1982) (Oxford: Oxford University Press, 1982); F. J. Furnivall, ed., *The Digby Plays*, EETS es 70 (1896; rpt. 1967) (Oxford: Oxford University Press, 1967); David Bevington, *Medieval Drama*, David Mills in *The Revels History*, 1:146–151 and other useful sections of the same volume.

16. On royal pageantry from Edward II to Richard III see Lancashire, *Dramatic Texts and Records*, xiv–xxiii, and individual entries; Withington, *English Pageantry*; Wickham, *Early English Stages*, vol. 1. See also John Lydgate, *The Minor Poems of John Lydgate*, ed. Henry Noble MacCracken, part 2, Secular Poems, EETS os 192 (1934 for 1933) (London: Oxford University Press, 1934). Lydgate's authorship of several of the mummings ascribed to him has been plausibly challenged.

17. On Robin Hood plays see David Wiles, *The Early Plays of Robin Hood* (Cambridge: D. S. Brewer, 1981); David Mills in *The Revels History*, 1:133–138; Joseph Quincy Adams, *Chief Pre-Shakespearean Dramas* (Boston: Houghton Mifflin, 1924), 345–49.

CHAPTER IV: THE SIXTEENTH CENTURY

1. For useful background information on early Tudor and Elizabethan England, see J. D. Mackie, *The Earlier Tudors, 1485–1558*, vol. 7 of *Oxford History of England* (Oxford: Clarendon Press, 1952); J. B. Black, *The Reign of Elizabeth, 1558–1603*, vol. 8 of *Oxford History of England* (1959); J. J. Scarisbrick, *Henry VIII* (Berkeley: University of California Press, 1968); Steven Ozment, *The Age of Reform, 1250–1350* (New Haven, Conn., and London: Yale University Press, 1980). Throughout this chapter I have of course depended heavily on a number of essential reference works, particularly Wickham, *Early English Stages*, vols. 1–3; E. K. Chambers, *The Elizabethan Stage*; David Bevington, *From Mankind to Marlowe*; Bevington, ed., *Medieval Drama*; Creeth, ed., *Tudor Plays*; F. P. Wilson, *The English Drama, 1485–1585* (Oxford: Oxford University Press, 1969); Phyllis Hartnoll, ed., *The Concise Oxford Companion to the Theatre* (1972; Oxford: Oxford University Press, 1986); and Lancashire, *Dramatic Texts and Records*.

2. On the English Reformation, see for instance Ozment, *The Age of Reform*; Scarisbrick, *Henry VIII*, especially chapters 7–8; Elizabeth L. Eisen-

stein, *The Printing Press as an Agent of Change* (Cambridge: Cambridge University Press, 1979).

3. On the sixteenth-century moralities see Happé, ed., *Four Morality Plays;* Bevington, ed., *Medieval Drama;* Bevington, *From Mankind to Marlowe;* Cawley, ed., *Everyman and Medieval Miracle Plays;* John Skelton, *Magnyfycence,* ed. Robert Lee Ramsay, EETS es 98 (1908 for 1906; rpt. 1958) (London: Oxford University Press, 1958); M. Pollet, *John Skelton: Poet of Tudor England,* trans. Warrington (Lewisburg, Pa.: Bucknell University Press, 1971); A. R. Heisterman, *Skelton and Satire* (Chicago: Chicago University Press, 1961); Bale, *The Complete Plays,* ed. Happé; T. B. Blatt, *The Plays of John Bale: A Study of Ideas, Technique, and Style* (Copenhagen: Gad, 1968); W. Murison, *Sir David Lyndsay, Poet and Satirist of the Old Church in Scotland* (Cambridge: Cambridge University Press, 1938). See also Joanne Spencer Kantrowitz, *Dramatic Allegory: Lindsay's Ane Satyre of the Thrie Estaitis* (Lincoln: University of Nebraska Press, 1975).

4. On Gosson, see Chambers, *Elizabethan Stage,* 1:253–60; 4:203–5.

5. On the end of the Corpus Christi cycles, see Gardiner, *Mysteries' End;* see also relevant discussion in Stevens, *Four Medieval Mystery Cycles,* and Cawley, ed., *The Revels History,* vol. 1.

6. On humanist drama see Bevington, *Medieval Drama;* Bevington, *From Mankind to Marlowe;* Creeth, ed., *Tudor Plays;* Lancashire, introduction to *Dramatic Texts and Records,* and relevant entries. See also F. S. Boas, *Introduction to Tudor Drama* (Oxford: Oxford University Press, 1933).

7. For court pageantry see Anglo, *Spectacle, Pageantry, and Early Tudor Policy;* see also F. S. Boas, *University Drama in the Tudor Age* (Oxford: Oxford University Press, 1914); David Bevington, *Tudor Drama and Tudor Politics: A Critical Approach to Topical Meaning* (Cambridge, Mass.: Harvard University Press, 1968); T. W. Craik, *The Tudor Interlude* (Leicester: Leicester University Press, 1958); Stephen Orgel, *The Illusion of Power: Political Theatre in the English Renaissance* (Berkeley: University of California Press, 1975); on the Inns of Court at a later date see P. J. Finkelpearl, *John Marston of the Middle Temple* (Cambridge: Harvard University Press, 1969); Dieter Mehl, *The Elizabethan Dumb Show* (London: Methuen, 1965).

8. On the rise of touring companies and stages, see Chambers, *Elizabethan Stage;* Bradbrook, *The Rise of the Common Player;* Wickham, *Early English Stages,* vols. 1–3; Lancashire, *Dramatic Texts and Records,* introduction and specific entries.

9. On major companies and their development, see Chambers, *Elizabethan Stage;* G. E. Bentley, *The Profession of Actor in Shakespeare's Time* (Princeton, N.J.: Princeton University Press, 1984); Henslowe, *Henslowe's Diary,* ed. Foakes and Rickert; Reavley Gair, *The Children of Paul's: The Story of a Theatre Company 1553–1608* (Cambridge: Cambridge University Press, 1982); Michael Shapiro, *Children of the Revels* (New York: Columbia University Press, 1977).

On European tours see Jerzy Limon, *Gentlemen of a Company: English Players in Central and Eastern Europe, 1590–1660* (Cambridge: Cambridge University Press, 1985), and refer to specific entries in Hartnoll, ed., *Concise Oxford Companion*.

10. On the debate over the Elizabethan audiences see Harbage, *Shakespeare's Audiences;* Cook, *The Privileged Playgoers of Shakespeare's London;* Butler, *Theatre and Crisis,* appendix 2:293–306. I am much indebted to this illuminating study.

11. On Munday and Greene see relevant entries in Chambers, *Elizabethan Stage,* vol. 3; Anthony Munday, *Pageants and Entertainments,* ed. David M. Bergeron (New York and London: Garland, 1985). See also G. E. Bentley, *The Profession of Dramatist in Shakespeare's Time, 1590–1642* (Princeton, N.J.: Princeton University Press, 1971).

12. On Christopher Marlowe, see Christopher Marlowe, *The Complete Plays,* ed. Irving Ribner (Indianapolis and New York: Bobbs-Merrill, 1963); Christopher Marlowe, *The Plays,* ed. R. Gill (Oxford: Oxford University Press, 1971); Bevington, *From Mankind to Marlowe;* M. C. Bradbrook, *Themes and Conventions of Elizabethan Tragedy,* 2d ed. (Cambridge: Cambridge University Press, 1952); Harry Levin, *The Overreacher: A Study of Christopher Marlowe* (Cambridge, Mass.: Harvard University Press, 1952); Michel Poirier, *Christopher Marlowe* (London: Chatto & Windus, 1951).

13. See also Chambers, *Elizabethan Stage,* vol. 3, for relevant entries; see also M. C. Bradbrook, *The Growth and Structure of Elizabethan Comedy* (1955; Harmondsworth, England: Penguin, 1963); Peter Saccio, *The Court Comedies of John Lyly: A Study in Allegorical Dramaturgy* (Princeton, N.J.: Princeton University Press, 1969); Thomas Nashe, *Works,* ed. R. B. McKerrow, 5 vols. (London: Sidgwick & Jackson, 1904–10); George Peele, *The Life and Works of George Peele,* ed. F. S. Hook, 3 vols. (New Haven, Conn.: Yale University Press, 1970); George Peele, *The Old Wives Tale,* ed. Patricia Binnie, The Revels Plays (Manchester: Manchester University Press; Baltimore: Johns Hopkins University Press, 1980). I am indebted to the editor's lucid introduction to this edition.

14. For Shakespeare I am continually indebted in the discussion that follows to the editors and contributors to *The Riverside Shakespeare,* ed. Evans. For a variety of critical comment on Shakespeare, see also C. L. Barber, *Shakespeare's Festive Comedy* (Princeton, N.J.: Princeton University Press, 1959); Alfred Harbage, *Shakespeare and the Rival Traditions* (Bloomington: Indiana University Press, 1952); Muir and Schoenbaum, eds, *A New Companion to Shakespeare Studies;* Norman Rabkin, *Shakespeare and the Problem of Meaning* (Chicago: University of Chicago Press, 1981); S. Schoenbaum, *William Shakespeare: A Compact Documentary Life* (Oxford: Oxford University Press, 1975).

15. See Thomas Dekker, *The Dramatic Works,* ed. Fredson Bowers, 4

vols. (Cambridge: Cambridge University Press, 1953–61); Chambers, *Elizabethan Drama*, vol. 3 and relevant entries; Ben Jonson, *Works*, ed. C. H. Herford and Percy and Evelyn Simpson, 11 vols. (Oxford: Oxford University Press, 1925–52); L. C. Knights, *Drama and Society in the Age of Jonson* (London: Chatto, 1957).

CHAPTER V: THE SEVENTEENTH CENTURY

1. For an overview of the seventeenth century to 1660, see Godfrey Davies, *The Early Stuarts, 1603–1660*, vol. 9 of *Oxford History of England* (1959); Basil Willey, *The Seventeenth Century Background* (1934; New York: Doubleday, n.d.); G. P. V. Akrigg, *Jacobean Pageant: The Court of James I* (Cambridge: Harvard University Press, 1963); C. V. Wedgewood, *The King's War, 1641–1647* (London: Collins, 1958) and *The King's Peace, 1637–1641* (London: Collins, 1955). The major sources for the theater up to 1642 are Bentley, *The Jacobean and Caroline Stage;* and Wickham, *Early English Stages*, vol. 2. See also Frederick S. Boas, *An Introduction to Stuart Drama* (London and New York: Oxford University Press, 1946). Throughout this chapter I am deeply indebted to Butler, *Theatre and Crisis.*

2. For the works of Shakespeare after 1603, see *The Riverside Shakespeare.* I am indebted in the extreme to the lucid introductions to the plays as well as Professor Levin's main introduction and the admirable edition as a whole.

3. For Jonson's Jacobean plays, see Jonson, *Works;* Knights, *Drama and Society in the Age of Jonson.*

4. See also Chambers, *Elizabethan Stage,* vol. 3 and relevant entries; Bentley, *Jacobean and Caroline Stage;* Robert Ornstein, *The Moral Vision of Jacobean Tragedy* (Madison: University of Wisconsin Press, 1960); Cyril Tourneur, *The Plays,* ed. George Parfitt (Cambridge: Cambridge University Press, 1978); Cyril Tourneur, *Works,* ed. Allardyce Nicoll (London: Fanfrolico Press, 1930); Thomas Middleton, *Selected Plays,* ed. David L. Frost (Cambridge: Cambridge University Press, 1978); Thomas Middleton, *Works,* ed. Alexander Dyce, 5 vols. (London, 1840); John Marston, *The Plays,* ed. H. Harvey Wood, 3 vols. (Edinburgh: Oliver & Boyd, 1934–39); John Marston, *The Selected Plays,* ed. MacDonald P. Jackson and Michael Neill (Cambridge: Cambridge University Press, 1986); Finkelpearl, *John Marston of the Middle Temple;* R. W. Ingram, *John Marston* (Boston: Twayne, 1978); Thomas Heywood, *A Woman Killed with Kindness,* ed. R. W. van Fossen, The Revels Plays (Cambridge, Mass.: Harvard University Press, 1961).

5. See Fredson Bowers, ed., *The Dramatic Works of the Beaumont and Fletcher Canon,* 11 vols. (Cambridge: Cambridge University Press, 1966); Ralph Berry, *The Art of John Webster* (Oxford: Clarendon, 1972); M. C. Bradbrook, *John Webster: Citizen and Dramatist* (London: Weidenfeld & Nicolson,

1980); John Ford, *Works,* ed. William Gifford and Alexander Dyce, 3 vols. (London: J. Toovey, 1869); John Ford, *The Selected Plays,* ed. Colin Gibson (Cambridge: Cambridge University Press, 1986); Donald K. Anderson, *John Ford* (New York: Twayne, 1972); Joan M. Sargeaunt, *John Ford* (Oxford: Basil Blackwell, 1935). Finkelpearl, *John Marston of the Middle Temple,* is also relevant for Ford's legal milieu.

6. See Butler, *Theatre and Crisis;* see also Philip Massinger, *The Plays and Poems,* ed. Philip Edwards and Colin Gibson, 5 vols. (Oxford: Oxford University Press, 1976); Philip Massinger, *Selected Plays,* Ed. Colin Gibson (Cambridge: Cambridge University Press, 1978); George Bas, *James Shirley (1596–1666): Dramaturge Caroléen* (Lille: Service de reproduction des thèses, 1973); James Shirley, *The Cardinal,* ed. E. M. Yearling, The Revels Plays (Manchester: Manchester University Press, 1986); James Shirley, *Hyde Park,* RSC Swan Theatre, commentary by Simon Trussell (London: Methuen, 1987); James Shirley, *Works,* ed. W. Gifford and A. Dyce, 6 vols. (London: John Murray, 1833); Richard Brome, *Dramatic Works,* 3 vols. (London: John Pearson, 1873).

7. For changes in companies and theaters see Bentley, *Jacobean and Caroline Stage;* Wickham, *Early English Stages,* vol. 2; Butler, *Theatre and Crisis;* Hartnoll, ed., *Concise Oxford Companion,* specific entries.

8. For the Stuart masque, see Jonson, *Works;* Chambers, *Elizabethan Stage,* 3: 352–94; Bentley, *Jacobean and Caroline Stage;* Wickham, *Early English Stages,* vol. 2; Allardyce Nicoll, *Stuart Masques and the Renaissance Stage* (New York: Benjamin Blom, 1968); and especially Stephen Orgel, *The Jonsonian Masque* (Cambridge, Mass.: Harvard University Press, 1967). See also Edith Welsford, *The Court Masque* (Cambridge: Cambridge University Press, 1927).

9. See Nicoll, *Stuart Masques;* Thomas Campion, *Works,* ed. Walter R. Davis (London: Faber & Faber, 1969); John Milton, *A Mask Presented at Ludlow Castle* in Merritt Y. Hughes, ed., *Complete Poetry and Major Prose* (Indianapolis: Bobbs-Merrill, 1957). Milton's character Comus derives from Jonson's masque *Pleasure Reconciled with Virtue.*

10. For university drama and the Inns of Court, see Bentley, *Jacobean and Caroline Stage;* Lancashire, *Dramatic Texts and Records,* specific locations; Finkelpearl, *John Marston of the Middle Temple;* Hartnoll, ed., *Concise Oxford Companion,* specific entries.

11. See Leslie Hotson, *The Commonwealth and Restoration Stage* (Cambridge, Mass.: Harvard University Press, 1928); Bentley, *Jacobean and Caroline Stage;* Butler, *Theatre and Crisis.*

12. For Davenant see Hotson; for his earlier career, see Butler.

SELECTED BIBLIOGRAPHY

PRIMARY WORKS

Baker, Donald C., John L. Murphy, and Louis B. Hall, Jr., eds. *The Late Medieval Religious Plays of Bodleian MSS Digby 133 and E Museo 160*. Early English Text Society (EETS) os 283 (1982). Oxford: Oxford University Press, 1982.

Bale, John. *The Complete Plays,* edited by Peter Happé. 2 vols. Cambridge: D. S. Brewer, 1986.

Beadle, Richard, ed. *The York Plays*. London: Edward Arnold, 1982.

Bevington, David, ed. *Medieval Drama*. Boston: Houghton Mifflin, 1975.

Block, K. S., ed. *Ludus Coventriae; or, The Plaie Called Corpus Christi*. EETS es 120 (1922 for 1917; rpt. 1960). London, New York, Toronto: Oxford University Press, 1960.

Bowers, Fredson, ed. *The Dramatic Works in the Beaumont and Fletcher Canon*. 11 vols. Cambridge: Cambridge University Press, 1966.

Brome, Richard. *Dramatic Works*. 3 vols. London: John Pearson, 1873.

Campion, Thomas. *Works,* edited by Walter R. Davis. London: Faber & Faber, 1969.

Cawley, A. C., ed. *Everyman and Medieval Miracle Plays*. London: J. M. Dent, 1956.

————, ed. *The Wakefield Pageants in the Towneley Cycle*. Manchester: Manchester University Press, 1958.

Clopper, Lawrence M., ed. *Chester*. Records of Early English Drama. Toronto: University of Toronto Press, 1979.

Creeth, Edmund, ed. *Tudor Plays*. New York: W. W. Norton, 1966.

Davidson, Clifford, ed. *A Middle English Treatise on the Playing of Miracles*. Washington, D.C.: University Press of America, 1981.

Davis, Norman, ed. *Non-Cycle Plays and Fragments*. EETS ss 1 (1970). London, New York, Toronto: Oxford University Press, 1970.

Dekker, Thomas. *The Dramatic Works,* edited by Fredson Bowers. 4 vols. Cambridge: Cambridge University Press, 1953–61.

Eccles, Mark, ed. *The Macro Plays*. EETS os 262 (1969) London, New York, Toronto: Oxford University Press, 1969.

England, George, ed. *The Towneley Plays*. EETS es 71 (1897). London, New York, Toronto: Oxford University Press, 1897.

Ford, John. *Works,* edited by William Gifford; revised by Alexander Dyce. 3 vols. London: J. Toovey, 1869.

————. *The Selected Plays,* edited by Colin Gibson. Cambridge: Cambridge University Press, 1986.

Furnivall, F. J., ed. *The Digby Plays.* EETS es 70 (1896; rpt. 1967). Oxford: Oxford University Press, 1967.

Galloway, David, ed. *Norwich, 1540–1642.* Records of Early English Drama. Toronto: University of Toronto Press, 1984.

Happé, Peter, ed. *Four Morality Plays.* Harmondsworth, England: Penguin, 1979.

Henslowe, Philip. *Henslowe's Diary,* edited by R. A. Foakes and R. T. Rickert. Cambridge: Cambridge University Press, 1961.

Heywood, Thomas. *A Woman Killed with Kindness,* edited by R. W. van Fossen. The Revels Plays. Cambridge, Mass.: Harvard University Press, 1961.

Ingram, R. W., ed. *Coventry.* Records of Early English Drama. Toronto: University of Toronto Press, 1981.

Johnston, Alexandra F., and Margaret Rogerson, eds. *York.* 2 vols. Records of Early English Drama. Toronto: University of Toronto Press, 1979.

Johnson, Ben. *Works,* edited by C. H. Herford and Percy and Evelyn Simpson. 11 vols. Oxford: Oxford University Press, 1925–52.

Lumiansky, R. M., and David Mills, eds. *The Chester Mystery Cycle.* EETS ss 3 (1974). London, New York, Toronto: Oxford University Press, 1974.

Lydgate, John. *The Minor Poems of John Lydgate,* edited by Henry Noble MacCracken. Part 2: Secular Poems. EETS os 192 (1934 for 1933). London: Oxford University Press, 1934.

Marlowe, Christopher. *The Complete Plays,* edited by Irving Ribner. Indianapolis and New York: Bobbs-Merrill, 1963.

————. *The Plays,* edited by R. Gill. Oxford: Oxford University Press, 1971.

Marston, John. *The Plays,* edited by H. Harvey Wood. 3 vols. Edinburgh: Oliver & Boyd, 1934–39.

————. *The Selected Plays,* edited by MacDonald P. Jackson and Michael Neill. Cambridge: Cambridge University Press, 1986.

Massinger, Philip. *The Plays and Poems,* edited by Philip Edwards and Colin Gibson. 5 vols. Oxford: Oxford University Press, 1976.

————. *Selected Plays,* edited by Colin Gibson. Cambridge: Cambridge University Press, 1978.

Meredith, Peter, and John E. Tailby, eds. *The Staging of Religious Drama in Europe in the Later Middle Ages: Texts and Documents in English Translation.* Early Drama, Art, and Music Monograph Series, 4. Kalamazoo, Mich.: Medieval Institute Publications, 1982.

Middleton, Thomas. *Selected Plays,* edited by David L. Frost. Cambridge: Cambridge University Press, 1978.

————. *Works,* edited by Alexander Dyce. 5 vols. London, 1840.

Munday, Anthony. *Pageants and Entertainments,* edited by David M. Bergeron. New York and London: Garland, 1985.

Nagler, A. M. *A Source Book in Theatrical History.* 1952; New York: Dover, 1959.

Nashe, Thomas. *Works,* edited by R. B. McKerrow. London: Sidgwick & Jackson, 1904–10.

Odenkirchen, Carl J., ed. *The Play of Adam.* Brookline, Mass., and Leyden: Classical Folia Editions, 1976.

Peele, George. *The Life and Works of George Peele,* edited by F. S. Hook. 3 vols. New Haven, Conn.: Yale University Press, 1970.

————. *The Old Wives Tale,* edited by Patricia Binnie. The Revels Plays. Manchester: Manchester University Press; Baltimore: Johns Hopkins University Press, 1980.

Shakespeare, William. *The Riverside Shakespeare,* edited by G. Blakemore Evans. Boston: Houghton Mifflin, 1974.

Shirley, James. *The Cardinal,* edited by E. M. Yearling. The Revels Plays. Manchester: Manchester University Press, 1986.

————. *Hyde Park.* London: Methuen, 1987.

————. *Works,* edited by W. Gifford and A. Dyce. 6 vols. London: John Murray, 1833.

Skelton, John. *Magnyfycence,* edited by Robert Lee Ramsay. EETS es 98 (1908 for 1906; rpt. 1958). London: Oxford University Press, 1958.

Smith, Lucy Toulmin, ed. *York Plays.* Oxford: Clarendon Press, 1885.

Tertullian. *Apology and De Spectaculis,* edited by T. E. Page. Trans. T. R. Glover. Loeb Classical Library. London: Heinemann, 1931.

Tourneur, Cyril. *The Plays,* edited by George Parfitt. Cambridge: Cambridge University Press, 1978.

————. *Works,* edited by Allardyce Nicoll. New York, 1923.

Webster, John. *The Complete Works,* edited by F. L. Lucas. 4 vols. London: Chatto, 1966.

————. *Selected Plays,* edited by Jonathan Dollimore and Alan Sinfield. Cambridge: Cambridge University Press, 1983.

SECONDARY WORKS

REFERENCE GUIDES AND BIBLIOGRAPHIES

Davidson, Clifford. *Drama and Art: An Introduction to the Use of Evidence from the Visual Arts for the Study of Early Drama.* Early Drama, Art, and Music Monograph Series, 1. Kalamazoo, Mich. Medieval Institute Publications, 1977. Essential introduction to the field.

Davidson, Clifford, and Jennifer Alexander. *The Early Art of Coventry,*

Stratford-upon-Avon, Warwick and Lesser Sites in Warwickshire: A Subject List of Extant and Lost Art Including Items Relevant to Early Drama. Early Drama, Art, and Music Reference Series, 4. Kalamazoo, Mich.: Medieval Institute Publications, 1988. Indispensable reference work on this subject.

Davidson, Clifford. *York Art: A Subject Index of Extant and Lost Art Including Items Relevant to Early Drama.* Early Drama, Art, and Music Monograph Series, 1. Kalamazoo, Mich.: Medieval Institute Publications, 1978. Indispensable reference work on this subject.

EDAM Newsletter. Edited by Clifford Davidson. Quarterly. Kalamazoo, Mich.: Medieval Institute Publications, 1979–. Especially useful for recent advances in the field of early drama, art, and music.

Harbage, A. *Annals of English Drama, 975–1700.* Revised by S. Schoenbaum. London: Methuen, 1962; supplements 1966 and 1970. Standard reference on the subject.

Hartnoll, Phyllis, ed. *The Concise Oxford Companion to the Theatre.* 1972; Oxford: Oxford University Press, 1986. A very helpful reference.

Lancashire, Ian. *Dramatic Texts and Records of Britain: A Chronological Topography to 1558.* Toronto and Buffalo: University of Toronto Press, 1984. Exceptionally useful reference work and commentary.

Logan, Terence P., and Denzell S. Smith, eds. *The New Intellectuals: A Survey and Bibliography of Recent Studies in English Renaissance Drama.* Lincoln and London: University of Nebraska Press, 1977. Indispensable reference work on this subject.

Stratman, Carl J. *Bibliography of Medieval Drama.* 2 vols. 2d ed. New York: Frederick Ungar, 1972. Indispensable reference work on this subject.

Wells, Stanley, ed. *English Drama: Select Bibliographical Guides.* Oxford: Oxford University Press, 1975. Excellent as a guide to further research.

GENERAL CRITICAL STUDIES

Chambers, Sir E[dmund] K[erchever]. *The Elizabethan Stage.* 4 vols. Oxford: Oxford University Press, 1923. Indispensable reference and critical work.

———. *The Mediaeval Stage.* 2 vols. Oxford: Oxford University Press, 1903. Still an essential reference in the field.

Gascoigne, Bamber. *World Theatre.* Ebury Press. Boston: Little, Brown, 1968. A well-illustrated overview of the topic.

Kahrl, Stanley. *Traditions of Medieval Drama.* London: Hutchinson, 1974. One of the key studies in the field.

Mill, A. J. *Medieval Plays in Scotland.* Edinburgh: W. Blackwood and Sons, Ltd., 1927. Still the standard work on the subject.

Nagler, A. M. *The Medieval Religious Stage: Shapes and Phantoms.* New Haven, Conn., and London: Yale University Press, 1976. An astute commentary on the available evidence.

Nicoll, Allardyce. *History of English Drama, 1600–1900.* 6 vols. Cambridge:

Cambridge University Press, 1952–59. One of the primary overviews of the field.

Potter, Lois, gen. ed. *The Revels History of Drama in English.* 4 vols. London and New York: Methuen, 1983. An exceptionally helpful series.

Rossiter, A. P. *English Drama from Early Times to the Elizabethans.* London and New York: Hutchinson's Universal Library, 1950. Readable and lively account of the topic.

Tydeman, William. *English Medieval Theatre: 1400–1500.* London, Boston, Henley: Routledge & Kegan Paul, 1986. One of the most useful recent studies.

———. *The Theatre in the Middle Ages.* Cambridge: Cambridge University Press, 1978. An astute overview of English and European evidence.

Wickham, Glynne. *The Medieval Theatre.* 3d ed. 1974: Cambridge; Cambridge University Press, 1987. An excellent concise history, especially good on staging.

Young, Karl. *The Drama of the Medieval Church.* 2 vols. Oxford: Clarendon Press, 1933. Still an essential reference in the field.

SURVEYS OF SOCIAL AND HISTORICAL CONTEXT OF DRAMA

Adams, Henry. *Mont-Saint-Michel and Chartres.* 1904; New York: New American Library, 1961. A classic both in American literature and medieval studies.

Greenblatt, Stephen. *Renaissance Self-Fashioning: From More to Shakespeare.* Chicago: University of Chicago Press, 1980. A provocative reassessment of the period.

Owst, G. R. *Literature and Pulpit in Medieval England.* Cambridge: Cambridge University Press, 1933. Still an essential reference in the field.

Willey, Basil. *The Seventeenth Century Background.* 1934; New York: Doubleday, n.d. Still a readable and informative account of the era.

SPECIALIZED STUDIES

Bakere, Jane A. *The Cornish Ordinalia: A Critical Study.* Cardiff: University of Wales Press, 1980. The standard critical work in the field.

Bergeron, David. *English Civic Pageantry, 1558–1642.* London: Edward Arnold, 1971. An essential study of the subject.

Brody, Alan. *The English Mummers and Their Plays: Traces of Ancient Mystery.* Philadelphia: University of Pennsylvania Press, 1969, 1970. An essential study of the subject.

Davidson, Clifford et al., eds. *Drama in the Middle Ages: Comparative and Critical Essays.* New York: AMS Press, 1982. One of the most useful collections of critical essays.

Helm, Alex. *The English Mummer's Play.* Folklore Society. Cambridge: D. S. Brewer, 1981. An essential study of the subject.

Homo, Memento Finis: The Iconography of Just Judgement in Medieval Art and Drama. Papers by David Bevington, Huston Diehl, Richard Kenneth Emmerson, Ronald Herzman, and Pamela Sheingorn. Early Drama, Art, and Music Monograph Series, 6. Kalamazoo, Mich.: Medieval Institute Publications, 1985. A valuable collection of essays on this key topic.

Nicoll, Allardyce. *Masks, Mimes and Miracles.* London: Harrap, 1931. A provocative reconstruction of the mime tradition.

Prosser, Eleanor. *Drama and Religion in the English Miracle Plays.* Stanford: Stanford University Press, 1961. A useful and provocative study of the subject.

Sheingorn, Pamela. *The Easter Sepulchre in England.* Early Drama, Art, and Music Monograph Series, 5. Kalamazoo, Mich.: Medieval Institute Publications, 1987. The essential study of the subject.

Southern, R. *The Mediaeval Theatre in the Round.* London: Faber & Faber, 1957. Presents a celebrated and provocative theory of staging.

Taylor, J., and A. H. Nelson, eds. *Medieval English Drama; Essays Critical and Contextual.* Chicago: University of Chicago Press, 1972. One of the best collections of critical essays in the field.

Whiting, B. J. *Proverbs in the Earlier English Drama.* Cambridge: Harvard University Press, 1928. An essential study of this important subject.

Wickham, Glynne. *Early English Stages, 1300–1660.* 3 vols. London and Henley: Routledge & Kegan Paul; New York: Columbia University Press, 1980. An essential reference work and analysis of the topic.

Wiles, David. *The Early Plays of Robin Hood.* Cambridge: D. S. Brewer, 1981. An essential study of the subject.

Withington, Robert. *English Pageantry, an Historical Outline.* 2 vols. Cambridge, Mass.: Harvard University Press, 1918–20. An essential study of the subject.

BRITISH DRAMA TO 1300

Axton, Richard. *European Drama of the Early Middle Ages.* London: Hutchinson, 1974. An essential study of the subject.

Beare, W. *The Roman Stage: A Short History of Latin Drama in the Time of the Republic.* London: Methuen, 1950. Useful as an introduction and a key reference.

Bieber, Margarete. *The History of the Greek and Roman Theater.* Princeton, N.J.: Princeton University Press, 1961. The standard overview of the subject.

Cawte, E. C. *Ritual Animal Disguise.* Cambridge: D. S. Brewer for the Folklore Society, 1977. An essential study of the subject.

Hardison, O. B., Jr. *Christian Rite and Christian Drama in the Middle Ages.* Baltimore: Johns Hopkins University Press, 1965. A revolutionary study, still essential.

Hobley, Brian, and Harvey Sheldon. "Big Bang Unearths London's Rich Past." *Illustrated London News,* May 1988, 40–45. Discusses the recent discovery of the London amphitheater.

Llewellyn, Peter. *Rome in the Dark Ages.* New York: Praeger, 1970. Useful for background of the last days of the Roman stage.

Maloney, John. "Fun and Games in Roman London." *Illustrated London News,* May 1988, 45–47. Discusses recent archaeology and stage history.

Ogilvy, J. D. A. "*Mimi, Scurrae, Histriones:* Entertainers of the Early Middle Ages." *Speculum* 38 (1963): 603–19. An essential study of the subject.

Wacher, John. *The Towns of Roman Britain.* Berkeley and Los Angeles: University of California Press, 1974. Essential and well-illustrated study of the field.

THE MYSTERY CYCLES

Collins, Patrick J. *The N-Town Plays and Medieval Picture Cycles.* Early Drama, Art, and Music Monograph Series, 2. Kalamazoo, Mich.: Medieval Institute Publications, 1979. Attractive attempt to apply evidence from art.

Davidson, Clifford. *From Creation to Doom: The York Cycle of Mystery Plays.* New York: AMS Press, 1984. An illuminating critical study.

Dutka, JoAnna. *Music in the English Mystery Plays.* Early Drama, Art, and Music Monograph Series, 2. Kalamazoo, Mich.: Medieval Institute Publications, 1980. An essential study of the subject.

Gardiner, H. C. *Mysteries' End.* Yale Studies in English, vol. 103. New Haven, Conn.: Yale University Press, 1946. Revolutionary and still extremely valuable work.

Kolve, V. A. *The Play Called Corpus Christi.* Stanford: Stanford University Press, 1966. Illuminating and influential study.

Salter, F. M. *Mediaeval Drama in Chester.* Toronto: Toronto University Press, 1955. An important precursor of much recent research.

Stevens, Martin. *Four Middle English Mystery Cycles: Textual, Contextual, and Critical Interpretations.* Princeton, N.J.: Princeton University Press, 1987. One of the most illuminating new studies of the topic.

Woolf, Rosemary. *The English Mystery Plays.* Berkeley: University of California Press, 1972. An essential study of the subject.

THE MORALITY PLAYS

Kelley, M. R. "Fifteenth-Century Flamboyant Style and *The Castle of Perseverance.*" *Comparative Drama* 6 (1972): 14–27. Penetrating stylistic analysis.

Miyajima, Sumiko. *The Theatre of Man: Dramatic Technique and Stagecraft in the English Medieval Moral Plays.* New York: Avon, 1977. A very useful investigation.

Potter, R. *The English Morality Play.* London, 1975. An essential study of the subject.

SELECTED BIBLIOGRAPHY

EARLY TUDOR DRAMA

Anglo, S. *Spectacle, Pageantry, and Early Tudor Policy*. Oxford: Oxford University Press, 1969. The definitive work in this important field.

Boas, F. S. *Introduction to Tudor Drama*. Oxford: Oxford University Press, 1933. Still a very helpful introduction.

———. *University Drama in the Tudor Age*. Oxford: Oxford University Press, 1914. A useful investigation of this key aspect of drama.

Bevington, David. *From Mankind to Marlowe*. Cambridge, Mass.: Harvard University Press, 1962. An essential study of the subject.

———. *Tudor Drama and Tudor Politics: A Critical Approach to Topical Meaning*. Cambridge, Mass.: Harvard University Press, 1968. An illuminating investigation of politics and theater.

Blatt, T. B. *The Plays of John Bale: A Study of Ideas, Technique, and Style*. Copenhagen: Gad, 1968. An important critical study of Bale.

Craik, T. W. *The Tudor Interlude*. Leicester: Leicester University Press, 1958. One of the key analyses of the interlude.

Heiserman, A. R. *Skelton and Satire*. Chicago: Chicago University Press, 1961. An essential study of the subject.

Murison, W. *Sir David Lyndsay, Poet and Satirist of the old church in Scotland*. Cambridge: Cambridge University Press, 1938. A standard work on this important writer.

Orgel, Stephen. *The Illusion of Power: Political Theatre in the English Renaissance*. Berkeley: University of California Press, 1975. An essential study of the subject.

Pollet, M. *John Skelton: Poet of Tudor England*, translated by J. Warrington. Lewisburg, Pa.: Bucknell University Press, 1971. An essential study of Skelton's life and work.

Wilson, F. P. *The English Drama, 1485–1585*. Oxford: Oxford University Press, 1969. A useful investigation of early Tudor dramatic forms.

ELIZABETHAN DRAMA

Bentley, G. E. *The Profession of Actor in Shakespeare's Time*. Princeton, N.J.: Princeton University Press, 1984. An essential study of the subject.

———. *The Profession of Dramatist in Shakespeare's Time, 1590–1642*. Princeton, N.J.: Princeton University Press, 1971. An illuminating analysis of the evidence in this field.

Bradbrook, M. C. *The Growth and Structure of Elizabethan Comedy*. 1955; Harmondsworth, England: Penguin, 1963. An essential study of the subject.

———. *The Rise of the Common Player: A Study of Actor and Society in Shakespeare's England*. Cambridge, Mass.: Harvard University Press, 1962. Still one of the most useful basic works in the field.

———. *Themes and Conventions of Elizabethan Tragedy.* 2d ed. Cambridge: Cambridge University Press, 1952. An essential study of the subject.

Finkelpearl, Philip J. *John Marston of the Middle Temple.* Cambridge, Mass.: Harvard University Press, 1969. Especially valuable on Marston's intellectual milieu.

Gair, Reavley. *The Children of Paul's: The Story of a Theatre Company 1553–1608.* Cambridge: Cambridge University Press, 1982. Illuminating analysis of this important company.

Ingram, R. W. *John Marston.* Boston: Twayne, 1978. An extremely helpful reference and analysis.

Knights, L. C. *Drama and Society in the Age of Jonson.* London: Chatto, 1957. An informative study of Jonson in his historical context.

Limon, Jerzy. *Gentlemen of a Company: English Players in Central and Eastern Europe, 1590–1660.* Cambridge: Cambridge University Press, 1985. An essential study of the subject.

Mehl, Dieter. *The Elizabethan Dumb Show.* London: Methuen, 1965. An essential study of the subject.

Saccio, Peter. *The Court Comedies of John Lyly: A Study in Allegorical Dramaturgy.* Princeton, N.J.: Princeton University Press, 1969. Penetrating and provocative analysis.

Shapiro, Michael. *Children of the Revels.* New York: Columbia University Press, 1977. An excellent study of this important company.

SHAKESPEARE

Barber, C. L. *Shakespeare's Festive Comedy.* Princeton, N.J.: Princeton University Press, 1959. An essential study of the subject.

Harbage, Alfred. *Shakespeare and the Rival Traditions.* Bloomington: Indiana University Press, 1952. A classic work, still of great importance to scholarship.

Muir, Kenneth, and S. Schoenbaum, eds. *A New Companion to Shakespeare Studies.* Cambridge: Cambridge University Press, 1971. A helpful introduction to research.

Rabkin, Norman. *Shakespeare and the Problem of Meaning.* Chicago: University of Chicago Press, 1981. An important critical study.

Schoenbaum, S. *William Shakespeare: A Compact Documentary Life.* Oxford: Oxford University Press, 1975. A valuable account of the biographical evidence.

JACOBEAN AND CAROLINE DRAMA

Akrigg, G. P. V. *Jacobean Pageant: The Court of King James I.* Cambridge, Mass.: Harvard University Press, 1962. An extremely readable account of James I and his court.

Anderson, Donald K. *John Ford*. New York: Twayne, 1972. A helpful concise overview of the subject.

Bas, Georges. *James Shirley (1596–1666): Dramaturge Caroléen*. Lille: Service de reproduction des thèses, 1973. An essential study of the subject.

Bentley, G. E. *The Jacobean and Caroline Stage*. 7 vols. Oxford: Oxford University Press, 1941–66. The primary reference for students of this field.

Berry, Ralph. *The Art of John Webster*. Oxford: Clarendon, 1972. An essential critical study of the subject.

Boas, F. S. *An Introduction to Stuart Drama*. London and New York: Oxford University Press, 1946. A helpful introduction to the field.

Bradbrook, M. C. *John Webster: Citizen and Dramatist*. London: Weidenfeld & Nicolson, 1980. An essential study of the subject.

Butler, Martin. *Theatre and Crisis, 1632–1642*. Cambridge: Cambridge University Press, 1984. An important and provocative reassessment of the field.

Nicoll, Allardyce. *Stuart Masques and the Renaissance Stage*. New York: Benjamin Blom, 1968. Especially valuable for staging, well illustrated.

Orgel, Stephen. *The Jonsonian Masque*. Cambridge, Mass.: Harvard University Press, 1967. An elegant and penetrating study of the masque.

Ornstein, Robert. *The Moral Vision of Jacobean Tragedy*. Madison: University of Wisconsin Press, 1960. An essential study of the subject.

Sargeaunt, Joan M. *John Ford*. Oxford: Basil Blackwell, 1935. A helpful introduction to the playwright.

DRAMA 1642–1660

Hotson, Leslie. *The Commonwealth and Restoration Stage*. Cambridge, Mass.: Harvard University Press, 1928. An important reference for the period.

INDEX

Index

THE AUTHOR

Jennifer R. Goodman, associate professor of English at Texas A&M University, received her B.A. in medieval history and literature from Radcliffe College, her M.A. in medieval studies from the University of Toronto, her M.A. in English from Harvard University, and her Ph.D. in English from Harvard. She is the author of *Malory and Caxton's Prose Romances of 1485* and *The Legend of Arthur in British and American Literature*. Her articles on Malory and Caxton, Chaucer, Captain John Smith, and theater history have appeared in such journals as *Studies in the Age of Chaucer, Virginia Magazine of History and Biography,* and the *Harvard Library Bulletin.*